RAISING MONEY

THE CANADIAN GUIDE
TO SUCCESSFUL
BUSINESS FINANCING

BOOKS BY DOUGLAS A. GRAY

Start and Run a Profitable Consulting Business

The Entrepreneur's Complete Self-Assessment Guide

Marketing Your Product (with Donald Cyr)

The Complete Canadian Small Business Guide (with Diana Gray)

Home Inc.: The Canadian Home-Based Business Guide (with Diana Gray)

Rai$ing Money: The Canadian Entrepreneur's Guide to Successful Business Financing (with Brian F. Nattrass)

Buying, Owning and Selling a Condominium: A Guide for Canadians

Making Money in Real Estate: The Canadian Residential Investment Guide

Mortgages Made Easy: The Canadian Guide to Home Financing

The Complete Canadian Home Inspection Guide (with Ed Witzke)

Home-Buying Made Easy

Marketing Professional Services

Risk-Free Retirement (with Graham Cunningham, Tom Delaney, Dr. Des Dwyer, Les Solomon)

RAISING MONEY

THE CANADIAN GUIDE TO SUCCESSFUL BUSINESS FINANCING

Douglas A. Gray
Brian F. Nattrass

McGRAW-HILL RYERSON
Toronto Montreal

RAISING MONEY: The Canadian Entrepreneur's Guide to Successful Business Financing

Copyright © 1993 Douglas A. Gray and Brian F. Nattrass

First published in 1993 by
McGraw-Hill Ryerson Limited
300 Water Street
Whitby, Ontario
L1N 3B4

Canadian Cataloguing in Publication Data
Gray, Douglas A.
    Raising Money

Includes index.
ISBN 0-07-551498-2

1. New business enterprises — Canada — Finance.
2. Small business — Canada — Finance.
3. Entrepreneurship — Canada.   I. Nattrass, Brian F.
II. Title.

HG4027.6G73 1993   658.15′0971   C92-095555-X

This book is sold with the understanding that neither the authors nor the publisher is engaged in rendering legal, accounting or other professional advice. If such advice or other assistance is required, the personal services of a competent professional should be sought.

Cover design: Stephen Baine/B&E Inc. Toronto
Text design: Dianna Little

Printed and bound in Canada

*To those wondrous and amazing persons, without whom
I would never have finished this book at all: my beloved
wife and daughter, Patricia and Sarah.*

BFN

*To Diana, my wife, friend and intrepid entrepreneur, for
her consistent encouragement and enthusiasm.*

DAG

ACKNOWLEDGEMENTS

A book like this which reflects the experience of entrepreneurs across the country, is really the expression — and acknowledgement — of a whole community of business and professional people. In fact, hardly anyone in Canada's entrepreneurial community who crossed our path during the writing of *RAI$ING MONEY* escaped without revealing to us their experiences and insights with respect to gaining access to investment capital in this country. We would like, however, to especially acknowledge the following people for their contributions to the creation of *RAI$ING MONEY*.

Chris and Phyllis Rob for generously providing a beautiful cottage on the Pacific Ocean as the perfect "writer's retreat" in which to keep this project on track; Ian and Judy Griffin for their unflagging friendship and enthusiasm for this work; John Lecky for his helpful personal recommendations; Dr. Lynn Tanner for his readily available and useful counsel; Gordon F. Dixon, legal entrepreneur for being an inspiring example of the "nine lives of a surviving risk-taker"; Keith Laws for remaining steadfast in his commitment to help us tackle new issues as they arose; and Joann Terry for being, and remaining, a constant source of love and support.

Peter Stone, a superb securities lawyer in Calgary as well as an expert on the federal investor immigrant program, for generously providing commentary on the investor program and on Canadian securities law; Greg Harris, entrepreneurial lawyer also in Calgary, for kindly reviewing material on the law and money raising; Ted Strocel of Abbotsford, B.C., a lawyer and expert on personal property security legislation, for his generous assistance; and Allan Shedlock, a Vancouver money-raising entrepreneur with a heart of pure gold, for all that he shared.

Dr. Andrew Wozny for acting as a regular sounding board for a work in progress; Ken Martin who helped unlock the Muse within; and Jim Quigley for always being there at the right time.

Our parents and family for providing the love and the inspiration which is ever sustaining.

Last, but not least, the staff of McGraw-Hill Ryerson for their ongoing support, encouragement and constructive ideas.

CONTENTS

Chapter Three: Understanding the Law and Money-Raising in Canada 30

Chapter Four: Structuring Your Deal 49

INTRODUCTION TO
RAI$ING MONEY

All highly successful entrepreneurs are obsessed with finding investors and raising capital for their ventures. It's not an obsession anyone teaches you. It's simply a matter of Learn or Die. Get the urge for raising capital into your blood.

Success Magazine

1. HOW THIS BOOK WILL HELP YOU RAISE MONEY AND SUCCEED IN YOUR BUSINESS

The purpose of this book is to empower you to succeed in business by funding your projects. We are going to lead you step-by-step through every major move that you will need to make in order to raise capital for your business. This is a very grounded and practical book about *how to actually do it!* Our "Money-Rai$ing Master Checklist" is the most complete and detailed guide to raising capital ever published in Canada for small to medium-sized business. Our "Sources of Financing Checklist" is a thorough outline of potential sources of financing. Both are located in the Appendix.

The emphasis in this book is on raising equity capital for independent business. We also analyze strategic partnering, bank, government and other sources of business funding including multi-level marketing and franchising. By following the steps explained to you in *RAI$ING MONEY*, you will be able to answer all of the vital questions about raising capital for your business or project, such as:

1. How do I find investors for my project?
2. How many investors can legally put money into my business?
3. To whom can I legally sell shares in my company?
4. How much money can I raise?
5. Is there any minimum amount that I need to raise?
6. Can I use the investment money as soon as I receive it?
7. What kind of documents do I need for:
   a. prospective investors, and
   b. actual investors?

8. Do I need to provide a prospectus or an offering memorandum to prospective investors? What is the difference between those two documents?
9. What is a strategic partner and how can I find one for my business?
10. How can I use multi-level or network marketing to finance my business?

There has never been a better time to launch a new business or sell a new idea in Canada provided that you have access to sufficient capital to achieve your goals. Today, there is a greater receptivity to new ideas in society generally, and in the marketplace in particular. Millions of Canadian "baby boomers" and "post-baby boomers" are dissatisfied with old ways of doing business and are continually demanding new and different services and products. From a global perspective, the ever-growing presence and pressure of international businesses and their products and services in Canada are creating both stresses and opportunities for our entrepreneurs. The entire business community is in a state of flux and transition the likes of which it has never before experienced. This provides a fertile environment for the entrepreneur with a likely story or a good idea to receive both a hearing for, and the financing of, his project — if he packages and presents his business proposal in an effective manner. *RAI$ING MONEY* will show you how.

2. SUCCESSFUL FINANCING: AN ONGOING PROCESS, NOT AN ISOLATED EVENT

Very little of value in life constitutes a single event, and certainly financing your business or project is not one of them. All businesses have a financial component all of the time. Like the constant ebb and flow of the tide, your business may be cash rich or cash poor at any particular time. Successfully predicting and satisfying the needs of your business for capital, whether in the form of debt or equity, is an ongoing process.

Do you treat your business's purchasing function as an isolated event? Or its production function? Or accounting for GST? In other words, do you only acquire inventory once every five years or so? Or make products, or generate services, once in a while? Or occasionally charge and remit GST as the whim occurs to you? Of course not (although, admittedly, it may be your fondest wish). Your mindset, your attitude, must be one of expecting to be engaged permanently with those functions as long as you are in business.

Likewise, your commercial survival today depends upon a similar readiness to be engaged in an ongoing process of financing your business. Successful financing is one of the key ongoing functions required for your business to thrive. Why do you think major corporations dedicate 100% of the time of many highly trained individuals to ensure the continuous satisfactory attention to the finance function? It's because they are both experienced enough and sophisticated enough to know that as their own cash resources fluctuate, they must be able to respond immediately to their financial needs as and when required. They know that they cannot afford the time required to start the money-raising process all over again each and every time they experience a need for capital. Very few major corporations would survive, and very little growth would occur, if they took such a piecemeal approach to financing their business. You can learn from that insight of major corporations. Remember: All businesses have a financial component all of the time.

3. FINANCING NEEDS CONTINUALLY CHANGE

Each business, each industry, has its own annual financial cycle. These cycles represent periods of relative capital need and relative abundance. From the retailer's need to acquire major amounts of inventory in the fall in preparation for the Christmas shopping season, to the farmer's need to acquire seed, fertilizer and other supplies in the spring in preparation for planting, the normal business cycle creates more or less predictable demands on financial requirements.

In addition, each stage of the growth process itself has its own unique capital requirements. From the planning stage, through start-up, to maturity, the need for capital is ever-changing. Furthermore, unpredictable events can also profoundly affect a company's financial requirements. Financial planning, flexibility and creativity are absolute necessities for today's businessperson in order to be able to cope with the ever-changing financial needs of his business within the rapidly changing business environment.

The nature of this environment was captured on the entire front page of the July 13th, 1987 issue of *Forbes* magazine with the boldly printed headline:

> *"CAPITALISM IS BY NATURE A FORM OF CHANGE*
> *AND NEVER IS, NEVER CAN BE, STATIONARY"*

This statement is a quote from Joseph Schumpeter's *Capitalism, Socialism and Democracy*. The article in *Forbes*, which expanded on the theme, went on to say:

> . . . capitalism is unruly and disconcerting, a system of flux rather than equilibrium. Change, however, is painful to many and disquieting to many more. . . . Progress, Schumpeter said, hinges on a process of "creative destruction." . . . Now, entrepreneurs, the agents of painful change, are heroes, while bureaucrats and stay-put management are suspect.

This message is abundantly clear and is made over and over by many authorities: "Learn or Die!" Change is constant and accelerating. We cannot effectively fight change. To be successful, we must embrace it, adapt to it, or perish. In the '90s, the key to business survival is access to capital. Yet the financial world itself is also in the midst of turmoil and great change.

4. FINANCING METHODS AND SOURCES CHANGE

Constant change in all aspects of business, including methods and sources of financing, requires that all successful players maintain constant vigilance. Business is a battleground, and today there are only two kinds of businesses, like there are only two kinds of combat soldiers — "the quick and the dead." In other words, business today demands that we be continually alert to changing conditions and new influences and practices. If the financing formula from the past worked in the present, commercial life would be much simpler for everyone. On the other hand, those individuals and companies which had mastered the old formula would continue to dominate their own spheres of business in the present.

Do you remember some of the highly publicized and high-flying Canadian financial institutions and real estate development companies from the '80s which were caught by rapidly changing financial conditions? Do you remember the leveraged buy-outs (LBOs) and the high-yielding, less-than-investment-grade debt instruments ("junk bonds") which were the financial "magic pills" of the '80s? Many of the prominent companies of that era are now bankrupt, or severely wounded, by the excessive debt taken on to finance their acquisitions, and the financial institutions which loaned them the funds are now weakened, some mortally so. If it can happen to them, and they were highly sophisticated, what about us? How can we successfully raise money for our projects today in a radical new era of finance and restricted credit? Answering these fundamental questions is precisely what we will be undertaking throughout most of this book.

5. STEPS IN THE PROCESS OF SUCCESSFUL FINANCING

In the chapters to follow, we will lead you step-by-step through each of the stages of a successful money-raising program with an emphasis on raising equity capital. The steps are basically the same, whether you wish to raise $25,000 or $2,500,000. We have divided the overall process into six stages as follows:

1. Creating Your Vision.
2. Preparing Your Business Plan.
3. Understanding the Law and Raising Money.
4. Structuring Your Deal.
5. Locating Your Prospective Investors and Lenders.
6. Marketing and Selling Your Deal.

The pursuit of capital in the '90s by Canadian businesses of all sizes in all industries will be relentless. Access to capital will be the major function in determining who will be the winners and who will be the losers in the business wars of this decade. The common denominator of the '90s, whether from franchised retail operations, to software developers, to hydrocarbon exploration, will be the ability to adapt to a constantly changing socio-economic environment with sufficient capital reserves to be able to meet all contingencies and to seize desired opportunities as they arise.

The process-oriented and proven approach to raising capital described in this book is remarkably effective. This is not only the "right stuff" — it's the "real stuff." Between us, we have successfully orchestrated the financing of dozens of projects, counselled thousands of money-raising entrepreneurs and raised tens of millions of dollars for our own and other people's projects in Canada. This stuff works! We sincerely hope that you will take the time to work through what may be new concepts and new attitudes in order to become familiar with the methodology that we are advocating.

This approach has worked successfully for thousands of other money-raising businesspeople in Canada; it can work for you. Our deepest intent in writing this book is that you utilize the insights and information that we have shared with you, get into action and make your dreams come true! We wish you great success and prosperity.

We always welcome candid and constructive feedback from readers to assist us in improving future editions of this book. Please write to us c/o Canadian Enterprise Institute Inc., #300–3665 Kingsway, Vancouver, B.C. V5R 5W2.

Vancouver, B.C.   Douglas A. Gray
March, 1993   Brian F. Nattrass

PART I

RAISING MONEY IN CANADA

Access to capital is emerging as the crucial factor in corporate success. The business world is dividing up into two tiers: those companies that can get capital and those that can't.

BUSINESS WEEK

CHAPTER ONE

CREATING YOUR VISION

Nothing happens unless first a dream.

Carl Sandburg

1.1 INTRODUCTION

The essence of raising capital is to enroll the prospective investor in your vision of the outstanding success that you will make of your business with an injection of his capital for your mutual profit. Your vision must be both enrolling and empowering in its impact. It must be so enrolling that prospective sources of financing will be motivated to join you by investing, lending or otherwise contributing to your project. It must be so empowering that you and your colleagues will persevere in pursuit of your vision in the long weeks and months of difficulty and darkness which usually plague even the most successful projects.

At its most fundamental level, successful capital-raising is a form of well-planned and well-executed evangelism. You must make a believer out of a sceptic, the targeted prospective financial source. He must come to believe in you and believe in your business proposal. You must win him over to your side. He must experience a kind of *metanoia*, a conversion, a change of heart, so that he sees things differently now: the way you wish him to see them. Another way of putting it is that the prospective investor must be brought to a point of believing that the share certificates in your hand are worth more than the money in his pocket.

In the years immediately after the Second World War, a man who came to be known as the "Billy Graham of the Needle Trade" began his business career in southern Alberta. The son of a lay minister, his missionary zeal perhaps came naturally. He began his business career as a manufacturer's sales representative selling blue jeans and work wear to retailers for what was then a tiny Alberta work wear manufacturer, the Great Western Garment Company Ltd. At that time, the company had approximately $2,000,000 in annual revenues. In the late 1940s, the western Canadian market for jeans and work wear was dominated by well-known American labels such as Levis, Lee and Wrangler. G.W.G. was struggling in its own home market just to maintain a foothold.

3

The young man developed a compelling two-fold vision. On the positive side, it was of high-quality Canadian clothing, made by Canadians for Canadians that would outlast and outwear anything else on the market. He also developed another side to the vision — a dark one. He showed the retail merchants how every time they sold an American product, they were cutting their own throats! This was because they were developing the consumer's taste for American products. So every time the customer was in the States he would naturally buy more of the same fine product, but at a much lower price and not from the Canadian merchant who sold it to him in the first place! In such a manner, the salesman demonstrated to the Canadian merchants how they were creating their own competition.

This approach proved highly successful. The merchants enrolled in G.W.G.'s vision of buying from a Canadian manufacturer as a means of ensuring their own survival as retailers. (In retrospect, given the flood of Canadian shoppers swarming to the USA today, this vision of almost a half-century ago seems brilliantly prophetic!)

The young salesman developed such a passion for his two-fold vision that after his first year on the road he became the number one producer in the company and achieved the highest per capita sales of his company's products in the country. He eventually went on to build the most successful sales force in Canada in the clothing industry for that time. G.W.G. achieved over $100,000,000 per year in sales, never before attained by any jean or work wear manufacturer in Canada. This was fundamentally due to a fierce evangelism in service of a clear vision.

If our use of emotionally loaded words such as "evangelical," "conversion," "win over," "believer," "change of heart," and even the reference to "Billy Graham" makes you uncomfortable, that is good. That is what we intended. The reason is simple: the investor's decision to invest in your business is rarely a rational process. If it were rational, it is almost certain that he would not invest with you, given the extremely long odds against the success of most independent businesses!

If you are to become successful in raising money for your business or project, you must stop thinking of the actions of the vast majority of private investors as a rational and reasoned process! Did you choose your spouse by a rational process? Why not? Did you prefer to "fall in love"? What about other important aspects of your life? Your house. Your vacation cottage. Your dog. Your cat. Do you like to fall in love? So does nearly everyone else! So do most investors. They particularly like to fall in love with their private investments!

It is critical to your future success in raising capital that you understand this. The decision to invest in your project, at its base level, is rarely a rational process! Just as "the Billy Graham of the Needle Trade" converted the scepticism, and in many instances the outright hostility, of the retail merchants to one of belief and support for him, his product and his company, you must also win over the prospective investor to you and your business. This is accomplished by your passionate and well-planned pursuit of *a clearly articulated and compelling vision.* You must go beyond your comfort zone if you are to succeed in enrolling people in your vision. Be passionate! Be both a lover and a fighter! This is about you creating your life the way that you really desire it to be!

However, unlike the usually accidental way in which most of us meet our future spouses, the passionate pursuit of financing your business must be as well-planned and as well-executed as a successful military campaign. Passions are never greater than they are in the heat of war, where we are engulfed in love and hate, fear and triumph, life and death. Yet in the midst of that high emotion, no endeavour of mankind is subject to as much detailed analysis, planning, preparation and discipline as the arena of warfare and combat. In similar fashion, your money-raising campaign must have a clear vision supported by a well-conceived business plan, meticulous financial projections and persuasive supporting material.

The essence of raising capital is *to enroll the prospective investor in your vision* of the outstanding success that you will make of your business with an injection of his capital for your mutual profit. Thus, creating your business vision is the *sine qua non* of the money-raising process, which means your vision is that without which the thing cannot be. In other words, "don't leave home without it!" In creating and articulating your vision, there is a highly effective threefold process as follows:

1. Declare Your Greater Business Purpose.
2. Define Your Core Objectives.
3. Determine Your Strategies.

1.2 DECLARE YOUR GREATER BUSINESS PURPOSE

An effective vision calls us forward to action. It speaks to our heart in some way, not just to our intellect or to our pocketbook. We can recognize a true business vision for ourselves because we feel somehow empowered by it. By that we mean that the vision somehow "calls us forth" in an evangelical sense to follow this particular path, whatever it may be. The vision gives us energy, it motivates us. For you to feel empowered by a vision means that you derive strength from that vision.

The first step in creating your vision is to state your "greater business purpose." This is sometimes referred to as your "mission statement." This statement will answer the "why" of your business, as in "Why are we in business?" A powerful vision was one of the driving forces behind the amazing success story of Apple Computer, a highly successful and profitable company. At the very beginning of the personal computer era, early employees of Apple were motivated and empowered by their opportunity to "change the way the world works." A hypothetical example could be that of a company set-up to make a profit from recycling CFCs (chlorofluorocarbons, which destroy the ozone in the Earth's atmosphere) from discarded refrigeration units. The highly motivating vision of such a company could be to "assure a liveable world for all mankind."

An effective vision statement answers the "why" of the business, not the "what" (as in "What does your company do?"). It answers the question, "Why is your company in business?" Ask yourself, "What is the vision of my organization?" Does that vision motivate you? If it doesn't, revise it until it does. Do you even have one? Then create one.

Lest you think that we overstate the vital importance of having a compelling vision for your business or project, we will quote directly from a recent annual report of the largest venture capital company in Canada, Vencap Equities Alberta Ltd. The significance for the money-raising entrepreneur of having and communicating a clear corporate vision is stated by Vencap as follows:

> Companies destined for success have a vision of what they intend to do. Communicating this vision is an important aspect of the business plan. While we may know your industry in general outline, only you can make clear what distinguishes your business from the competition.

In addition, the vision can give you a sense of participating in the quest to achieve some greater purpose, something more than merely making money. This kind of vision can be the source of great strength to an entrepreneur in difficult times. In many instances, your vision may be the critical element in your generating the will to persevere with a business or project. For example, writing a book is a long, solitary and often tedious process. In drafting this book, the authors were inspired by the vision which we have for this book and how it will benefit Canadian entrepreneurs all across our country. The mission statement for this book could therefore be, "To empower Canadian entrepreneurs to succeed in business by funding their projects successfully." That vision of being able to make a genuine difference in the business success of some fellow Canadian entrepreneurs, almost all of us struggling in a strange new economic world, regularly drew us back to continuing and completing this project.

1.3 DEFINE YOUR CORE OBJECTIVES

The next step after making a clear statement of your greater business purpose is to define the core objectives for your business. Defining such objectives will answer the "what" of your business, as in "What does the business do?" Objectives can be of either a quantitative or a qualitative nature.

A quantitative objective is something measurable, such as "recycling 10,000 kilograms of CFCs in our first year of business." A qualitative objective is not, by its very nature, subject to calculation (although our society attempts to quantify everything, including the artistic merit of figure skaters in the Olympic Games). This element of objectives has to do with the very quality of something, its essence. A qualitative company objective might be "to increase the well-being of all Canadians."

Defining objectives, in its qualitative aspect, is very similar to goal setting. There are many books written on this topic and its absolute necessity in business is beyond dispute. Without objectives, you don't know where you are going, and perhaps worse, you don't know if or when you've arrived. The classic formulation of this is by Alice in her adventures in Wonderland from *Through the Looking Glass* by Lewis Carroll:

> "Would you tell me, please, which way I ought to go from here?"
> "That depends a good deal on where you want to get."

"I don't much care where."

"Then it doesn't matter much which way you go."

The very worst thing possible for you to communicate to a prospective investor is that you do not know where you are going. Money likes certainty. Certainty breeds confidence. Confidence breeds trust. Investment money is attracted to trust. You convey certainty by communicating your sense of direction for your business or project. To do this, you need to know where you are going and how.

In writing this book, the authors had both quantitative and qualitative objectives in mind. An example of a qualitative objective is "to establish *RAI$ING MONEY* as the primary reference source for entrepreneurs raising money in Canada." An example of a quantitative objective is "to achieve first-year sales of 10,000 copies." Each of these objectives requires strategies by which the objectives are to be attained.

1.4 DETERMINE YOUR STRATEGIES

After you have defined your core business objectives, the next step in this process of articulating your vision is to determine the strategies by which you will achieve your objectives. Determining your business strategies will answer the "how" of your business, as in "How will the business attain each of its objectives?"

For the purpose of being very clear about the strategies that you intend to employ to realize your objectives, and particularly so that you can communicate without confusion those strategies to potential investors in your company, we highly recommend that you summarize the strategies to be used to attain the individual objectives in no more than three or four key points. The purpose of this exercise is not only to help focus your own thinking, but to be able to communicate to your listener a word picture of your greater business purpose, your core objectives and the strategies to achieve those objectives. In sum, to be able to communicate effectively your overall vision for the company.

1.5 CONCLUSION

The essence of raising capital is to enroll the prospective investor in your vision of the outstanding success that you will make of your business with an injection of his capital for your mutual profit. In order to create that vision which we believe to be critical to your success as a money-raising entrepreneur, we urge you to engage in the three-fold process of creating your company's vision as discussed above. Creating your vision consists of the following steps:

1. Declare Your Greater Business Purpose.
2. Define Your Core Objectives.
3. Determine Your Strategies

In order to be able to communicate your business vision effectively, you should be able to condense all three elements down to no more than one page in length. Strive for clarity and simplicity. When you have a clear vision of where you are going with your business, it is then time to prepare the document which will be the base from which to launch your successful money-raising program — your company's business plan. This is covered in Chapter Two.

CHAPTER TWO

PREPARING YOUR BUSINESS PLAN

Long-range planning does not deal with future decisions,
but with the future of present decisions.

Peter F. Drucker

2.1 INTRODUCTION

"You never have a second chance to make a first impression." This old adage attains a new significance when applied to the highly competitive process of raising money. The first time that you approach a potential investor or lender with your project, you must have everything right. If you fail, through naivety, sloppiness, ignorance or lack of attention to detail, you are very rarely graced with a second chance. Just as a successful attacking general never commits his army to an offensive without a detailed battle plan, a successful businessman never commences a money-raising campaign without a thoroughly prepared business plan. In money-raising, as in war, you've got to get it right the first time!

In the eyes of the financier, your business plan is you. Whether you are perceived to be businesslike, well organized, effective and credible will be determined in his first thirty seconds of handling and scanning your business plan. If the impression is positive, he'll take the next step and read the executive summary of your plan. This must also be excellent. If it is, he'll go on to the body of your plan. If is not sufficiently enticing, the plan over which you may have laboured for weeks, or even months, will be cast into the "out basket" or the garbage after only a few seconds of cursory review, and you'll likely never know why you were never granted an appointment to present your proposal. You were betrayed by your own written presentation without the investor even examining the merits of your business!

The purpose of this chapter is to provide you with an overview of what is involved in the complex task of creating an *effective* business plan and to impress upon you the critical importance of generating an *excellent* business plan (not "adequate," "fair" or "acceptable") for your proposed business or project. Competition for the investor's dollar has never been tougher or more intense. The average wealthy individual sees dozens of proposals designed to separate him from a portion of his cash every year. Professional venture capitalists see many hundreds of such plans and proposals in the same period. The standard of quality set by

9

your money-seeking competition is getting higher and higher. Anything short of excellence in presenting and communicating to potential investors or lenders is a guaranteed failure in today's competitive world of raising money.

Please be aware that this chapter does not purport to be either a full or adequate description of how to construct an effective and excellent business plan. Because of the number of individual topics, the specific kinds of information and the amount of coaching that you require to produce a genuinely winning business plan, the intent of this chapter is simply to alert you to some of the really critical matters which are of particular significance to using the plan for raising money. You are strongly advised to initially purchase a book on the subject of preparing your written business plan, then consider engaging a consultant to help you complete your plan. It should be such a well-finished document that it will be perceived as a credit to both you and your business and open the financing doors that you want it to.

Project Feasibility Analysis vs. Business Plan Preparation

We must assume, for purposes of this chapter, that you have taken the necessary steps to prove the feasibility of your proposed project. The rigour of the analysis to which you have subjected your proposed enterprise will then be demonstrated in the business plan. Remember, this is about your life! Have you satisfied yourself that this is truly a project which is worthy of expending a significant portion of your life on? Do not be seduced by a sexy idea that does not perform under close scrutiny!

The preparation of a business plan is no substitute for undertaking the prior and fundamental step of establishing the feasibility of your project as a viable and profitmaking enterprise. You must be so confident of the proposed project by the end of your analysis that you feel *drawn* and *compelled* to proceed with it. If you have not been totally convinced, if you still have doubt, do not proceed. You will be amazed at how soon another idea or opportunity comes along to catch your interest. As a seasoned observer of the new venture scene once observed, "New deals and business opportunities are just like city buses; there's another one every fifteen minutes."

Not only can you make the sometimes difficult decision not to proceed with a project that appears attractive or urgent on the surface, you must let it go if it fails to pass the objective criteria that you establish to evaluate its feasibility.

The project feasibility analysis of the challenge or opportunity facing you is your own personal study of whether and how your proposed project can be achieved as a viable business enterprise. It will include a number of factors, all leading you to be in a position to be able to affirmatively answer five fundamental questions:

- Does a satisfactory market exist for me to profitably serve with my proposed product or service?
- Is my proposed product or service of a high enough quality to be able to properly serve the market that I have identified?
- Can I put together a highly capable management team along with the necessary resources to be able to effectively create the product or service and deliver

it in a manner so as to satisfy the market and make a profit for our business? (If this is going to be a one-person business initially, can you truthfully say to yourself that you are capable of doing everything necessary on your own, or in conjunction with support that you can afford and can conveniently access?)

- Is my financial plan sufficiently comprehensive such that it will meet all projected financing requirements including a reasonable provision for contingent expenditures?
- Have I identified all of the risks inherent in the proposed project and determined how to successfully manage each of these risks?

In contrast to your personal feasibility study, which is intended for your eyes only and the purpose of which is to determine if there really is in fact a viable business opportunity, a business plan is a formal document intended to be read and acted upon by others.

2.2 YOUR BUSINESS PLAN

Prelude to Money-Raising

Money-raising is about marketing and selling your proposal to others. Marketing and selling. And not much else. Do you remember what every real estate salesman you ever met told you were the three secrets to making money in real estate? In case you've forgotten, the stock answer is "Location. Location. And location." Similarly, the three secrets of money raising are:

A. Marketing and selling.

B. Marketing and selling.

And just in case you haven't anticipated it, the other secret is:

C. Marketing and selling.

Insofar as the money-raising process is concerned, everything else is merely supportive of the financial marketing and selling functions.

Those of you who are inventors, scientists, engineers and other species of technocrats will be deeply offended by that, because you are always so mesmerized by the product or technology that you like to believe that "this product is so fantastic, it will just sell itself to investors." Wrong. Actually you are wrong on two counts. Creators of better mousetraps also like to believe that "this product will just sell itself to consumers in the marketplace." That's why so many product-oriented companies go so rapidly into bankruptcy, despite the elegant technology. No product in the history of the known universe ever successfully "just sold itself, either to investors or to consumers."

Infatuated with your product as you are, you enjoy the delusion of believing that investors will simply line up to invest in the launch of your new product. Wrong again. You won't even get past the investor's assistant, or the security alarm system, to open your mouth about the product that was supposed to sell itself. After about a dozen failures of this sort, you may (if you are highly intelligent) come to the conclusion that your infant product isn't talking too well; in fact, the little rascal hasn't even opened its mouth yet! Unfortunately, you will by now have blown your credibility with about a dozen good sources of financing (and they aren't always as easy to come by as you may have earlier believed). At this point, you may pick up this book again and start reading where you originally got turned off! Now, if you just simply keep reading, we can save you a great deal of wasted time and effort by guiding you in a way that should greatly enhance the speed and success of your money-raising campaign.

What Is a Successful Business Plan?

A successful business plan is a document that is so well organized and so well written that it motivates and enables the prospective financier to make a positive decision in favour of putting money into your project without ever having met you!

In content, a business plan is a document that fully describes all aspects of your business or project. It includes information on the purpose and objectives of your business, details of the company and its structure, the history of the business, an in-depth analysis of your chosen market, your marketing strategy, your sales and distribution strategies, your management team, your products and services, your competition, the risk factors and a discussion of how you plan to overcome them, financial history, current financial position, financial forecasts, growth potential, capital requirements and other details of the business.

Uses of a Business Plan

Besides its primary use as a marketing tool in order to raise equity capital for your business or project, your business plan has several other uses and benefits. However, just as none of us can successfully be all things to all people, neither can your business plan. Consequently, most successful entrepreneurs keep a current version of their business plan on their personal computer and modify it as circumstances and their audience change.

For example, the requirements and lending criteria of a banker are normally significantly different than the investment criteria of a venture capitalist. The lender is very interested in your cash flow to ensure that he receives his regular interest payments. In addition, your assets are of fundamental importance because he wants the assurance that in the (unlikely) event that your business should fall on unfortunate times, his loan will be secured against those assets. Consequently, his concern for these two areas will cause you to emphasize and document them in your approach for a loan facility. On the other hand, the venture capitalist is looking for a major capital gain and usually wants to see a minimum average compound rate of return of from 30% to 40% and frequently higher. His focus will be heavily on the evidence of upside potential rather than current cash flow or security for a loan. While the sophisticated equity investor is prepared to take a risk on the money that he puts into your business and is looking for you to hit a home run for him, the lender is not. The lender will be happy to see you make a number of base hits and keep on making your payments!

Another valid reason for you to go through the laborious exercise of creating a business plan, then revising it on a regular basis, is that it really forces you to think about and analyze where your business actually is now and why; where it has been and where it is going; how is it going to get there and who is going to make it so. In other words, the business plan is like the road map that you will keep nearby at all times and will follow on your business journey. It is frequently said that if you can't put a plan to paper, then you really haven't thought it through. If you haven't fully thought out a plan for your business with a firm goal and methodology clearly defined, then chances are very high that it doesn't matter what you say your goal is, you won't be achieving it. Putting down on paper your total business plan can be one of the most eye-opening and rewarding uses of your time imaginable. As Sir Francis Bacon, who is recognized as having had one of the greatest minds in the history of the English-speaking world, once said, "Writing makes an exact man."

Integrity of Your Business Plan

It is extremely important that your business plan be factual and truthful throughout. The "selling function" of the business plan is accomplished by describing the genuine competitive advantages and market opportunities that exist for your company, definitely not through exaggeration or deception of any kind. Accordingly, it is important to be able to "back-up" any factual assertions, particularly about the industry and the marketplace, with references or citations to the source of the information. If you are making an assumption, rather than a known statement of fact, it is important to the honesty and integrity of your business plan that you identify the statement as an assumption. By so doing, you will sharpen your own ability to analyze your business and may surprise yourself as to how frequently what you had previously thought to be fact turned out to be an unsupported and even false assumption.

Format of a Comprehensive Business Plan

The proper design, layout and contents of your business plan are extremely important in creating the right impression of both your business and yourself. You must objectively ask yourself, "Is it, and therefore am I, logical or illogical, easy to read and understand or incomprehensible, thorough or careless, interesting or boring, realistic or impractical, true or false, strong or weak?" As you can see, very strong opinions can be formed of you and your business in a frighteningly short period of time. Remember this: the prospective investor is looking for any excuse to throw your plan in his "circular file"! Don't give him this chance! Start with a highly professional appearance and order to your business plan. Use the "Model Business Plan Outline" in Appendix A as the format for your business plan, with such modifications as are appropriate to your particular circumstances. We will discuss each of the main elements now, but first briefly review the "Model Business Plan Outline" at the back of this book.

Elements of a Comprehensive Business Plan

The "Model Business Plan Outline" is very comprehensive. It is neither necessary nor expected that your particular plan would need to comply with every single item. Common sense should be your guiding principle when applying the outline to your specific situation. It is clear that a start-up restaurant will have considerably different functional elements than the expansion of a manufacturing company with proprietary products. The restaurant will have neither patents nor manufacturing processes to protect, nor research and development plans and budgets to contend with. Whatever your circumstances, the outline will help you to effectively focus your thinking on each of the major functional areas of your business so that you will have a better plan as an operating guide for yourself and a better document to show to others when you are seeking financing.

A. PLAN PRELIMINARIES

For presentation to financial sources, the appearance of your business plan must comply with the "Porridge Test" of Goldilocks and the Three Bears. It must not be "too hot"; it must not be "too cold"; it must be "just right." Do not go to the expense of having your plan bound with a hard cover and embossed, as some over-achievers have tried. It can be a turn-off for investors because it looks as though you have a "money to burn" attitude. On the other hand, do not present the potential investor with an unkempt version either as that indicates a careless attitude. Ensure that your plan is on crisp, clean white bond, a standard 8-1/2″ x 11″ in size. It is helpful, but not mandatory, to use a clear plastic cover (it keeps the document clean and looks professional) and to have it bound with a plastic coil spine, such as Cerlox, which enables the reader to lay the document flat yet have it all held together. Most instant copy shops can provide both the clear plastic cover and the coil binding for a modest price.

The cover page should include the name, address and telephone number of the business, and the names and telephone numbers of the contact persons with whom the potential investor can follow-up. It has happened more than once that the covering letter has been detached from a business plan and lost before the investor has a chance to see it. If that happens and there is no adequate information on the document, even if he liked your document the financier could not pursue it.

In addition, your business plan should never be used as, or construed as being, a legal offering document such as a prospectus or an offering memorandum. Accordingly, it is highly recommended that you insert a *legal disclaimer* at the bottom of the cover page of your business plan or, alternatively, on its own as the first page immediately after the cover page. (See section 2.2(I), entitled "Financial Plan and Information.")

The table of contents should be well-organized and have accurate page numbering. Avoid excessive detail. Make the reader's life easy. Do not give him an early and nonsubstantial reason to throw the document away.

The covering letter that is to be sent out with your business plan is a very important document. It should be personally addressed to the intended recipient by name. If you do not know to whom it should be sent, then find out; telephone for the information if you must. Do not make it an anonymous looking "broadcast letter" that has the appearance of having been sent to every financial source in the country. If it's addressed to someone by name, he may actually receive and read it. Make the letter short and to the point, not more than one page. Let your business plan do the talking. Remember our definition of a business plan above.

B. EXECUTIVE SUMMARY

The executive summary is arguably the most important section of your business plan. You have from thirty seconds to five minutes in which to interest the reader or lose him forever!

Therefore, this critical component of your business plan must be appealing, convincing and to the point. It should in no case exceed four pages in length. Shorter is better. This part of the document should be prepared last, after you have analyzed, anguished, soul-searched and finally written each part of the main body of your business plan. As you work on the main part, make note of the key points, the most important financial figures and unique features that concisely summarize your business. Organize them under the topics suggested above in the "Model Business Plan Outline."

Your objective here is to succinctly state the business opportunity represented by your project; why does it exist; how will it be exploited; who will execute it; and what and when is the pay-off to the investors. You achieve this by describing the most significant aspects of your business and the opportunity.

Really make the executive summary "sing your song" for you! Show it to people whose business judgement you respect and ask them for their objective response to reading your summary. Were they enrolled? If not, then why not? Make as many changes and rewrite it as many times as necessary until it is as perfect as you can make it. Then apply that standard to your whole business plan!

As a final note, at the top of the first page of the executive summary, be sure to include your full company name, address, telephone number and contact person(s). Sometimes only your summary will be copied and passed around, so it is helpful to have that information right up front on the first page in the event that someone wishes to obtain additional information or otherwise contact you.

C. THE COMPANY

This is where you have the opportunity to really state "This is me and this is why I'm special." What business are you in and what is your "uncommon competence?" In other words, what is it that makes your business unique and exceptional, and will lead to your success in the marketplace?

This is another chance for you to whet the appetite of the reader by describing what a dynamic and special enterprise this is with a unique market opportunity. Briefly give the history of the formation of the company and its development to date. Describe why and how it entered the industry that it did. What products or services does it presently offer and what does it intend to offer by way of new developments in the foreseeable future?

D. THE INDUSTRY

Provide an overview of the industry which you are currently in or intending to enter. Describe the present status of the industry, along with current issues facing the industry and foreseeable trends. Refer to your sources of industry information.

Describe your company's opportunity within your chosen industry. Where do your products or services fit within the industry? What is your particular niche in the marketplace? How will your uncommon competence enable you to exploit your perceived opportunity? How will industry trends affect your company, either positively or negatively?

E. PRODUCTS AND SERVICES

This is the section where you can explain exactly what it is that you sell to the marketplace. What do you produce or provide? What is unique or uncommon about your product or service? Why is it special?

Sophisticated investors understand the importance of proprietary assets, such as patents, trademarks and copyrights. Describe any advantages that you have in this regard. Do you have a head start or some other preferred position in your industry? If so, it is important to clearly describe why.

Beware of getting into too much detail in this part of the business plan. Potential investors want to have a clear idea of what it is that you are selling but do not want to get bogged down in a technical description of your product or service. Create an appendix at the back of the business plan to show such diagrams, drawings, photographs, patents, copyrights, trademarks and other items that you consider highly persuasive in presenting your product or service. If your product is of an advanced and highly technical nature, you could in fact organize all of the product back-up documentation in a separate document and agree to provide it to the prospective investor or his representative at such time as negotiations reach an advanced stage.

You should also be aware that it is a truism in the venture capital industry that it is not the product, but rather management, that ultimately makes a project or company successful. Inventors and engineers in particular need to heed some advice here: make this section relatively short and to the point. Remember our comments above on the topic "Prelude to Money-Raising." Intricate elaboration of the product, if it is needed at all, should be made in the appendix to your business plan or in a separate document entirely. It would be better to elaborate on how you will obtain sales of the product. In other words, provide a detailed breakdown on how the product will be marketed and sold for the purposes of interesting your future investors.

F. MARKETING AND SALES

This is an extremely important section of your business plan. So frequent is the tragic story of companies with brilliant ideas and innovative products who have never become a success due to a lack of competence in "marketing and sales." Do you remember our introductory comments that "no product ever sells itself?" You may not believe that, but sophisticated investors certainly do! They want clear evidence that you have a very concrete plan, based on solid market analysis, as to how your product will enter the marketplace and be sold at a profit.

The Market Share Assumption Error

Probably the most significant error and the one most frequently seen in business plans is what we may call the "market share assumption error." It is a sure sign of incompetence and will usually send the sophisticated investor racing, not walking, away from you and your proposal. The lure and danger of this trap is particularly odious because the entrepreneur generally thinks that he is being eminently conservative and reasonable while at the same time he is falling straight into a pit from which he will never be rescued.

The market share assumption error occurs whenever the business person assumes that he can accurately predict what his future sales will be by determining the sales figures for the overall market or industry which he is targeting, then projects a share of the total market for his own company by stating that he "assumes we will achieve a very conservative X% of the total market." You can take a very large market — for example, the world-wide sales of personal computers — and show well-documented figures from impressive journals that the total world market is, say, $50,000,000,000 per year. You then state that with your fantastic new technology and your incredibly bright and capable management team, if you just obtained "a very conservative, infinitesimally small" 1/10th of 1% of worldwide computer sales in your first year, you would do "a very conservative" $50,000,000 in sales! "Conservatively!" At that point, the dust that you see on the horizon is from the wheels of the financier's Porsche retreating at maximum speed down the highway in any direction as long as it's away from you!

You may ask then, "How do you make forecasts for revenue?" First of all, you must indicate in detail your methodology for determining your sales forecasts. A good book on business planning, or on sales and marketing, is a place to start if you have little experience in this area. Another approach is to hire a consultant experienced in developing sales and marketing plans. You must be able to substantiate your assumptions! These include items such as data on which market segments you will be targeting; how customers in these target areas currently satisfy their purchase requirements; why they will switch to your product (show user economics); what are the changing buying patterns in the marketplace and how do your products or services address them; and many other related topics.

Secondly, you must break your revenue figures down into monthly "number of units sold." By showing numbers of units sold, your performance can be measured. You need to do this with every major product line if you are dealing in a low number of products at relatively high cost, such as a computer manufacturer; alternatively, with major categories of products, if you are dealing in a high number of products at a relatively low cost, such as a retail store.

Thirdly, you must be very specific about your actual sales strategy and how you will implement your sales program. Many, many business plans fall apart in this area, particularly those prepared by individuals with a technical background who tend to be biased towards describing the attributes of the product rather than on the selling of it to customers in the real world. Remember the sales truism: *"Customers buy need satisfactions, not products."*

Get right down to the grassroots in your description of the sales program. How will you determine who your prospective customers are? Who specifically in your organization is going to do the selling? What will be his method of operation? What will be his sales quotas, if any? What are these quotas based on? What will be the size of initial customer orders? What will be the size of repeat orders and when do you expect these to occur? If you multiply the number of sales people times their monthly sales quotas, does that equal the monthly revenue figures in your financial forecasts? If not, why not? What is the commission structure for your sales people? How does this compare to the industry? When do the sales people receive their commissions? Have you made an allowance for warranty and returned goods? What is your warranty and refund policy? Who will bear the cost of returned merchandise? What evidence and corroborating data do you have to support all of your responses to the above questions?

G. PRODUCTION AND OPERATIONS

The prospective investor needs to be convinced that you can produce and deliver what you promise on time and on budget. Who will be responsible for this and how will it be achieved? What is the status of your current technology? Are you truly in the production stage, or is your product still in development? What proprietary elements do you have in your technology and how have you protected them? Does your present production capacity tie in to your projected revenue figures? If they don't, you have a problem!

What are the vulnerabilities of your product sourcing? What are the critical components? Are these single or multiple sourced? Do you have back-up sources? Are you vulnerable to many elements outside of your control, such as production delays due to inferior quality control, collective action or political instability? How much of your production is under your direct control and how much is subcontracted? Is that to your advantage or disadvantage? Why? These questions go to the very heart of your ability to survive as a start-up, small or emerging manufacturer.

The unfortunate demise recently of two very young and very promising Canadian high-technology manufacturing companies is sadly illustrative of this issue. Both of them failed because they depended 100% on Taiwanese suppliers to custom design and custom manufacture key components for their products. One was a new consumer electronic goods manufacturer in central Canada which had orders on their books for millions of dollars of their products. The other company was a Western Canadian manufacturer of specialty vehicles which had raised millions of dollars of development money from a wide number of investors and likewise had millions of dollars of orders on the books. Both failed because they had no alternate source of supply when their offshore suppliers let them down badly.

Young companies, typically thinly capitalized and dependent on sales from only one or two product lines, cannot afford to expose themselves to the caprice or ineptitude of single-source suppliers. They are especially vulnerable to the risks inherent in undertaking offshore manufacturing, especially when the business risk is compounded by significant cultural differences. What seems initially like a dream come true of promised savings in tooling and manufacturing costs, can turn out to be a real-life nightmare.

In the case of the consumer electronic goods manufacturer, their sales were so successful and so far exceeded original expectations, that the Taiwanese parts manufacturer demanded "a piece of the action." In fact, a very big piece of the action. When negotiations did not bring the Canadians to their knees, as was the plan, the offshore manufacturer completely cut off the supply of essential components and intentionally put the Canadian company out of business. A short time later, the Taiwanese began marketing the product under their own label in the USA.

With respect to the Western Canadian company, their entire product launch was aborted on two separate occasions because essential components custom manufactured in Taiwan proved fatally flawed. In the end, the company did not have the financial reserves to sustain the delays and their credibility had been irreparably damaged in the marketplace. In both cases, what had originally seemed a logical and businesslike move, going to a low-cost manufacturer in a low-cost country, proved fatal to corporate survival.

There are undoubtedly a number of lessons to be derived from the preceding accounts. However, for our purposes here with respect to your own vulnerability to suppliers, you can see the potentially fatal danger of relying on a single source of key components, particularly when they are offshore. When preparing your business plan, it is clear that there should be other considerations than just attempting to minimize costs. If you are a single-product company — and most start-up, small and emerging companies are — then reliability of supply and consistency of quality is even more important than finding the lowest cost supplier.

Describe your quality assurance (QA) and reliability programs. What are your QA standards and reliability objectives? How will these be satisfied? Who is responsible? Are you vulnerable to product-liability litigation? Describe your product liability defence planning? Do you have product-liability insurance? If not, why not?

H. MANAGEMENT TEAM AND CORPORATE ORGANIZATION

For many sophisticated investors, this is the only section of your business plan that really counts. Great management can take a failing company in a non-glamorous industry, turn it around and make it a star! The fundamental question is, does top management really know what it is doing and does it have a track record of having successfully done it before in this same industry?

To illustrate the significance of this, it is instructive to note that top management of both of the young Canadian manufacturing companies discussed above had no prior experience in small company manufacturing start-ups. Although they had successful backgrounds in sales, marketing and manufacturing with major corporations, the problems faced in a start-up with very limited resources and short time frames for critical decision-making are very different. If even one of the key members of each management team had a strong and successful background in new-product development and manufacturing in a small company start-up environment, it is highly possible that both companies would be healthy and thriving today, rather than being more sad statistics on the list of business obituaries.

For you, in preparing your business plan, your focus should be on the key players of your team. Ordinarily, a small company has no more than three key players and a large company no more than six. Even transnational companies with thousands of employees frequently have at their core no more than a half dozen truly *key* employees.

Your potential investors are extremely interested in the background, training, and relevant experience and success of your key players. These are the champions on whose shoulders the success of your company depends. In the main body of your business plan you can write up to four or five paragraphs on each of the key players describing how they contribute powerfully to the advancement of your business. In the appendix, you can then include a full resume on each of these people. It is compelling to see even more of the human being than normally is evident in a standard executive resume. For example, with respect to a Director of Sales and Marketing, it is useful to know that he has had a lifetime love and interest in selling, from a paper route as a child, to working as a sales clerk in a clothing store in high school, to working as a commission salesperson during summers between terms at university so that he could pay his own way through college. He then started his formal business career where he experienced growing responsibility and success in business directly relevant to his role in your company. You must convince the reader that the executive that he is reading about is, indeed, the right person for the role that he plays on your team! If you are not convinced, then you will not convince the reader.

You also need to look especially closely and objectively at yourself. Are you, in fact, the right person for the job that you have in your business? If not, can you replace yourself, or hire someone who has the credentials and delegate the responsibility to him?

It is an amazing fact, yet little known outside the venture capital industry, that many venture capital firms force the replacement of the chief executive officer in more than 75% of the companies in which they invest. This usually occurs within eighteen months of their initial investment! Thus, if you are the CEO of an investee company which is the recipient of funds from one of those venture capital companies, there is a 3:1 chance that you will be replaced within two years after the initial venture investment. This should either tell you that you need to be brutally honest with yourself about your own talents and abilities and be prepared to take whatever steps are necessary as a result of that ongoing assessment, or you should avoid professional venture capital companies, or both! The corporate coup d'état may well await the unfortunate chief executive officer of an investee company who does not deliver what he promises to a venture capital investor!

The compensation formula is also of very keen interest to financial backers. They like to see founders and other key players rewarded on the basis of performance. Income, bonuses and stock options all tied to profitability make investors smile and give them confidence, because they see that you are willing to put your money where your mouth is. If you produce what you promised, you will be rewarded. If you don't, you won't. Since the investors will be putting their own real money into your company now, as a result of your promises about earning projected money sometime in the future, such a compensation scheme seems eminently fair and reasonable to them.

I. FINANCIAL PLAN AND INFORMATION

For sophisticated sources of financing, second only in importance to the section on the management team is the section on your company's financial situation and plans for the future. In fact, for an established company, the financial section is actually a direct commentary on management because your numbers tell the bottom-line story of how management has actually performed to date. The numbers are nakedly barren of excuses, rationalizations and justifications. They also enable direct comparison between the performance of your company and other companies in the same industry, including your competitors. Industry ratios tell an investor what the average return on investment is for other companies in your industry; what the average net profit is as a percentage of gross revenue; what the average ratio of current assets is to current liabilities; and so on. Thus, your bottom line is of critical importance and interest to the prospective investor. It is of even more concern to a prospective banker. Historical figures provide objective evidence of your capacity to generate profits in order to retire a loan. We will be discussing ratios later on in this chapter as well as in Chapter Four.

For a start-up company, the cash flow projections and the cash flow break-even point are of paramount importance. Refer to Example 2 in Appendix A. Young companies live or die on their cash flow. In the Battle of Business Survival, this is mission control: radar, telemetry and altimeter all in one! Young companies produce not just monthly or weekly cash flow projections, but often daily ones, depending on how tight their circumstances are. Sophisticated investors know this. That is why they will take a very hard look at your projected expenditures and revenues, your performance to date, how long it will take you to reach break-even and, particularly, what hoops are you going to have to jump through in order to get there. What are the odds of your succeeding? Do we believe you? Convince us!

In your financial projections, everything flows from your assumptions. These should be explained and laid out in great detail. Sophisticated investors want to follow your total train of thought, all the way from forecast labour costs to monthly deliveries per product line. Do not stumble here. Your assumptions should be so carefully explained that even someone who knows nothing of your business can follow your logic and your numbers into the cash flow projections. You must be able to defend each and every one of your assumptions under questioning. If you are the person responsible for meeting with prospective investors, but did not prepare the projections, it is essential that you personally work through all the numbers yourself so that you understand how they originated and can explain them clearly. If you cannot do this, you will look like a fool and lose all credibility.

As a final recommendation, we strongly suggest that you do not attempt to set any terms in the business plan for the investment that you are seeking. In other words, do not try to establish the terms of the deal in advance. There are three reasons for this.

Firstly, the potential financier is either himself sophisticated in structuring financial transactions or has ready access to advisors who are. In the event that he wishes to proceed with an investment, he will then want to have a say in how the deal is to be structured. In fact, he may insist on dictating absolute terms if you are to receive his money. His own personal or business financial needs may be such that he will want you to create a form of tax-advantaged flow-through share, or a form of convertible debenture which will give him advantages of both debt and equity including a charge on your assets. If you attempt in advance to determine the terms and conditions of a proposed investment for a sophisticated investor, such as a venture capitalist, it is almost certain that you will not create the precise structure that he would want and therefore he will reject your proposal as inappropriate. You are beaten before you have even begun — ironically, not on the merits of your business itself, but because you jumped the gun on setting the terms of the investment.

Secondly, in the event that you decide to pursue more unsophisticated investors, you will very likely not know until some time after you have completed your business plan and have taken advice from financially sophisticated individuals exactly what the terms of your offering should be. This topic, including how to obtain expert advice on structuring your financing, is discussed further in the next chapter in section 3.5 under the title "When Is It Selling or Not?"

Thirdly, your business plan should never be used as, or construed as being, a legal offering document such as a prospectus or an offering memorandum. There is a large body of law dealing with this whole issue and the next chapter, entitled "Understanding the Law and Money-Raising in Canada", is devoted to this topic. Accordingly, it is highly recommended that you insert a *legal disclaimer* at the bottom of the cover page of your business plan or, alternatively, on its own as the first page immediately after the cover page, as follows:

FOR INFORMATION PURPOSES ONLY

THE INFORMATION CONTAINED IN THIS BUSINESS PLAN IS CONFIDENTIAL AND IS INTENDED ONLY FOR THE PERSONS TO WHOM IT IS TRANSMITTED BY THE COMPANY. THIS BUSINESS PLAN IS NOT AN OFFERING MEMORANDUM AND DOES NOT CONSTITUTE AN OFFER TO SELL OR SOLICITATION TO BUY ANY SECURITIES OF ANY KIND WHATSOEVER. WHILE THE INFORMATION SET FORTH HEREIN IS BELIEVED BY THE COMPANY TO BE RELIABLE, IT MUST BE RECOGNIZED THAT PREDICTIONS AND PROJECTIONS AS TO THE COMPANY'S FUTURE PERFORMANCE ARE NECESSARILY SUBJECT TO A HIGH DEGREE OF UNCERTAINTY AND NO WARRANTY OF SUCH PROJECTIONS IS EXPRESSED OR IMPLIED HEREBY.

J. APPENDIX (SUPPORTING DOCUMENTS)

This is the section to affix all of the useful supporting documentation which, if it had been inserted in the main body of the business plan, would have distracted the reader and interrupted the flow of the document's presentation. These documents include such items as:

1. Historical financial statements and corporate tax returns (see Example 3, "Balance Sheet" and Example 4, "Income Statement" in Appendix A).
2. Detailed biographies of the principals.
3. Intellectual property documentation, such as patents, copyrights and trade marks.
4. Marketing support materials, such as letters of intent from prospective customers, third-party testimonials, market studies and articles from trade journals.
5. Copies of additional documents relevant to the plan, such as licensing agreements, leases and other contracts

It may be that you are sufficiently concerned about trade secrets or industrial designs and that you want no circulation of the information whatsoever, yet you would be willing to show the material to a serious prospective investor under controlled circumstances. In that case, you could put the restricted material together under a separate cover and allow the financier to examine it in your presence, or alternatively, he could send his due diligence investigator to your office where he could examine it under the watchful eye of someone close to you.

Who Should Write the Business Plan?

Having now examined all of the elements of your plan, the $1,000,000 question (or greater if you are going for more money) is, "Who should write the business plan?" Would you be very surprised if we said, "You should?" You knew that all along! The correct answer is that each of the people who is responsible for executing the plan should be heavily involved in its creation. However, the plan is too important to be left entirely to amateurs. That is, amateurs in the art of creating excellent and effective business plans. You can start the process by setting up a draft document in the format which we have outlined above. Then set out to create and compile all of the documentation which you think that you will require in order to create a persuasive and winning plan.

When you have done all of the ground work, retain a consultant to produce a superb business plan working in partnership with you and your team. The consultant will ideally be expert in drawing out of you all of the elements required for an excellent plan and also in arranging and writing the document in a highly effective manner. However, you must not delegate the entire task to him. You are the expert in your business. In that regard, the consultant is the amateur. He should be the expert in compiling, writing and presenting your story. You should be just as careful in selecting the consultant to assist you in this project as you would be in selecting your family lawyer, doctor or accountant. As we have pointed out one or two times above, the business plan is an exceedingly important document for you and your business future. Your entire money-raising program can stand or fall on the quality of your business plan. The best approach to finding someone good is by referral from someone you know who was well satisfied with the services of such a consultant. Other good sources are your accountant or your lawyer. All of the major accounting firms have consulting divisions which assist clients in preparation of business plans. As with most professional services, fees and quality of work vary widely. Shop around.

Differentiating a Business Plan from a Loan Package, Financing Plan, Financial Proposal, Concept Paper or Mini-Business Plan

By now, you have a pretty clear idea of what a business plan is. There are, however, a number of similar documents that you may hear referred to in the course of business and you should understand what they are in the interest of avoiding confusion. The focus of our approach here, in our use of a business plan, is the raising of money. This is not to downplay the other important uses of a business plan as mentioned above; it is simply that this book is about raising money, mainly for start-up, small and emerging businesses. By their very nature, these kinds of businesses should mainly be seeking infusions of equity, not debt. The burden of regular interest payments and the risk of non-repayment of both principal and interest are fundamentally too onerous for small and emerging companies to take on significant debt to fund their early growth. Accordingly, we assume that a business plan is basically preparatory to raising equity.

However, in the event that a company is seeking what for it is significant bank financing, which means lending, it will normally be asked by the bank to provide documentation for a loan package. This consists of the particular selection of documentation that the bank in question requires of you. It may consist of an updated personal financial statement, a list of accounts receivable showing age of accounts, a search of the government companies office showing the presence or absence of liens registered against your company, and other related materials. As part of that documentation for the loan, you may be requested to provide a financing plan.

A financing plan is an abbreviated form of business plan which you put together to support your loan application. It emphasizes past performance over future potential. It emphasizes assets over cash flow. Bankers are interested in your current and near-term ability to make your interest payments and repay your debt to the bank. They look to your past performance as documented in your historical financial records to see what you have actually accomplished. This is in direct contrast to the risk-taking investor, who looks to future promise. That is the direct opposite of your banker's approach. He is exceedingly interested in your history. The other focus of a financial plan is to substantiate any assets that your business may have in order to provide collateral for your bank loan. Consequently, you will describe in detail your company's assets, their value, location and any current charges against them. As a result of that emphasis, you need only very short sections on production, marketing and personnel. Be sure to obtain specific guidelines from the bank which you are dealing with as to exactly what they want to see in your financing plan.

Another type of document with a similar name is the "financial proposal" or "concept paper." It is also occasionally referred to as a "mini-business plan." Regardless of which one of the three names is employed, it is mainly used when you are really pressed for time, have an important appointment with a potential investor, yet have not completed your full business plan. You produce a document with financial projections, yet they may not be as solid as you intend to develop later; perhaps they are lacking in certain details, and all the sections of the business plan are substantially abbreviated. The document is usually from ten to twenty pages in length. You should be very careful to point out in the document and also in person, that this is indeed a concept paper, a bare bones document, for the purpose of initiating discussion and that you intend to flesh it out shortly.

Money-Raising Points of Persuasion

Remember that for our purposes here, a business plan is a document with the ultimate purpose of persuasion. Reflect on our definition of a successful business plan:

A successful business plan is a document that is so well organized and so well written that it motivates and enables the prospective financier to make a positive decision in favour of putting money into your project without ever having met you!

In order that it may fulfil its purpose, there are a number of important items that should be adopted as fundamental principles in creating your business plan.

A. **Be impeccably honest throughout**. There is no greater tragedy in business life than the day that your investor comes to the realization that he has made his investment based on your misrepresentation, either innocent or intentional. He will never trust you again. He will never speak well of you again. Your relationship will be permanently impaired, if not altogether destroyed. It does not matter whether the investor was your own son or a complete stranger. No short-term gain is worth this price.

You must also have the courage of intellectual honesty as well. Do you, in your heart of hearts, truly believe your own projections? Your own assumptions? Have you researched them thoroughly, checking them against industry norms and discussing them with others who are experts in the industry? Many entrepreneurs, by their nature enthusiastic and optimistic, when emotionally captivated by a great opportunity are blind to facts which are quite contrary to the new vision which they have captured (or been captured by). Your vision must be impeccably rooted in the soil of thorough research, study and investigation.

A very worthwhile attitude of self-preservation to adopt when approaching a new deal, no matter if it looks like your opportunity of a lifetime, is to be prepared to walk away from any new business opportunity at any such time that the facts do not support the assumptions, or at the first sign of a lack of honesty amongst any of the participants in the project. Getting romanced by a deal is very similar to getting romanced by someone intimately. What you thought was love may turn out to have been a brief infatuation based on a little chemistry and not much else. Reputations can be damaged forever when that happens in business.

In addition, as you will learn in the next chapter, should you proceed with a formal money-raising program using either one of two legally required formal disclosure documents, a prospectus or an offering memorandum, your business plan will be the basic source of the information that needs to be generated for either one of those two lengthy documents. Of utmost significance is the reality that you will have a legal obligation to be scrupulously factual in those documents. In most instances, the law will deem that the investor relied upon the information provided by you in an offering memorandum or a prospectus. An omission to state a *material fact* is a misrepresentation and carries legal consequences. A material fact is one which, if it had been known by the investor, may have caused him to change his mind about proceeding with the investment. Does the financing source to whom you show the business plan deserve any less rigorous standard? Why would you not simply adopt that as your standard policy right from the start in your business plan? We recommend that you do so.

B. **Make your business plan highly readable and attractive**. Follow the guidelines noted throughout this chapter as to lay-out and appearance. Ensure that you use grammatically correct English written in non-technical layman's language. Definitely use a laser printer. A document prepared on a dot-matrix printer isn't even in the same galaxy in terms of projecting a professional appearance as a competing business plan prepared on a laser printer. Remember, your document should be so inviting that it seems to be shouting, "Read me, read me!"

C. **Sell the company, not the product or service**. As stated earlier, do not be meserized by the product or service that you are providing. Emphasize the ability and successful experience of all the key players on your team. You are selling many things besides a product, including service, effectiveness, consistency, integrity and all the other attributes of a successful business.

D. **Identify, explain and be reasonable in all of your financial assumptions**. Explain how your assumptions were derived. Provide back-up for them wherever possible. Do your research. Be thorough. Do not be unrealistically optimistic. There's nothing more exciting to a venture capitalist than doing his due diligence research, reviewing your calculations and projections, when, to his great dismay, he finds your projections too conservative and concludes that you will do much better than you predicted! He has discovered that rare and wondrous beast: the honest and reasonable money-raiser! Remember that sophisticated investors know how to use standard industry ratios to compare the actual results of companies operating in your industry with your projections to see if you are in the world of reality. Industry ratios are published by Dun and Bradstreet, Robert Morris Associates, Financial Research Associates and others, and are available for you to examine in most major city and university libraries.

E. **Forecast wonderful profitability**. Despite the fact that you are reasonable, factual and honest, your business must show tremendous profit potential. If your company is a start-up or early-stage business, to warrant attention as a private investment, your business plan should predict a compound return on investment of 30% to 40% or better over the next five years. Certainly nothing less than 25% at the very worst. Remember some things about sophisticated investors. Firstly, practically all business plans crossing their desks will have projections in that magnitude, so yours will appear not even worth reading if it is not in the same league. Secondly, the experience of many professional venture capital companies is that a surprisingly high 80% or more of all of their venture capital investments either fail outright or simply muddle along showing little or no profits! Therefore, the remaining 20% or less needs to show magnificent yields in order that on the totality of their investments the venture capitalists can show an overall profit. Can your projections support being in the winning 20% of investee businesses? Thirdly, the financier will often cut your revenue projections in half and multiply your costs by two as an opening gambit because, as a famous Dean of the Harvard Business School used to pontificate to his first year MBA students, "You will soon learn two fundamental principles of existence. First, life is not fair. And second, all business plans are wrong!" Therefore, to get and keep the attention of the potential investor, you and your business plan must have the look, the feel and the sense of a real financial winner!

F. **Demonstrate market demand for your product or service**. Orders in hand, preferably with deposits, are very persuasive to potential investors. They are compelling evidence that you actually have the basis of a real business! They prove that there truly is a market for what you have to offer and that you have been successful in accessing that market. Do you have letters of commitment or purchase orders? Can you get third-party testimonials from people who are active in your business stating that they would buy your product or service if it were available? This sort of documentation goes a long way in assuring the potential investor that there is a real business at hand. This type of evidence should be visible and available. It can usefully be included in the appendix to your business plan.

In summary, your mission is to persuade. Your weapons are impeccability, honesty, integrity, a highly readable and attractive business plan, a great management team and a superior business opportunity with proven market demand.

Money-Raising Points to Avoid

As opposed to the items in the previous section, there are a number of matters that you should most emphatically not do in the preparation of an effective and winning business plan. We have discussed a number of them in the body of this chapter. However, we particularly caution you to beware of the following four elements:

A. **Do not set the terms of the sought-for financing in the business plan**. Allow the terms to emerge through the process of negotiation with the proposed financial sources. You should only state the amount of money that you are seeking. The cash flow projections will indicate a company with the potential to generate a great deal of cash over the next five years. Allow the creativity and needs of the investor to be expressed and to influence the ultimate structure of your financing. Let the proposed investor make a specific proposal to you rather than you attempting to guess what would work for him. See our comments above under section 2.2(I) "Financial Plan and Information."

B. **Do not pursue more than one, or at the most two, lines of business in the beginning**. You must demonstrate to potential investors that you have a clear focus on a particular market niche and are going full-out to capture a segment of that specific market. For example, if you decide to set up your own software development company, you would not be very credible if you stated that no project is beyond you, from the mainframe computer software used by global media corporations to control unmanned communications satellites to the new generation of small business applications which will be required for RISC-based computers to be produced by the IBM-Apple joint venture. In fact, probably no software company is equipped to do that! Experienced business people know that success in business does not usually come easy. It takes concentration and real effort directed at a specific target market, especially in the early stages of an enterprise. Do not spread and diffuse your efforts and energy. You will lose credibility if you show a plan to enter several markets or lines of business at once. In the military, the principle of "concentration of force" is known to be fundamental to success. On the other side, enemies have attempted to "divide and conquer" their opposing forces since the dawn of history. Do not be your own worst enemy.

C. Do not use unsupported growth projections. All sophisticated investors will be highly sceptical of your projections. The only way to make believers of them is to be able to document, demonstrate and verify your forecasts. We have discussed this fully above under the heading "Marketing and Sales," particularly warning you against the market share assumption error.

D. Do not ignore the risk factors inherent in your business. You know there are risks and we know there are risks. Not surprisingly, so do your potential investors. Most days, the financial sections of large daily newspapers look like financial obituaries. Therefore, deal with the risks of your business in an upfront manner in your business plan. It is to your advantage to take the offensive by identifying the areas of risk as you see them and then prescribe your own solutions. Do not put yourself in a position of being on the defensive and forcing the potential investor to have to confront you with his concerns. You look more credible and gain in stature by openly acknowledging the risks and then showing how you have them under control. Facing and overcoming risk is what entrepreneurs get paid for!

There are two effective ways of identifying and dealing with the issues of risk. The first way is to deal with risk under each topical area of your business plan. In that way, you would handle the marketing risks under the marketing section, the production risks under the production section, and so on. Alternatively, you could simply create a separate section with its own heading, "Risk Factors," and list all of the most significant risk factors. The latter method is the approach used in prospectuses and offering memoranda and is familiar to most investors. By reviewing a few prospectuses of public companies, readily obtainable from any stockbroker, you will quickly see how the issue of risk factors is dealt with in those documents. Particularly useful for you in this regard would be prospectuses from the initial public offering of young, technology-based companies. They are all exposed to significant risk factors.

A final advantage of including full disclosure of the risk factors in your business plan is that it will give you at least some comfort if your business subsequently fails after you have put a financing deal together without a prospectus or offering memorandum. You will at least know that the investor came in with his eyes open and there were no surprises that he had not been apprised of from the beginning. While your business reputation may suffer, your reputation for honesty and integrity would not. That, in itself, is worth a very great deal. Furthermore, it would enable you to start over again!

2.3 CONCLUSION

Understanding the concepts and strategies outlined in this chapter is essential to obtaining business financing for most businesses. Your business plan is one of the key weapons in your arsenal to win financing and build a business. Used effectively, this document will help carry you to victory. Well researched, well prepared and well utilized, it will greatly support you in winning the battle for funding. The forces against you are many: other entrepreneurs scrambling for the same prize — the investor's dollar; the investor's scepticism and defensiveness which must be overcome; a general economic climate of uncertainty and wariness that might be present at the time; and, in many cases, your own lack of confidence and lack of experience. However, take heart; thousands upon thousands of other entrepreneurs have defeated similar forces in the past and continue to do so today. So can you! The key to advancing effectively in the intense competition for financing is to progress in a methodical manner, one stage at a time, pursuant to *The Plan*. Your business battle plan!

CHAPTER THREE

UNDERSTANDING THE LAW AND MONEY-RAISING IN CANADA

The energy and ambition of the money-raising entrepreneur must be contained within the boundaries of the law. To do otherwise turns the businessperson into an outlaw.

B.F. Nattrass

3.1 INTRODUCTION

The money-raising entrepreneur functions within two principal contexts: that of the market and that of the law. The enthusiasm and energy of the entrepreneur as directed at the challenge of financing his business enterprise in Canada must be channelled into activity permitted by the laws of each of the provinces in which he seeks to raise money.

The law cannot guarantee to an investor the success of any investment, and that is not its purpose. It basically seeks to ensure that the potential investor has disclosed to him a certain *standard of information* concerning the business and financial affairs of the enterprise for which his investment is being solicited in order that he can make an *informed investment decision*. In addition, the law requires that selling be undertaken only by registered personnel who are subject to a special disciplinary regime.

The required investment information is contained within a detailed disclosure document called a "prospectus," the purpose of which is to provide to the prospective investor "full, true and plain disclosure" of all information material to his investment. The investment information is to be provided by a salesperson who is "registered" to sell securities in the province in which the securities are sold. The law provides an exemption from the prospectus disclosure requirements for certain specified categories of persons who are deemed not to require a prospectus and also for certain specified kinds of transactions. The law also provides an exemption from the provincial registration requirements for salespersons in the case of certain special categories of persons who have a special relationship to the enterprise in which the money is to be invested. In order to keep the money-raising entrepreneur's costs to a minimum and also to move ahead at the greatest possible speed with money-raising activities, it is necessary to understand what the various categories of exemption to the prospectus and registration requirement are and how to qualify for them.

Lawyers sometimes refer to the "delicate balance" in public policy which exists between the need for investor protection on the one hand and the need for efficient access to capital in the marketplace on the other. Maintaining this balance is an important issue of government policy right across Canada. Some businesspeople would argue that this delicate balance has already been upset by the law becoming over-regulated in the interests of protecting the investor and now represents a serious impediment to the efficient raising of the capital so vital to generating new business activity in Canada. Conversely, other serious-minded people would argue that the pendulum has swung too far in the opposite direction, with the result that Canadian investors are inadequately protected from irresponsible and even un-scrupulous promoters.

3.2 THE LAW AND MONEY-RAISING

The law pertaining to the activities of money-raising for business entities is generally referred to as "securities law," and the form of legal instrument exchanged for the investor's money is a "security," such as a common share, a preferred share or a corporate bond. The word "issuer" refers to the company, or other entity such as a partnership or syndicate, which "issues" securities in order to raise money for itself. The Glossary at the back of this book contains definitions of some of the securities and other financial terminology found in the text.

It is absolutely mandatory that the money-raising entrepreneur understands a few basic principles of securities law. Otherwise, he may find himself, at best, expending significant time and money after the fact anxiously attempting to correct legal oversights or errors made by him in the process of fund raising, or at worst, facing the wrong end of a civil law suit, or a quasi-criminal or criminal prosecution under securities legislation.

Entrepreneurs often make the serious mistake of assuming that since they do not have a "public company," or since they are "only selling a few shares," they do not need to comply with any particular securities law requirements. Nothing could be further from the truth! It is the self-policing nature of securities law in Canada which contributes to this frequent misapprehension of the business-person. Our system of separate provincial securities laws, and the consequences of failure to comply with their individual requirements, is somewhat analogous to our Canadian system of income tax law and its filing requirements, where the responsibility is on the individual taxpayer to police himself and prepare and file his income tax return as required by law. In other words, it is not the government's responsibility, *it is your responsibility* to ensure that you comply with both the provisions of the Income Tax Act as a money-earner and the provincial securities laws as a money-raiser. Just as a plea of personal ignorance is not going to assist the errant taxpayer who has failed to file his income tax return, neither is ignorance of the securities law requirements in any particular province going to assist the money-raising entrepreneur. In fact, the exact opposite is true. Ignorance of the prevailing provincial securities law can lead to very serious legal and financial problems for the money-raiser, including being required to return money to investors which might otherwise have been kept by the money-raiser if he had complied with the law.

The purpose of this material is simply to introduce you to some significant legal concepts of vital concern to anyone raising money for business in Canada and to alert you to the self-policing nature of this important area of the law. The concepts discussed here are a gross oversimplification of a very complex body of law that is often difficult to interpret precisely. Securities law in Canada is a matter of provincial jurisdiction and the law varies from province to province in many important respects. This material is definitely not a substitute for current advice from a lawyer competent in matters of securities law.

As a money-raiser, you need to be able to satisfy yourself that you have the answers to several critical questions, including the following:

1. How many investors can I get to put money into my company?
2. To whom can I sell the securities?
3. How much money can I raise?
4. Is there any minimum amount that I am required to raise?
5. When can my company use the investment money that it receives?
6. What kind of documents do I need for:
    a. prospective investors, and
    b. actual investors?
7. Do I need to provide a prospectus or an offering memorandum? What is the difference between those two documents?
8. What is supposed to go into such offering documents such as an offering memorandum or a subscription form?
9. Can the investor sell his shares whenever and to whomever he wants?
10. What government agency, if any, needs to be advised of the sale of shares in my company?

A very significant issue with serious consequences is at what point in organizing your money-raising campaign do your actions begin to have legal significance for you. You are strongly advised to consult with a lawyer well-versed in Canadian securities law at such time as you are ready to begin planning your money raising campaign. See the "Money-Rai$ing Master Checklist" in Appendix B. We recommend strongly that you consult with a securities lawyer at a point no later than when you reach item "D" on the Checklist.

3.3 TWO CANADIAN LEGAL REQUIREMENTS: PROSPECTUS AND REGISTRATION

The first general principle that needs to be understood by everyone raising money for business in Canada is this:

Every sale by an issuer of its own securities, and every sale by a controlling person of his securities of the issuer, will require a prospectus unless a specific *statutory exemption is available or an exemption ruling is obtained from the relevant provincial securities regulator.*[*]

This clearly states that it is only in exceptional cases that a prospectus is not required. In other words, *a prospectus is always required* unless the transaction falls within one of the stated categories of exemption provided under the relevant provincial securities law or, alternatively, unless an exemption is expressly granted to the issuer by the relevant provincial securities regulator. One of the main purposes of the exemptions is to permit an entrepreneur to raise funds for a venture without incurring the costs and delays that are encountered when using a prospectus. The material in this book deals primarily with those exemptions.

The second general principle that needs to be understood is this:

Every person selling the securities of an issuer must be registered with the securities regulator in the province in which the securities are sold unless a specific statutory exemption is available or an exemption ruling is obtained from the relevant provincial securities regulator.

This clearly states that it is only in exceptional cases that a provincially registered salesperson is not required when securities are being sold. In other words, *a registered salesperson is always required* unless the seller falls within one of the stated categories of exemption provided under the relevant provincial securities law or, alternatively, unless an exemption is expressly granted to the issuer by the relevant provincial securities regulator.

3.4 EXEMPTIONS FROM THE PROSPECTUS REQUIREMENT, OR "WHO CAN BUY THE SHARES OF MY COMPANY?"

The prospectus standard of "full, true and plain" disclosure of all information material to a proposed investment originally developed for offerings of securities to the public and sets a very high standard of information in order to provide a certain level of protection to the investing public. This standard has been reduced, and in some instances eliminated, for a type of money-raising activity known as a "private placement." This term generally refers to an offering of securities tightly aimed at a small target of prospective investors as permitted by specific exemptions to the prospectus requirements in each province. The actual words "private" and "placement" by their very nature contrast sharply with "public" and "offering." To "place" something implies a specific location or destination, as contrasted to the much broader term "offer." "Private," of course, is the very opposite of "public" and implies something personal, confidential and not affecting the community. Thus, the term "private placement" accurately reflects the nature of the intention underlying exemptions to the prospectus requirement. By reason of their relation-

---

[*]Except in Quebec, where there is no requirement that a control person file a prospectus before he sells his securities.

ship to the issuer or their own wealth or sophistication, certain categories of investor are deemed not to require the protection offered by a prospectus.

The private placement exemptions permit money to be raised through the sale of an issuer's securities, such as shares in a company, without a prospectus in very precisely defined circumstances as specifically permitted by the law of each province. The law varies significantly from province to province, so the following descriptions are very general and must not be relied upon in any particular instance of money-raising. It is important to note that an issuer who is in breach of securities law requirements (such as the filing of required reports of certain trades) may be precluded from relying on the exemptions which are otherwise generally available, and may, as a result, commit further significant breaches of securities law requirements. Legal advice should always be sought at the beginning of any money-raising program as to the current state of the law in your province and the most effective legal means for you to achieve your objectives.

The "Seed Capital" Exemption

This exemption from the prospectus requirement is one of the most useful and frequently utilized by entrepreneurs in the course of funding their enterprise, and is currently available in the provinces of Alberta, Saskatchewan, Ontario, Nova Scotia and Quebec. "Seed capital" refers to start-up capital. It is to the process of raising the initial money for an enterprise that this exemption is addressed. An issuer is allowed to engage in a limited sales of its securities in order to obtain the seed capital that it requires to get started.

The key elements of the seed capital exemption, with the requirements within each province where it is available varying somewhat, are as follows:

A. Each purchaser must "purchase as principal" the securities he acquires, meaning that he is not acting as an agent for someone else.

B. Each purchaser must be a "sophisticated purchaser" as defined by the securities regulations. This means that each investor must by virtue of net worth and investment experience, or by virtue of consultation with or advice from a registered securities dealer, be able to evaluate the prospective investment on the basis of information respecting the investment presented by the issuer. If the investor is a director or senior officer of the issuer, or a parent, spouse, child, sister or brother of a senior officer or director, then the "sophistication" requirements may not have to be met.

C. Each purchaser must be given, depending on the province, either an offering memorandum that complies with the securities regulations, or access to substantially the same information that a prospectus would provide, prior to entering into an agreement to purchase the securities.

D. All purchases must be completed within a fixed time period (usually six months) from the date of the first purchase of the issuer's securities.

E. The total number of investors permitted under this exemption varies from twenty-five to fifty people, depending on the province, and there is a limit in some provinces to the number of people who can be approached or "solicited" to purchase the securities.

F. In some provinces, no selling or promotional expenses may be paid or incurred except for professional services or for services performed by a registered dealer.

There is a significant difference between Alberta and the other provinces with respect to the availability of this exemption. The seed capital exemption may be used again and again by the same issuer in Alberta in successive rounds of financing provided that twelve months has elapsed since one distribution has been completed before the next one commences. It is much more restricted in Ontario and Quebec where the seed capital exemption may only be utilized once by any issuer.

The "Private Company" Exemption

The private company exemption is available in several provinces and is also one of the most frequently utilized. In fact, the average person causing a company to be incorporated often is not aware that he is using this exemption as it includes within its scope the kind of corporation known to most people: the closely-held, family company. A "private company" is defined in most provincial statutes as one whose incorporation documentation limits the number of shareholders to a specified maximum (varying provincially from a low of five people in Quebec to a high of fifty people in some other provinces), restricts the transferability of its securities and prohibits any "invitation to the public" to purchase its securities. To qualify for this exemption in the provinces where it is available is very simple: the issuer must be a private company and the securities must not be offered for sale to the public.

However, to determine who is a member of the "public" is not as easy as one would prefer. There is not a precise line clearly separating "public" investors from "private" investors with respect to any particular issuer. Two key issues considered by the courts in Canada in determining who is a member of the public are as follows:

A. Does the prospective purchaser *need to know* the information that would otherwise be provided in a prospectus in order to make an informed investment decision? (This is in contrast to someone who is already so close to the issuer or one of its promoters that he already has access to this information or can easily obtain it.)

B. Are there *common bonds* of interest or association between the prospective purchasers and the issuer or its promoters so that the purchasers have easy access to all of the information that would otherwise be provided by a prospectus?

In order for you to have some sense of the approach of the courts in determining whether or not shares have been offered to the public, we will examine briefly an important Canadian case on the subject, *R. v. Piepgrass*, a decision of the Alberta Court of Appeal on a prosecution under the old Alberta Securities Act. The accused person was being prosecuted for trading in securities to the public without being registered as an investment dealer. The accused relied upon the private company exemption in his defence. Only five people purchased shares in the company. Of those, only one had no previous business dealings with the accused, and the other four had purchased shares in another company from him. In rendering his judgement, Mr. Justice Macdonald stated:

> It is one thing for an individual or group of individuals to disclose information to friends or associates, seeking support for a private company being formed or in existence, pointing out its attractions for investment or speculation as the case may be, but it is quite another thing for a private company to go out on the highways and byways seeking to sell securities of the company and particularly by high pressure methods, that is by breaking down the sales resistance of potential purchasers and inducing them to purchase . . . [The investors] were not in any sense friends or associates of the accused, or persons having common bonds of interest or association.

It is also instructive to note that in the *Piepgrass* case, only five persons actually purchased shares in the issuer company. It is apparent, then, that it is not just a question of the number of persons who purchase securities of the issuer, but in addition it is *their relationship to the issuer* which is so critical in the eyes of the law.

Unless you are very confident about your relationship and that of your fellow promoters to prospective purchasers of securities in your enterprise, including your *common bonds* to the purchasers, and also that you have satisfied each purchaser's *need to know* sufficient information about the issuer in order to make an informed investment decision, then you would be wise to consult with legal counsel as to whether the private company exemption would actually apply to any particular person.

The "Wealthy Purchaser" Exemption

This exemption is available to those investors who purchase the securities as principal (rather than acting as agent for someone else), and who purchase at least a specified minimum amount which varies across the country depending on each province's regulations. The minimum cost of the investment must currently be at least $97,000 in most provinces and $150,000 in Saskatchewan, Ontario and Quebec. There have been discussions amongst securities regulators in several provinces with respect to significantly raising the minimum purchase amount necessary to qualify for this exemption, possibly to as high as $250,000, but so far no change in the law has occurred. The rationale behind this exemption to the prospectus requirement is that by virtue of the size of their investment, the purchasers in this category have sufficient financial clout to be able to obtain whatever business and financial information they require before making their investment decision.

"Pooling" the Investors' Funds

A frequently asked question is whether two or more prospective investors could join together and pool their money in some manner, such as a partnership or syndicate, in order to meet the mandatory minimum investment amount under the various provincial regulations. Provincial securities regulators have taken the view that unincorporated entities, such as partnerships or syndicates, do not qualify for the exemptions when their sole purpose is to facilitate two or more people pooling their money for the purpose of qualifying for the exemption. It may still be open for prospective investors in some provinces to join together and create a new corporation with the intention of utilizing the "wealthy investor" exemption to invest in another company. This manoeuvre has been expressly disallowed in certain provinces but may remain available in others. Current legal advice is required before undertaking this procedure.

On the other hand, it is quite acceptable for a number of individuals to pool their money in an unincorporated entity, such as a partnership or syndicate, to invest together in an issuer under this exemption and to appoint one of their group to administer their investment and to take actions on behalf of the group, provided that each of the investors on his own has contributed the required minimum statutory amount. In other words, each member of the syndicate must have contributed at least $97,000 or whatever is the full exemption amount required in that province. Where an unincorporated entity is utilized to make an investment under this section, the securities regulator will require that a special certificate be filed by the issuer indicating that it has exercised reasonable diligence in its enquiries and is of the belief that each member of the group has contributed the $97,000 or other amount required under the exemption.

There are various reasons, including privacy, why someone may not want to appear as a shareholder in a corporation in which he has invested money. In that case, it is common for the shares to be held in the name of another person and to utilize a document called a "Share Declaration of Trust." In that document, the person who becomes the registered holder of the securities is the "Trustee" and the person advancing the funds and for whom the shares are held is the "Beneficiary."

Other Statutory Exemptions

In addition to the three commonly used exemptions described above, there are a number of other statutory exemptions available in specific circumstances which vary from province to province. One such exemption is known as the "institutional investor" exemption. This exempts financial institutions such as banks, trust companies, insurance companies and other regulated institutions. It is relatively easy to ascertain from the securities regulator or from official lists distributed by the provincial and federal governments which particular institutions qualify under this exemption in any one province. Another prospectus exemption has been created in several provinces for a category known as "exempt purchasers." The provincial securities regulator grants this status to applicants who can satisfy the following three requirements: investment expertise, a pooling of contributions from a large number of people, and a substantial amount of assets being administered. The type of investor that typically meets this criteria is a large, sophisticated fund such as a mutual fund or a pension fund. The exemption is not restricted to those kinds of organizations though, and there is some latitude for the securities regulators to recognize other sophisticated organizations as exempt purchasers for the purpose of completing a fund-raising program.

Although there are other exemptions, the final one which we will bring to your attention is the "government incentive securities" exemption, more commonly known as a "tax shelter." Examples of investments which have been included in this exemption include oil, gas or mineral resource exploration or development program; statutory small business development corporations (SBDCs) in Ontario and their other provincial counterparts such as the small business venture capital corporations (VCCs) in British Columbia; motion picture and videotape productions; and scientific research program. The kinds of investment program which qualify for the "tax shelter" exemption are in continual flux as amendments are made to the Income Tax Act of Canada and to provincial legislation. Current legal and tax advice will be necessary in order for you to determine whether it is possible to structure such a program for your particular project.

There are a number of other exemptions which can be utilized in certain specific circumstances. These are particularized in the securities legislation of each province. In addition, the specific facts of any particular money-raising program may justify an application for a discretionary ruling from the provincial securities regulator which would allow the financing to proceed without a prospectus and without falling within one of the specified categories of exempt transactions as discussed above.

The Discretionary Ruling

The provincial securities regulators have a certain discretionary authority, varying from province to province, to grant a ruling unique to the facts of each case such that a particular issue of securities is exempt from either the prospectus or registration requirements. In order to grant such a request, the regulator must satisfy himself that it would not be prejudicial to the public interest to grant the discretionary ruling. In those provinces where there is a very limited range within which the regulators can exercise any authority respecting discretionary exemptions, the regulators regularly issue "no action" or "comfort" letters confirming that the regulator will take no action to prevent the proposed transaction from taking place.

How Many Investors?

An extremely important consideration for anyone raising money for a project is how many investors are permitted by law to invest in the enterprise. By determining the amount of your financing needs, for example $500,000, and dividing that by the number of allowable investors, for example 40 persons, you will arrive at the average amount that you will have to target to raise from each individual investor. In this example, the average amount per investor must be $500,000 ÷ 40 persons = $12,500 per person.

In the example shown, you would then know in advance that you would be extremely unwise to sell 36 people investments of $1,000 each, because that would leave $464,000 to be divided among the four allowable investors remaining to you under the exemptions. That would mean that you would need to receive an average of $116,000 from each of the remaining four investors in order to raise the $500,000 that you require. Is that realistic for you?

"Stacking" the Prospectus Exemptions

The method of determining how many investors you can obtain for your project is to ascertain which of the exemptions from the prospectus requirements in your province apply to your project. See Item F on the "Money-Rai$ing Master Checklist." You are permitted to utilize all of the exemptions available to you and to add together all of the exempt purchasers in each category in order to reach the grand total of allowable investors. This process of combining categories of exemptions is called "stacking." Money-raising entrepreneurs regularly stack the exemptions, not only to maximize the total number of investors who can purchase securities in their enterprise, but also to maximize both their flexibility and their financing options. However, it should be noted that the stacking rules are complex, especially when used in more than one province. Armed with the knowledge that stacking may be possible in your particular circumstances, you should obtain current legal advice from an experienced securities lawyer in your province to confirm which exemptions are available to you.

An example of stacking exemptions for a financing, in this case in Alberta, is shown as follows:

Category of Exemption	Solicitations Permitted	Investors Permitted
1. Seed capital	Not Applicable	50
2. Close friends, relatives, business associates, etc.	Not Applicable	50
3. Over $97,000	Not Applicable	Unlimited
	TOTAL	<u>100+</u>

The result in the example shown above is that there can be 100 investors in total in the first two exemption categories plus an unlimited number of $97,000 investors. In addition, the issuer could also request a discretionary ruling from the provincial securities regulator to allow certain other sales if there were special circumstances to be pleaded.

3.5 EXEMPTIONS FROM THE REGISTRATION REQUIREMENT, OR "WHO CAN PROMOTE THE SHARES OF MY COMPANY?"

As stated above, every person selling the securities of an issuer must be "registered" with the securities regulator in the province in which the securities are sold unless a specific statutory exemption is available or an exemption ruling is obtained from the relevant provincial securities regulator.

The purpose of the requirement for registration of everyone who sells the securities of an issuer is to ensure that there exists in the marketplace some basic standard of proficiency and competence in respect of trading in securities. This typically applies to a person working as a registered dealer (stockbroker) with one of Canada's several firms of investment dealers. In addition, exemptions from the registration requirement have been created so as not to unduly encumber the entrepreneur raising money for his own enterprise by way of private placement. The registration exemptions have very specific conditions and must be strictly observed.

The two key issues on this topic that confront anyone raising money for a project are:

A. Who can sell the securities of the issuer?

B. When does the "selling" of the securities actually occur?
(Can it be distinguished from incidental presale conduct?)

As a practical matter, it is extremely important that you establish a system to monitor and record your contacts with prospective purchasers. These issues will be discussed below.

Who Can Sell the Securities?

Under most provincial securities regulations, directors, senior officers and promoters of the issuer can raise money for the issuer by selling its securities. They are not allowed to charge a fee for this service. It is a question of fact whether a person was a director, senior officer or promoter of the issuer at the time when that person was engaged in selling its securities. That is one of the many practical reasons why companies and other issuers should maintain accurate and current corporate records, such as minutes of directors' meetings and changes in the ranks of the company's senior officers and directors. Proper corporate records will be of great assistance in providing evidence of who in fact was a director, senior officer or promoter at any particular point in time should that ever become a contentious legal issue for the company.

As stated above, registered securities dealers can sell the securities of an issuer at any time.

When Is It "Selling" or Not?

The issue of when the securities are actually sold is a critical one because so many legal ramifications flow from the act of selling the securities. Incidental presale conduct by an issuer is not considered to have legal significance. For example, it is normal for the senior officers, directors and promoters of an issuer to initially research the market to ascertain what kind of securities, on what terms and in what quantities would be saleable in the current market. Thus, preliminary discussions with potential investors, *prior to the fixing of the terms of the deal*, would likely escape any legal consequences.

However, once the issue has proceeded beyond the planning and formulation stage, to the stage when the directors have made the decision to really go ahead with a financing and know what the terms of the securities will be, any actions "in furtherance" of a sale would have legal significance. At that stage, even if the prospective purchaser did not buy any securities, he would be considered to have been "solicited" by the issuer. In those provinces where there is a limit on the number of solicitations allowed under each exemption, such as with the seed capital exemption in Ontario where an issuer is allowed only fifty solicitations and twenty-five actual purchasers, that one contact would count as one solicitation out of the fifty permitted.

Monitoring Your Contacts with Prospective Purchasers

It is very important and relatively simple to pay close attention to, and keep a record of, the issuer's contacts with prospective purchasers for the reasons discussed above. Included in Appendix B is a sample "Prospective Investor List" which is a model of the type of form that you could use to monitor contacts with prospective investors. When the individuals become actual purchasers of securities of the issuer, you will need to ensure that they have received various documentation. We refer you to an additional form in Appendix B, the "Shareholder List," which will allow you to easily monitor the status of your contacts with your investors. You can only be sure that you are in compliance with your province's legal requirements, and those of any other province in which you are raising money, by summarizing in an organized manner the nature of all of the issuer's contacts with prospective and actual investors.

We strongly recommend that you prepare summary documents along the lines of what we have suggested and that you appoint one person associated with the issuer to be clearly responsible for keeping the summaries both current and accurate. It's not difficult, *it just has to be done*.

Investment Dealers

We highly recommend that at the outset of any money-raising program, not later than Item B on our "Money-Rai$ing Master Checklist," you have a discussion with at least three different registered securities dealers about your proposed project, obtaining their individual views on the type of securities currently most saleable in the marketplace and how each of them may be able to assist you. We have found that registered dealers can be helpful in several ways, some of which include:

A. They can sell your securities for you. These are the people who are "registered" as required by law and are therefore allowed to solicit investors without relying on exemptions. The policies of some investment dealers will not permit their registered representatives to sell your securities for you unless the issuer and the size and nature of the issue meet specific criteria and have been approved by a more or less formal procedure within the particular firm of investment dealers. However, they may be able to assist in alternative ways.

B. They can act as financial "middlemen." Stockbrokers, by the nature of their business, have clients with money and they know of many other people and businesses in the community with money. Your business may represent a real opportunity for someone with funds to invest. A stockbroker may be able to make the connection and even help you to negotiate the transaction.

C. They may be able to act as "financial architect" for your deal. As they should be familiar with current trends in the financial marketplace, brokers can often be very helpful in suggesting the most appropriate structure for your financing and the type and terms of the securities. See discussion to follow in Chapter Four: "Structuring Your Deal."

D. They may be able to help you develop a long-term financial strategy for your business. As we have emphasized, money-raising for a business is an ongoing process and a registered dealer may be able to assist you in seeing the current financing as a step on the ongoing road of your long-term needs. It is important that the issuer's capital structure be flexible enough so that your current financing does not cause difficulties for subsequent rounds of financing which may be required at a later date.

3.6 RESTRICTIONS ON RESALE OF THE SECURITIES

It is extremely important to know that the legal right of your investor to resell the securities that he has bought in your enterprise is restricted, and in the provinces of Alberta, Saskatchewan, Ontario, Nova Scotia and Quebec is severely restricted. Your purchaser cannot simply turn around and immediately offer the securities to anyone in order to divest himself of his investment in your project. The intent of the regulatory policy on this issue might be summarised by saying, "that which cannot be done directly (i.e., issue shares to the public without a prospectus) is not to be done indirectly (i.e., through an immediate resale by an exemption purchaser of the same securities to a third party)."

The right of resale may also be restricted (independently of any securities laws) by the charter documents of the issuer. A typical restriction is that no transfers are permitted without the approval of the board of directors, which may be granted or withheld at the board's discretion. The existence of a restriction of this type (if applicable) must be disclosed to a purchaser.

Alberta, Saskatchewan, Ontario, Nova Scotia and Quebec

An investor in securities of an issuer pursuant to a private placement exemption cannot resell those same securities without also either relying on one of the categories of exemption as discussed above, or actually preparing, filing and having a prospectus accepted, unless all of the following three requirements are satisfied:

A. The enterprise which originally issued the securities must become a "reporting issuer." A reporting issuer is an issuer who either voluntarily agrees, or is required, to comply with the regular and extensive public financial and other financial disclosure obligations as specified by law. The reporting requirements of a reporting company are intended to provide potential investors with sufficient information to make an informed investment decision. The exact requirements to become and remain a reporting issuer are prescribed in the statutes of each of the provinces which utilize that concept.

B. "No unusual effort" can be made in Alberta, Saskatchewan, Ontario or Nova Scotia to prepare the market or create a demand for the securities which are being sold, and in Quebec "no effort" can be made.

C. The "hold period" which exists with respect to the securities in each of the five provinces must have been satisfied. The proposed reseller of securities in Alberta, Saskatchewan, Ontario or Nova Scotia must have held the securities for set periods ranging from six, twelve or eighteen months from the date that the securities were purchased or, alternatively, from the date when the issuer became a reporting issuer, whichever is later. The proposed reseller of securities in Quebec must have held the securities for either six or twelve months from the date of their original transfer. The foregoing principles are stated in a very general manner and you are advised to obtain current legal advice with respect to the hold period in any specific situation.

British Columbia, Manitoba, New Brunswick, Prince Edward Island and Newfoundland

An investor in securities of an issuer pursuant to a private placement exemption outside the provinces of Alberta, Saskatchewan, Ontario, Nova Scotia and Quebec is much less restricted in reselling his securities. The basic restriction in the other five provinces — British Columbia, Manitoba, New Brunswick, Prince Edward Island and Newfoundland — is that there is a statutory hold period before the purchaser can resell his shares unless he, in turn, sells pursuant to one of the statutory exemptions as discussed above. As soon as the hold period has expired, he is free to sell his shares to whomever will purchase them. In most of these provinces, the hold period is twelve months calculated from the time the securities were originally purchased or from the time when the issuer becomes a reporting issuer (whichever is later). It is therefore important for a purchaser that the issuer have and maintain the status of a reporting issuer.

Sales by "Control Persons"

The reselling of securities held by "control persons" is additionally complicated in all provinces except Quebec. In most provinces, the concept of a control person refers to someone who either alone or in combination with others holds a sufficient number of securities of an issuer to materially affect the control of the issuer. The special policy relating to control persons is a result of the fact that because of their particular influence over the affairs of the issuer, such control persons would be privy to information either not yet disclosed or else poorly disseminated, such that they could use this information to their advantage in trading the securities of the issuer.

The rules relating to control persons are beyond the scope of this book. We simply want to alert you to the fact that control persons are treated quite differently than ordinary persons in securities law. Accordingly, you and your investors should be aware of that. Current legal advice should be obtained if this issue becomes relevant to you in your business dealings.

3.7 THE OFFERING MEMORANDUM

The term "offering memorandum" is generally used to describe any written information describing the target company, and the uses to which it will apply invested funds, which is given to a prospective investor. An offering memorandum may therefore be in many different forms.

The most important thing for you to know about offering memoranda is that *there are serious legal ramifications attached to every single document that you give to a prospective investor*. Because of the self-policing nature of securities laws, no one is going to be looking over your shoulder at each document that you give to the purchaser. It is usually only when the investment turns sour and your former friend is looking for his "pound of flesh," or at least his money back, that his lawyer will examine everything that you gave to the investor in order to determine if there has been a misrepresentation, or fraud, or breach of contract on your part. Every single document that you provided to the investor will be carefully examined to determine whether it provides helpful evidence in his case against you. Accordingly, you should appreciate now the significance which your documents may attain later.

In addition, some provinces grant the investor the right to demand his money back if you did not provide him with an offering memorandum containing certain particulars within a specified time after he purchased the securities. In the absence of the issuer delivering an offering memorandum to an investor who has advanced the purchase funds to the issuer, in some provinces the investor has two days to withdraw, whereas in other provinces he has a full sixty days in which to give you notice of his intention to withdraw and demand his money back.

The "Standard Form" of Offering Memorandum

There is no such thing as a "standard form" of offering memorandum that is required by law. However, certain of the exemptions, for example the seed capital exemption, require specific information to be included, sometimes to a level that is "substantially the same information" as that which a prospectus would provide. In actual practice, most issuers raising money imitate the form of a public offering prospectus which does have a prescribed form and content.

To obtain samples of such public offering prospectuses, simply contact a stock broker working with any of Canada's investment dealers and ask to be given a half-dozen or so current prospectuses. The broker receives these free of charge and normally has access to hundreds of them. In fact, you can particularize your request and ask if he has any prospectuses relating to your specific type of business, be it real estate development, manufacturing, retail sales, oil and gas exploration or any other area of commerce, as these can provide you with additional insights into how you can most effectively present your own material.

The practice in business is that most offering memoranda include information on the following topics:

1. A title page showing the issuer's name, how much money is being raised, the nature of the securities offered and the minimum subscription amount, if any.

2. A brief history of the enterprise to-date.

3. A summary description of the issuer's business.

4. The names of the issuer's directors, officers and promoters.

5. The occupation and prior business experience of the directors, officers and promoters.

6. The reason that the issuer is raising money and a description as to how the money raised will be used (usually referred to as the "use of proceeds").

7. How the securities are being sold (usually referred to as the "plan of distribution").

8. The specific characteristics of the securities being sold.

9. Whether there is an existing market for the securities.

10. The principal current holders of the issuer's securities.

11. A summary of the issuer's share and loan capital structure.

12. Current financial statements (preferably not less than ninety days old).

13. All of the reasons why there is risk attached to this investment (usually referred to as "risk factors"). It is important to be thorough here because the failure to mention an important risk could later give credence to an allegation of misrepresentation if the project fails.

14. The issuer's advisors: including accountants, lawyers and banker.

15. All contracts material to the business of the issuer (usually referred to as "material contracts").

In addition, many offering memoranda provide certain other information found in public offering prospectuses such as:

16. The interest of management, directors and promoters in the material contracts and in any material transactions.

17. The compensation of directors and officers.

18. A description of the assets of the issuer.

In preparing your own offering memorandum, you should first consult with a securities lawyer to determine your province's specific legal requirements. You can then prepare a "rough draft" of the offering memorandum for presentation to the lawyer to finalize. This will normally save you both time and money. Do not be misled by blindly following the format of someone else's earlier offering document. Note: In some cases the law prescribes the minimum contents of an offering memorandum.

One caution on drafting: Be factual. The offering memorandum is not the place for hyperbole, wishful thinking or exaggeration. In most instances, the law will deem that the investor relied upon the information provided by you in the offering memorandum. An omission to state a material fact is a misrepresentation. A "material fact" is one which, if it had been known by the investor, may have caused him to change his mind about proceeding with the investment. The offering memorandum requires a sober, concrete, realistic description of all matters enumerated above.

"Can I Avoid Using an Offering Memorandum?"

Some exemptions in some provinces provide for the discretion of the issuer as to whether or not an offering memorandum is used. In other words, it is not always legally mandatory to use such a document. In those cases where one is not *legally* required, it will then be a question of *business judgement* as to whether the prospective investors will demand one or not. If not, then what should you give them?

The answer probably depends on to whom you are selling, how complex the transaction is and how much you are raising. In the situation where you decide that your intended audience will not demand an offering memorandum, and it is not required by law, then a simple "term sheet" or what some people refer to as a "non-memorandum" will suffice. More importantly, a simple term sheet will not be considered to be an offering memorandum and therefore not attract the statutory compliance requirements.

The contents of a "term sheet" or non-memorandum reflect its name; that is to say, it simply gives the "terms" of the deal (hence "term sheet"). The document can be one page only and it should just provide the financial details of the investment. Two sample term sheets from two specific money-raising programs, one for a private company and one for a public company, are included in Appendix A. As you can see, each document simply summarizes the financial terms of the particular deal in question. Other than providing a useful format, the terms of these particular transactions likely have very little in common with the terms of your own deal. The contents of a term sheet are unique for each separate money-raising program. There is no legally required format or content.

Some further guidance may be found in the statutory language of Ontario (and similar language in Alberta and Saskatchewan) where an offering memorandum is defined as follows:

> a document purporting to describe the business and affairs of an issuer that has been prepared primarily for delivery to and review by prospective investors so as to assist those purchasers to make an investment decision in respect of securities being sold in a distribution . . . *but does not include* [emphasis added]:
> (i) a document sending out current information about an issuer for the benefit of prospective purchasers familiar with the issuer through prior investment or business contacts, or
> (ii) . . . an annual report, interim report, information circular, takeover bid circular, issuer bid circular, prospectus, or other such document the content of which is prescribed by statute or regulation.

This indicates that so long as you provide the purchaser only a term sheet or documents prepared for other purposes and publicly filed, then you are not utilizing an "offering memorandum." However, if you provide any more than is permitted, you may have unintentionally provided an offering memorandum; it is not necessary that a document actually be called an "offering memorandum" in order to be an offering memorandum under the law.

It is important to understand that in the situation where an offering memorandum is not required, if you do in fact create one, either intentionally or accidentally by providing more than you should have, then the memorandum must include contractual rights of rescission and damages similar to the ones for misrepresentation required in a prospectus. If you fail to provide this to the investor, you may be in violation of provincial securities legislation and therefore subject to quasi-criminal or criminal penalties under the statute. Where an offering memorandum is not required under the statute, in your choice of documents to be given to the prospective purchaser of your securities, remember that this is clearly a situation where "less is better than more."

3.8 INVESTOR RIGHTS OF ACTION AND RESCISSION

In most provinces of Canada, in the case where a purchaser of securities has been given an offering memorandum, securities legislation provides the purchaser with contractual rights of rescission and damages similar to those contained in prospectuses for misrepresentation. Rescission, in this case, refers to the remedy of revoking or cancelling the purchase contract and obtaining a refund of the purchase monies. In addition, the purchaser has a number of rights and remedies at common-law. Two of the principal remedies are an action for damages or rescission based on misrepresentation and an action for damages based on deceit.

Prior to completing your offering memorandum and distributing it to prospective purchasers, it is important that you consult with your lawyer as to the various outstanding questions which you will have with respect to the issuing of securities. In particular, you must obtain the correct form of the notice of contractual rights of action which is legally required to appear in the offering memorandum in each province where securities are being distributed.

3.9 THE SUBSCRIPTION AGREEMENT

The issuer must also prepare a "subscription agreement" which documents the issuer's sale and the investor's purchase of the securities. This document will create certain legal rights for both parties. It is a contract which can be sued upon for specific performance by the issuer if the purchaser does not provide all of the purchase monies as agreed. Similarly, the purchaser can enforce the contract against the issuer. Among a number of other matters, the issuer will want to include in the subscription agreement the purchaser's representations that are necessary for him to qualify for certain exemptions. Such representations would address issues such as the purchaser's sophistication, wealth and access to professional advice to confirm that the issuer has exercised "due diligence" in his examination of the affairs of the purchaser to ensure that the purchaser does qualify for the exemption.

The subscription agreement is a very important document as serious legal ramifications flow from it. It is crucial that you have a lawyer write your own unique subscription agreement, or at least review the one that you may have acquired from another source, to ensure that:

A. Your purchaser is legally committed to purchase the amount of securities, at the price, and on the terms, that you both intend; and

B. You are in compliance with the legal requirements of the particular categories of exemption that you are utilizing in the province(s) in which you will be raising money.

3.10 CLOSING AND POST-CLOSING REQUIREMENTS

The moment when the investor pays the purchase funds for the securities is called "the close" or "the closing." The close necessitates the preparation and delivery by the issuer of a number of documents. In a straightforward private placement, with no unusual complications, the documents required would be the following:

1. Subscription agreement as discussed above fully executed (signed copies for both purchaser and issuer). (Note: The purchaser normally acknowledges in the subscription agreement that he has received a copy of the offering memorandum in those instances where one is utilized. It is good practice to confirm again with the investor that he has a copy of the offering memorandum and if he has not, or is unsure, provide him with a new copy.)

2. Purchaser's cheque as payment for the securities.

3. Certificate from the issuer evidencing the securities sold (e.g., a share certificate).

4. A signed receipt from the purchaser for the securities certificate.

5. The form(s) required to be filed with the provincial securities regulator(s). (Note: In some provinces this form is to be signed by the purchaser, while in others it is the issuer.)

A legal obligation to file a notice with the provincial securities regulator, as noted in item 5 above, may arise on the sale of securities pursuant to a private placement. As the rules vary from exemption to exemption, and from province to province, current legal advice on the notice and filing obligations is a necessity.

3.11 CONCLUSION

The purpose of this chapter is simply to alert you to the key securities law issues facing the money-raising entrepreneur. You must be aware of and beware the reality that the actual legal rules in force at any particular moment in any particular province are in a constant state of revision as adjustments are made to changing market conditions. One must not simply charge ahead raising money like "a bull in a financial china shop." The resulting damage could be very costly to you in both money and reputation. The best usage of this material is for you to understand the issues and then make a list of questions for which you require answers in order to legally and responsibly undertake your current money-raising programs. Armed with your own list of questions and the procedures outlined in the "Money-Rai$ing Master Checklist," you will be in excellent shape to have a relatively short, efficient and very productive meeting with your own securities lawyer in order to set you on your path to lawful and successful money-raising in the provinces of your choice.

CHAPTER FOUR

STRUCTURING YOUR DEAL

Money is like a sixth sense without which you cannot make a complete use of the other five.

Somerset Maugham

4.1 INTRODUCTION

You are now ready to determine how much you are going to ask from your prospective investors and what you are prepared to give up in order to get it. The two basic questions that you must ask yourself at the outset of your money-raising program are:

1. "How much money do I need to raise for my business?"
2. "What am I willing to give for the money that I get?"

The first thing that you need to understand is that there is no set formula. This is strictly making it up as you go along. You create the deal through negotiation. One of the reasons that there is no magic formula is that sources of capital, be they private investors, venture capitalists, investment dealers, banks or other sources will all differ in their requirements as to what is an acceptable deal for them.

That is why it is incumbent on you to also determine at the outset which specific sources of financing you are first going after so that you can tailor your proposal appropriately to the particular sources of financing. You may approach an investment source with no fixed structure on your agenda and be prepared to generate the form of the transaction through negotiation; or, on the other hand, you may create a specific proposal whereby you offer the same investment opportunity to all persons to whom you present it.

An example of the former is the suggested methodology when approaching a professional venture capitalist, where through a process of negotiation you arrive at a mutually acceptable arrangement. Conversely, an example of a fixed proposal is the situation where you offer shares in a private company pursuant to a private placement offering memorandum. In the latter case, each investor is offered the same investment opportunity at the same price in your company, such as common shares at $1.00 per share. Thus, you need to understand the interests and requirements of the particular sources of capital which you will approach.

Although there is no set formula that will appeal to all investors, it is imperative to realize that there are four basic elements that must be handled to the satisfaction of every investor no matter what form the deal eventually takes.

4.2 FOUR KEY ISSUES FOR THE PROSPECTIVE INVESTOR (THE "SLIP TEST")

It is vitally important to your success as a money-raiser that you understand that each investor, whether or not he has ever articulated it, requires a satisfactory answer to four fundamental issues. Before he will invest, he must be comfortable as to the following:

1. The **security** of his investment;
2. The **liquidity** of his investment;
3. The **income** to be earned from his investment; and
4. The **potential upside** to be gained from his investment.

Taken together in the form of an acronym, investment professionals refer to the above factors as the "SLIP Test," from "Security," "Liquidity," "Income" and "Potential upside."

We have emphasized throughout this book that money raising is a marketing exercise and, as such, deals at a base level of human emotions and psychology. Accordingly, the four factors of the SLIP Test are totally subjective and different in every person. For example, some sources of capital, such as banks, widows and retired people, will predictably place very high value on the security of their investments. Investments with high security usually will generate a modest income but not much, or any, capital gains. Examples of this would be Canada Savings Bonds or Treasury Bills. Thus, for many investors, a relatively low return is acceptable when the paramount importance is the safety of the invested capital.

On the other hand, some investors will not value security highly at all because they want to go after a big capital gain; they want the "big score," the large potential upside. These types of investors can be found amongst venture capital firms, affluent professional people in their early to mid-years of practice, successful independent entrepreneurs and various other sources.

It is thus incumbent on you, the money-raiser, to understand the four elements of the SLIP Test and how your business opportunity will be able to satisfy them for any particular investor. As a corollary to that, you will save yourself a great deal of time, expense and anxiety if you know beforehand that it is highly unlikely that your business could meet the SLIP Test for any particular investor or class of investors and therefore leave these prospective investors out of your money-raising program, or at least at the initial stages of it. You want to maximize the odds of success in your favour. Therefore, you are advised to first target those financial sources where you will have the highest likelihood of satisfying their SLIP Test.

1. Security

To an investor, the security of his investment refers to how safe his investment is perceived to be. At its most basic level, this really means how strong is his feeling of certainty that he will get his money back. It deals with the question, "How safe is my money?" Before he will invest in your project, the investor must be brought to the point of feeling comfortable with the likelihood that he will experience the return of his capital. The opposite of "security" or "safety" is "risk" or "peril." If a totally safe investment represents one end of a continuum, a totally risky investment represents the other. (On a statistical basis, there is no such thing as either a totally safe or totally risky investment, although on a practical basis there most definitely is such.)

SCALE OF DEGREE OF RISK

TOTAL SAFETY _____ TOTAL RISK

0%   50%   100%

For example, investing in Canada Savings Bonds has historically been considered to be a no-risk investment; that is to say, a totally safe investment. The purchasers of these bonds do not generally consider the risk of inflation, the risk of devaluation of the dollar or the risk of potential failure of the Bank of Canada to be of any practical significance. These factors are not given any appreciable weight in the decision-making process. The investors fully expect to receive the return of their capital any time that they choose to sell or redeem the bonds.

Is your business proposal as risk free for the investor as Canada Savings Bonds? We assume not. But fear not, you are not alone. Given that your proposal is not without some risk, you need to introduce factors which compensate for the lack of objective, real world security. You will need to either provide additional, more intangible assurances as to security with respect to the investment, or alternatively, diminish the importance of security in light of the enormous expected upside to the transaction.

A. TWO COMPENSATING FACTORS

There are two factors in your favour as a money-raiser that will compensate for the lack of objective security in your project. The good news is that many investors will in fact accept a high degree of risk, yet actually feel quite secure and satisfied with their investment, when two factors exist which compensate for the lack of objective security. Although the presence of just one of these factors may be enough, the presence of both is often quite powerful. These factors are: **1.** Intangible security; and **2.** Potential upside.

1. Intangible Security

Although you would think that the security aspect of an investment is a black and white, objective sort of issue, that most definitely is not the case. Security can be very much intangible as well as tangible. The issue here is having the prospective investor feel comfortable with the proposed investment. Where the business, on an objective basis, definitely involves a degree of risk, even a high degree of risk, this may be compensated for by the presence of other factors, some of which are listed below.

Relationship with Family. The trust and confidence in, plus the desire to help, a family member very frequently takes precedence over the fundamental risk of the proposed investment. The emotional bonds between the investor and the money-raiser will very frequently override appreciation of the inherent risk of the investment. For example, how many parents have invested in losing ventures of their children? Most likely, we believe, many more than have actually made money on their offspring's projects. Will then, the flow of money from the older generation to the younger slow down or cease? Only when there are no more children!

Relationship with Close Friends. Similar motivations operate with friends as with family. Sometimes friends will even be more inclined to invest than family members because in some cases they may see the money-raiser on a more regular basis and feel more attuned to the money-raiser's current life interests.

Good Reputation. It is an interesting phenomena that people often assume that someone will become successful in one field if they have been successful in another, even if they have little or no experience in the new endeavour. For example, star athletes frequently are successful in obtaining investors for their business ventures, one of the main reasons being that the investor believes that the same qualities of drive, determination, competitive spirit, and so on will enable the athlete to be successful in an entirely new arena.

Successful Relevant Experience. Although the proposed investment may be in a young or start-up company, if the money-raiser has a successful track record in the same or a related industry, this can engender a strong feeling of investor confidence in his probability of current success. This is an even stronger and more credible expression of the phenomena described under "Good Reputation."

Religious Affiliation. It is a fact that people frequently let their guard down and feel less sceptical when they are with others who share their same, deep personal beliefs. The bonds of trust and affinity that develop within a spiritual or religious context can sometimes be stronger than any other ties. In this environment, a money-raiser often meets with support and cooperation from investors who would otherwise not invest in the type of project being proposed.

The above examples illustrate just some of the ways of compensating for an investment being of an inherently risky nature. These are merely a handful of the countless unique ways in which potential investors come to become actual investors through the process of developing a sense of comfort with the money-raiser and his project. The other factor that can compensate for a lack of real security in a deal is that the proposed investment shows a fabulous potential upside. This was perfectly described by an outrageous Canadian investor and sport fisherman who loved to fish in Mexico when he once said, "I don't mind going out in a leaky boat, if I think I'm going to catch me the Great White Shark!"

Upon reflection, you will see that the boat and fishing scenario is a perfect metaphor for the entrepreneurial money-raising process. Normally, the fisherman demands a totally watertight vessel, fully equipped with life preservers, and will have a fixed destination or voyage plan in mind. However, little by little, he may feel increasingly comfortable, then enthusiastic, and then even excited, about giving up one, then two, then more components of that safe and secure feeling if the voyage promises sufficient other attractions, inducements or rewards. The ultimate expression of this is the impassioned fisherman who embarks out to sea in a leaky boat, with no life preserver, in stormy weather in longing pursuit of that magnificent yet elusive prize, the Great White Shark.

2. Potential Upside

Which brings us to the "Big Upside." This basically translates as "large capital gains." This is the gain which is made from buying low and selling high. The issue is, does the investor think that your investment offers the potential for an exciting capital gain, otherwise known as a "major upside," a "big score," a "home run," or a Great White Shark?

Great White Shark   It is constantly amazing to us what people have, and continue to, put their money into if they think that they will "hit the jackpot." What this means for you as a money-raiser is that investors have often been willing to give up much of the security value in a proposed investment if the amount of the potential upside is attractive enough to them personally.

What is really fascinating about this, is that the potential upside actually has no direct or causal relationship with the safety of the investment. Yet many people will consistently attach a greater value to the upside potential than they do to absolute security. Carried to an extreme, this is, of course, the essence of gambling. However, it is not only the source of "the action" in Las Vegas, but also to much of the activity in stock exchanges across Canada and around the world. In its most primitive form, this is just plain greed.

Consider, for example, the purchase of penny stock in a private offering of a brand new company incorporated to exploit raw mineral property in the Yukon. To a sceptical, yet uninformed member of the public, the degree of risk might be considered to be about 99% or higher. It looks like just another "spec mining stock." Nevertheless, to an interested investor, this might still be an acceptable risk because of what he perceives to be the absolutely outstanding potential upside. (Remember, these things *do* get funded with amazing regularity.) The prospective investor may first hear the story about a booming metals market, the very positive indicators from aerial surveys, and the fact that this property is immediately adjacent to the property on which a major ore body had already been discovered and which has made all of the investors in the adjacent mining property a fortune practically overnight. Incredibly, the adjacent stock went from $1.25 to $125 in six months! He thinks this could too! Add to this some intangibles, such as the prospector's passionately described "gut feeling" about the property and the fact that this prospector has been right before. In addition, the investor has casually known of the company promoter for years because he went to school with the investor's kid sister . . . well, before long, the investor gets a cosy feeling about the deal: "I just feel kind of good about this one," he says. And so it goes.

One more junior mining project gets financed, yet providing no security of investment at all, little liquidity and no income. But with one heck of a good story and dreams of $100 stock! "So what if the boat is a little leaky!" After all, vaguely discernible, through the mist of the early morning fog, that tell-tale ripple in the water, that movement in the shadowy light — it just might be, it almost certainly is . . . the Great White Shark!

In addition to handling the issue of investment security, there are three other aspects of the SLIP Test that need to be satisfied to an acceptable degree before an investor will put money into your project. The next one to be considered is the issue of once the investor gets into your deal, how does he get his money out again?

2. Liquidity

When an investor refers to the "liquidity" of an investment, he is referring to the ease with which it can be converted into cash again. This is generally a function of whether there is a ready market for the investment. For there to be good liquidity, two conditions must be fulfilled: **1.** that there are ready buyers for the investment; and **2.** that there are no legal restrictions or impediments to its sale.

For example, the common shares of Bell Canada Enterprises, Inc., one of Canada's largest corporations, trade principally on the Toronto and New York Stock Exchanges and are considered to be one of the most liquid investments in this country. Tens of thousands of BCE common shares worth millions of dollars are traded every day. There are always willing buyers at the current market price, and for all intents and purposes, there are no restrictions on the rights of ordinary investors to buy and sell the stock.

Contrast this with purchasing a large piece of undeveloped recreational real estate in northern Ontario. At times the market may be very weak, there may be few buyers and there may be legal restrictions affecting what a potential new purchaser is able to do with the property. This would be considered to be a relatively illiquid investment, particularly during a major downturn in the economy, compared to the publicly traded shares of a large company on a large stock exchange.

Investors like to have liquidity in their investments. More liquidity is better than less liquidity. It is incumbent on the money raiser to have an answer to the prospective investor's question, "How do I get my money back?" or, "How can I sell my investment?"

There are basically three ways for the investor in a private company to divest himself of his investment:

A. Private Share Transfer. He must locate someone willing to purchase his shares privately, subject to provincial securities law restrictions as discussed above in Chapter Three on the topic, "Understanding the Law and Money-Raising." This could also include a purchase of the shares by the original entrepreneur who arranged their sale in the first place, or, if funds were available, repurchase by the company itself.

B. Go Public. If the company eventually arranges to have its shares listed for trading on a stock exchange in Canada or elsewhere, the investor may eventually have some liquidity for his shares. However, for more than 99% of the private companies incorporated in Canada, the shareholders' high hopes will never lead down the road to successfully going public. See our comments on this complex process in section 5.10 below on the topic, "The Initial Public Offering (IPO)."

C. Sell the Company. If the company is sold to a third party, what money that remains after paying off all of the company's creditors, and the expenses of the sale, will be distributed to the shareholders. One real advantage to this route is that there is currently a $500,000 lifetime capital gains tax exemption for each person on his gains made from the sale of shares in a qualified small business in Canada (compared to a $100,000 lifetime capital gains tax exemption with respect to shares held in a public company). The allure of this kind of tax-free treatment acts as a powerful incentive to some investors. Tax laws relating to treatment of capital gains can change at any time of course. Obtain timely professional tax advice.

As is apparent from the above, liquidity of investment in a private Canadian company is normally rather limited. Nonetheless, many entrepreneurs succeed in bringing investors into such investments based mainly on the strategy described above under the heading "Security." That is, compensate for the lack of liquidity by the intangible factors and by the large potential upside. In addition, if the company is profitable, it can pay dividends to shareholders, pay directors' fees, pay salaries to employees and grant bonuses to officers and employees. Depending on the role of any particular investor, he may qualify for some or all of those sources of income. And income is the third element to consider in any investment.

3. Income

The income from an investment simply refers to the financial return on that investment which is received by the investor as a result of holding the investment. Income can take many forms. It is often of a recurring or periodic nature. With a bank savings account, the income is in the form of interest payments. With common stocks held in a profitable public corporation, the income is in the form of dividends. In the context of this discussion, it would be the earnings that the investor receives by virtue of simply holding the investment, as opposed to a gain that he makes on the sale of the investment. With respect to an hypothetical apple grower, for example, the income from his orchard would be derived from the sale of the apples grown on the trees. In the event that he sold his farm, including all of the trees, after some years and made a gain from that sale, that gain would be his capital gain.

For some investors, income is of prime consideration. An example would be anyone who relies on the income generated from investments to pay his living expenses, as is the case with many retired people. If you intend to raise money from such people, we recommend that you consider structuring the investment so that the investor receives regular income from it. This is typically achieved through borrowing the money from the investor and paying interest on it. There are a number of variations on this theme which we will discuss below. You are not limited to a simple unsecured loan, which nowadays can often be a hard sell, even to your loving friends and family members. You may well have to enhance the attractiveness of the loan, for example by somehow giving security for the loan, or by creating a loan which can be converted into equity at the option of the lender. This is discussed further below in section 4.3 under the heading, "What to Give for the Money You Get."

4. Potential Upside

This is the real hook for the investor in most private investments. It is that which draws him in. This is the Great White Shark! This is the reason, above all, why the investor is willing to venture out with you in your leaky vessel. This is where professional venture capitalists look for a capital gain which, when averaged over the years that the capital investment was held, will yield a compound rate of return which works out to at least 30% to 40% per annum. The potential upside had better be good! The investor needs to see a very pretty picture here to make up for all those leaks in your boat.

Most private investors in Canada will tolerate a lack of iron-clad security, will also tolerate uncertainty as to how they will achieve liquidity (because you cannot be certain in the early stage of a business), will tolerate even very modest income, but you had better really show in your financial projections how you are going to achieve a dynamite upside. It has been said of many Canadian entrepreneurs that they "sell mystery, not history." That is very true for many money-raising entrepreneurs, particularly in the start-up or early stages of their business where there is no prior operating history.

4.3 FIVE KEY ISSUES FOR THE MONEY-RAISER

With respect to your own needs and concerns, five important questions that you must ask yourself at this stage are:

1. "How much money do I need to raise?"
2. "How am I going to use the money that I raise?"
3. "When do I need the money that I raise?"
4. "What am I going to have to give (up to the investor) in order to get the money that I want?"
5. "What sources of capital am I going to approach and in what order?"

1. Amount of Money to Be Raised

Money-raising is not an end unto itself. The funds are being raised for the purpose of enabling you to achieve specific business objectives. How much you need will be revealed by preparing a good set of financial projections, such as we discussed in Chapter Two on the topic "Preparing Your Business Plan." A carefully prepared cash flow projection is the key document in determining your money needs.

A. CASH FLOW PROJECTIONS

Your cash flow projections will reveal for how long and by how much your business will be in a situation of "negative cash flow." This is the condition experienced by your company when the total of the money flowing out of the business exceeds the total of the money flowing in. If you expect to remain in business, the day must eventually arrive, the sooner the better, when the money flowing into the business exceeds the money flowing out. That desirable condition is known as "positive cash flow." It is also sometimes known to an entrepreneur as "Bliss," "Nirvana" or "Heaven." Many an overstressed independent business person has discovered and adopted the motto: "Happiness is positive cash flow!"

The cumulative total of your projected negative cash flow plus a reasonable amount set aside for contingency planning will show you the absolute minimum amount of money which you need to raise for your business (see further comments on this topic below under "Worst-Case Scenario"). It is essential to your success that the assumptions and information that go into the preparation of your cash flow projection be as accurate as possible. The numbers that you use should be well researched and be defensible under scrutiny by interested third parties, such as prospective investors. Almost any investor of sophistication will demand that you explain in detail how you arrived at the figures in your cash flow projection. Be prepared.

There are very important ramifications which flow from these calculations. If you badly underestimate your capital needs, you will run out of money before achieving your goals — in other words, the business will go bust. That is, unless you are successful in raising an additional round of financing to make up for your errors, and that is nothing to count on, especially since your credibility would be badly affected by failing to meet your original projections. On the other hand, if you significantly overestimate the need of your business for capital, you will likely wind up parting with much more of your business to investors than was really necessary.

Experienced investors, such as professional venture capitalists, look sceptically at even the most prudently prepared financial projections. Long experience has proven that many unforeseen variables, including pure bad luck, almost always surface in almost every business. Murphy's Law: "Whatever can go wrong will go wrong," seems to be universally applicable. This is especially so in start-ups.

B. UNFORESEEN KILLER VARIABLE (UKV)

To be particularly feared is the infamous "UKV." This is the "Unforeseen Killer Variable." By definition, the introduction of a UKV is sufficient to put you out of business. This is always a risk in any business and in some more than others.

By way of example, let us look at an unfortunate period that occurred for syndicators of tax shelters in Canada. In the early 1980s, many real estate investors were financially wiped out, including many upper-income professionals such as doctors, lawyers and accountants who thought they were investing in a "sure thing" when they invested in land on which to construct multiple unit residential buildings, or "MURBs" as they were then called, otherwise known as apartment buildings. When the federal government, in November, 1981 completely changed the tax laws thereby eliminating most of the tax benefits of constructing MURBs, investment properties dropped precipitously in value almost overnight. In the aftermath, many development companies went out of business and many individuals and companies went bankrupt. The UKV in this case was taxation legislation. Any highly regulated industry has a similar vulnerability to changes in government policy. Indeed, almost every industry is potentially subject to the UKV inherent in revolutionary change nowadays, whether from technological, political, economic or environmental causes.

C. WORST-CASE SCENARIO

As a result of all of the risk factors inherent in almost any entrepreneurial investment, many sophisticated investors take the view that once you have conservatively determined from your cash flow projection how much money you need to raise, you should then go back and redo the calculations creating what many refer to as a "worst-case scenario." One approach to that is to take what you think is your weakest likely scenario, then arbitrarily double your expenses for the period in question; for example, the first two years. Then halve the revenues for the same period. How deep in the red is your negative cash flow then? That total amount of red ink is arguably what you should be seeking to raise in order to give both you and the investors a comfortable margin of safety. Again, this is particularly so in start-ups, where you do not have any historical operating figures upon which to base your financial projections.

While this may seem like an extreme approach to determine how much money you should raise, and admittedly somewhat discouraging when you look at the size of the figure, "lack of sufficient capital" is cited as the chief cause of countless business failures. It is right at the top of almost all lists of why businesses failed. It is because entrepreneurs are invariably either too optimistic in their original cash flow projections upon which they determine their money needs, or too inexperienced (even if they are trying not to be optimistic) to really know what the operating results are really likely to be during the critical early stage. To assist you in your initial rough calculations as you make exploratory cash flow projections for a new or expanding business, we have included a sample format for making cash flow projections in Appendix A.

2. Use of the Money Raised

Your financial projections will also show how the money that is raised is going to be used. This will answer your question, "How am I going to use the money that I raised?" The two most common general purposes for raising money are to start or to expand a business. In addition, many companies also attempt to raise equity in order to retire their current debt. Such an infusion of capital would have the effect of reducing their interest payments and is much faster, and frequently easier, than retiring debt out of retained earnings.

On a prospectus or offering memorandum, the information on how the money is to be used is summarized in specific categories under the heading, "Use of Proceeds." It may show the money being utilized in such categories as:

1. Debt retirement.
2. Research and development.
3. Working capital.
4. Capital equipment.
5. Marketing.
6. Acquisition or takeover.

The specific uses for the money raised should all be laid out in your financial projections with supporting assumptions, as discussed in Chapter Two on "Business Plans."

3. When the Money Is Needed

This issue deals with your question, "When do I need the money that I raise?" The timing of the receipt of funds is crucial to the advancement of your plans. No money, no business. Again, your cash flow projection is the key. It will show you month by month what your expenditures are forecast to be, and what funds you need to operate and to fulfil your business plan.

Spreading the Investment. Timing is an important issue for a significant reason beyond the obvious matter of your project's need for capital. The knowledge as to when you actually need the funds can allow you to be flexible with potential investors and permit them to spread their investment over time — thereby making it easier for them to invest. The concrete result for you is that you may enable more people to invest in your project.

For example, if an investment in your business is to be in units of $15,000 each, and if the prospective investor does not have that amount immediately available, you may still be able to salvage him as an investor and give him the opportunity to participate in your business by permitting him to write three cheques spread over an agreed time period in the amount of $5,000 each. Often people who genuinely want to invest with you cannot because of insufficient funds at the current moment. But if you can show them how they can invest over time, you can solve a problem for both of you. You need the money and they need the time. You can thus expand your base of potential investors.

Important Tip. When preparing the monthly columns on your cash flow projections, rather than pick a named month, such as July, for example, as the starting month in the first column, then August for the second column, use numbers instead, as in "Month 1, Month 2," and so on. The reason is that your cash flow projections will very quickly look dated as soon as you are a little bit behind in your start-up or money-raising plans. If you have any of the delays that are normal to any project, a potential investor examining your cash flow projections will immediately see that you are already behind schedule and this can cause him to have doubts. Instead, if you start with "Month 1" on the cash flow projection, then it doesn't matter whether you actually start in July, August or September. It gives you more leeway, a kind of tolerance factor. See Example 2, "Cash Flow Projection," in Appendix A.

4. What to Give For the Money You Get

Here at last, we come to the "bottom line" question, "What do I have to give to the investor in return for the money that he is putting into my project?" As we alluded to at the beginning of this chapter, any deal could be sliced one hundred different ways or more. There is no pat answer. However, in money-raising as in music, there are many variations on a theme. In raising money for a company, the two main themes are equity and debt. There are also a number of important minor themes, mainly dealing with the specific promises made between the entrepreneur and the investor or lender with respect to operation and control of the company.

While the money-raising entrepreneur wishes to go forward with his investors in a spirit of cooperation and good will, the reality is that each side will usually attempt to advance its own interests at the negotiating stage. In the end, for the investment to proceed, both sides must find that it is an acceptable arrangement. Sometimes there is naiveté on either side of the deal, but generally at the time that the contract is to be consummated, both sides will have retained professional advisors, such as a lawyer and an accountant skilled in commercial matters, to help plan and negotiate the transaction. It would be extremely foolish of an entrepreneur not to consult with skilled professional advisors before settling on the terms of the investment contract. Indeed, as we discuss several times in Chapter Three on the topic of the "Law and Money-Raising," before instituting any money-raising program it is imperative to determine with an experienced securities lawyer that your program remains within the confines of the law in the provinces in which the money is being raised.

Accordingly, we will simply introduce some of the major issues that will need to be discussed with your legal and financial advisors and be settled, either in the course of your open-ended negotiations with a financing source, or before you fix the terms of a specific offering which you will make on the same terms to several parties pursuant to a private placement offering memorandum.

A. THE DEBT-EQUITY DECISION

The question as to whether to raise money for your project by way of debt, or alternatively by way of equity, or by some chosen combination of both, is of primary and fundamental importance to the future success of your business. The nature of the financing will strongly determine the company's very chances of survival, as well as the rate at which it can grow. The basic distinction between debt and equity is that a person who contributes money to a company by way of equity becomes an owner of the company, whereas a person who contributes money to a company by way of debt becomes a creditor of the company. We strongly suggest that you obtain wise counsel from experienced professional advisors before making the ultimate decision as to the form of financing.

In any case, as you will see from the comments to come in the section in Chapter Five on the "Initial Public Offering," the form of financing is very often market driven. By that we mean that sometimes it may be almost impossible to raise money by one route, so you are in practical terms forced to raise money another way. An example would be the start-up of a new company. Banks will almost never lend money to new company on its own, without personal guarantees from the founder, whereas it may be eminently possible to raise equity for the same business without personal guarantees. That is the market telling you what is possible.

When we refer to "debt" we are referring to money borrowed. Debt comes in many forms, and may be secured or unsecured, whereas "equity" refers to the money invested in a company by purchasing shares in the company. Although there are many different types of shares that it is possible to utilize, equity normally refers to voting, common shares, which are the most frequently used form of shares. When you hear a businessperson say that he is "raising equity" for his business, it means that he is selling shares in his company to obtain capital for the business. If you hear someone say, "Mr. Canuck has 25% of the equity in the business," it usually means that Mr. Canuck owns 25% of the voting, common shares of the company.

1. Key Factors in the Debt-Equity Decision

Some of the key factors to consider in determining whether to raise money by way of debt, by way of equity, or a combination of both, are the following:

a. Stage of business development. Is your business a start-up, is it well established and sustaining itself, or is it rapidly growing? As a general rule, the earlier the stage of development, the less likely you are to either want to finance the business by way of debt, or be able to finance through debt. For your own good, the higher the risk involved in your business, the less likely you should be constrained by interest payments, the need to pay the money back or the pressure of the uncertainty of your being able to do so. In addition, as we will discuss further on, banks are not in the venture capital business, so institutional debt funding is limited or rare for start-ups, depending on various factors, such as the amount of money involved, nature of business, owner's equity, owner's experience in industry, degree of risks, quality of security pledged, etc.

b. Required amount of money. The size of the desired amount of money is also a factor. The smaller the amount, relative to your own financial capacity or the capacity of the business, then the easier it will be to repay. Depending on your personal comfort factor, you may wish to assume the risk of the loan in the business and borrow the money needed, rather than give up ownership in the business for want of a relatively small amount of money. Conversely, the larger the amount, the more difficult it may be to repay, and secondly, the higher would be the monthly service charges on a loan.

c. Intended purpose of the money. The higher the degree of uncertainty in the enterprise, the less it is a candidate for debt financing.

d. Length of time that the money is required. The longer the anticipated payback period, the less appropriate is it for debt financing, particularly in the early years of a business. The exception would tend to be fixed-asset financing, such as a mortgage, where the loan is secured against the fixed asset.

e. Method of repayment of money. How is it intended that the money raised be repaid? What are alternative sources of repayment in the event of something going wrong? If you do not anticipate that the revenues are going to be high enough to pay back the principle amount of the funds invested, then you should raise the money by way of equity. If the only way that the money can be repaid is to sell the business, or bring in future equity financing, then you should start with equity. The fact is, many businesses are viable but marginal. This usually means that if the businesses are started with equity they will be able to remain in operation, probably earning the entrepreneur and the employee(s) a living but not contributing much as a return on investment to the investors. Whereas, if the same company were founded with debt, it would likely become insolvent because the interest payments would drain too much cash out of the business.

f. General economic conditions. Current interest rates, availability of money and the attitude of prospective investors all have a lot to do with whether you ought to proceed by way of debt or equity. A small business may be able to handily sustain paying interest at 10%, but would pound the nails into its own coffin at 20%, as many businesses experienced in the early 1980s when interest on demand loans, and even term loans, exceeded that figure. On the other hand, during very tight economic times and a period of general fear and pessimism, such as occurred immediately after the stock market crash in October, 1987, it may be necessary to offer an income inducement to investors. In such a case, a form of preferred share or a convertible debenture may be most effective because they offer both income and potential upside.

In addition to the foregoing general factors which you must consider, there are a number of specific advantages and disadvantages to utilizing either debt or equity.

2. Debt-Equity Comparative Advantages and Disadvantages: The "Capital Quality" Issue

Equally as important as the quantity of financing that is obtained for your business is the issue of the "quality" of the financing. "Quality" in this sense refers to the characteristics or qualities of the type of financing utilized. The qualities of either debt or equity financing have a number of ramifications for both the entrepreneur and his company.

A. DEBT — ADVANTAGES
Does not dilute ownership of the business. If you own 100% of a business, no matter how much you borrow, your ownership remains 100%. This is contrasted to raising money by way of equity, where you sell part of the business with every share that you sell to raise money.

Gives you financial leverage. For example, if you have $100,000 of equity in your business, you may be able to borrow another $100,000 against it for certain purposes; for example, to purchase inventory. Therefore, you would have $200,000 in assets, with only $100,000 in net worth. This is financial leverage of 2/1. In real estate, the leverage can be much greater. For example, when putting a mortgage on a piece of real estate. With 10% equity, you may be able to borrow 90% of the purchase price. That is much greater leverage: 10/1. In the latter example, if the total property goes up just 10% in value, you have made 100% on your money.

B. DEBT — DISADVANTAGES
You have to pay it back! And usually within specific time limits. And usually there are unpleasant ramifications for your company, and also for you if you have personally guaranteed the debt, if the money is not repaid pursuant to the terms of its borrowing.

You have to pay interest on it. This not only cuts into working capital, it can put the company out of business if times are difficult for the company and if the interest payments are high enough.

You may have to encumber corporate assets by allowing the lender to register a lien against one or more of the assets. This cuts down your options with respect to dealing with those assets and therefore being able to undertake certain desired courses of action.

You incur more risk in difficult times. If your business is slow or having a difficult time, you may lose the business if your bank calls the loan.

You may have personal financial exposure. If you had to give a personal guarantee in order to obtain financing for the company. In the event that the business fails to repay the loan, you could be financially wiped out with the resulting hardship on your family.

C. EQUITY — ADVANTAGES

Adds to the net worth of the business, therefore makes the business stronger and better able to withstand downturns of any kind.

Makes the business more creditworthy by increasing the net worth of the business, therefore enabling the company to obtain better terms from some suppliers, thereby increasing revenues.

Increases the financing options open to the business, including borrowing against the strength of the increased net worth of the business.

Does not have to be repaid like a loan. It enables the company to be more flexible and also more long-term in its planning because there is no time-fuse burning with respect to fixed pay-back term.

Does not incur interest payment obligation. This increases the cash flow, as well as the net income, of the company and therefore the enterprise is better able to withstand business downturns. (This provision applies to common shares and may not apply to preferred shares depending on how their terms are drafted.)

Does not require encumbering corporate assets in order to obtain the equity financing, therefore leaving all assets of the company, including inventory and capital assets, free to be dealt with by the company as it chooses.

D. EQUITY — DISADVANTAGES

Risk of loss of capital. The equity that is invested in your company by the purchase of shares is sometimes referred to as "contributed capital." That is, it is the capital that you and any other investors contribute to the company. If the business fails, you and your investors will likely lose all of your capital. This is the inherent risk in any business.

Dilution of ownership. By the very nature of the act of selling shares, you are bringing in additional shareholders, which means additional owners, into the company. You therefore will own less of the business. The more other people own an interest in the business, the more your interest is said to become "diluted." In the event that the business is successful, this simply means that less of the dividends, on a distribution of profits, and less of the capital gain, on the sale of the company, will be available to you.

Dilution of control. The size of the portion of the company that these new owners, that is shareholders, own, will determine their rights in law. Depending on whether they own 10%, 25%, 33-1/3% or 51%, there will be specific company law ramifications in each province, with the basic premise being that the more of the company they own, the more power they acquire. It is also fair to say that as soon as you bring in even one shareholder into the company beyond yourself, you must take that person into consideration and are accountable to that person under a number of circumstances. For more information on this point, consult a lawyer or read up on the subject of shareholders' rights in any book on company law, particularly Canadian company law.

Reporting to shareholders becomes mandatory. Stockholders become very unhappy when they are not kept abreast of corporate developments in the company in which they have put money. Additionally, most provinces have strict requirements under the law with respect to the need for reporting to shareholders.

3. Methods of Debt Financing a Business

Raising money for your business by means of borrowing money is called "debt financing." There are numerous forms such financing can take, as debt financing generally has evolved into a very flexible vehicle. Each financial source generally provides only a limited number of methods of debt financing. Therefore, you will need to learn the sources of the various modes of debt financing should you choose to utilize debt in one or more of its forms. Some of the most commonly used forms of debt financing are briefly described below. In Chapter Six, we will briefly discuss the forms of security that lenders sometimes require to protect them for their loan of funds to you.

a. Demand Loan   The simplest form of loan is generally referred to as a "demand loan." The reason it is so named is that the loan is immediately repayable by the borrower "on demand" from the lender. This type of loan is available from Canadian chartered banks for many different purposes, and generally has no fixed repayment schedule. It is generally intended for a shorter term than many other forms of debt and usually has a floating interest rate that varies with the prime rate. Very established businesses which are considered extremely creditworthy by lenders may be charged interest as low as the current bank prime rate (which is the lowest interest banks charge their most creditworthy customers), while others may pay as much as 5% to 6% above prime in interest to the bank. In addition, higher interest rates than those may be charged by other financial sources, usually involving a perceived higher-risk business enterprise.

b. Shareholder Loan   A company may borrow money directly from its shareholders, as a proprietorship may borrow money from its owner(s). After all, who better to believe in the prospects of the business? A bank will often not lend money to a start-up business, but it may loan money to a shareholder against his personal assets as security, then he can inject money into his company either in the form of equity through purchasing shares or in the form of debt through making a shareholder loan to the company. There are a number of advantages to the shareholder in contributing money through a loan rather than equity. Some of these reasons include the following:

- it is easier for the shareholder to withdraw his money from the company when he needs it for another purpose than if it were contributed in the form of shares;
- the company can deduct as an expense for tax purposes the interest it pays to the shareholder on his loan, whereas dividend payments to shareholders are not tax deductible;

▪ the shareholder lender may be able to create a preferred position for his loan, as against the claims of unsecured creditors of the company in the event of the failure of the business, if he loans the money to the company as the company's initial source of funds then registers a security document against the company in order to secure his loan.

c. Interim Financing ("Bridge Financing") "Bridge financing" is so named because it functions as a "bridge" during an interim period between the start-up of a project and the moment that the project receives some form of longer-term financing. It is a generic name that can be applied to many different types of financing for many different types of projects. For example, it may refer to some interim financing arranged for a growing company during the period between the initial contribution of seed capital and the point where the company went public and received equity funding through an initial public offering. In real estate projects, it is often the debt financing (i.e., a loan) that is added onto the owner's equity in order to finance the completion of construction. It is ultimately repaid by the owner who obtains long-term financing from a mortgage company. This long-term financing is sometimes referred to as "take-out" financing because it pays back or "takes out" the bridge financing and often pays back or takes out some or all of the owner's original equity contribution. Depending on the type of project, bridge financing may be available through chartered banks, venture capital companies, the Federal Business Development Bank (FBDB), private investors and other sources.

d. Line of Credit (Operating Bank Loan) Lenders will make available to a wide variety of businesses which they consider to be creditworthy a line of credit up to a set maximum amount. As long as all of the conditions of borrowing are satisfied, the borrower is free to borrow money up to that agreed maximum. This form of loan is generally to provide working capital to a business and the outstanding balance will rise and fall with the cyclical needs of the business. For example, retail stores frequently utilize most of their available line of credit in purchasing inventory for the peak Christmas season. The loan will be repaid as stock is sold and converted into cash. You should be aware of the policy that is sometimes applied by the banks through what is known as a "clean-up provision." The bank may require you to "clean-up" the loan by reducing the outstanding balance to nil at least once a year and maintain a nil balance for a certain period of time, for example, one month.

e. Floor Planning This is a method of borrowing frequently used by retailers of large-ticket merchandise, such as automobiles, recreational vehicles, boats and appliances. The lender is frequently a finance company associated with the manufacturer of the goods, such as Chrysler with automobiles or Bombardier with recreational vehicles, or alternatively, another form of large financial institution. The interesting thing about this method of debt financing is that the lender frequently maintains legal ownership of the merchandise being "floored" (i.e., financed while the merchandise is physically on the dealer's showroom or warehouse "floor") until the merchandise is sold. This method enables the merchant to acquire a significant inventory of merchandise without the requirement of providing purchase funds in advance of selling the merchandise.

f. Inventory Financing This form of financing is a close cousin of floor planning but differs significantly in that title to the goods transfers to the merchant because he has paid for the goods. He then uses the goods as collateral for a loan. The financing is usually secured by the lender, normally a chartered bank or commercial finance company, by entering into formal security documentation and arrangements. Depending on the specific circumstances of the borrower and the current lending practices of the financial institution, the borrower can typically obtain approximately 50% of the wholesale value of the inventory as a loan.

g. Accounts Receivable Financing In this type of financing, the borrower's accounts receivable from his own customers become the collateral to support a loan from a financial institution. In Canada, financial institutions will sometimes loan as much as 75% of the value of the outstanding accounts receivable which are not more than 60 days old. As security, the lender will usually take a security document which covers an assignment of book debts (i.e., accounts receivable). In the event of default by the borrower, the lender can take steps to realize payment by obtaining from the customers of the borrower the accounts receivable owed to the borrower. This type of debt financing is more readily obtained and is available from chartered banks, factoring companies and commercial finance companies. It is sometimes combined with inventory financing to help a business get through a period where its capital needs are high, such as is often the case in cyclical industries.

h. Conditional Sales of Goods A businessperson needing to acquire a capital asset, such as equipment of one kind or another, and who requires financial assistance in the purchase, may often obtain debt financing from the manufacturer of the equipment in the form of a conditional sales arrangement. The business owner gets possession, yet the sale is "conditional" upon the purchaser finally paying in full for the merchandise of which he has had possession. The creditor receives security documentation which is filed in the appropriate provincial registry. As a rule of thumb, many manufacturers require that 25% to 33% of the full purchase price be paid as a down payment, therefore leaving 67% to 75% of the price available to be financed.

i. Letter of Credit This is an interesting device frequently used by a domestic purchaser (in any country) to obtain credit from a foreign supplier. An "L/C," as a letter of credit is called, is a form of guarantee issued by a bank on behalf of a client (such as a domestic purchaser) to a third party (such as an overseas supplier). The L/C represents a guarantee by the bank to the supplier that when the purchaser receives the goods ordered, the supplier will be paid. For the enterprising Canadian entrepreneur, if he does not have the financial resources to back a letter of credit for himself, then he could approach a third-party investor to put up the L/C in return for some remuneration. The investor may be able to obtain the L/C very easily on the strength of his own credit with the bank, so will only have to pay a modest fee to the bank as a service charge in arranging the L/C. It can be a very important piece of financing for the entrepreneur/purchaser who will work out an appropriate compensation to the investor for obtaining the L/C.

j. Factoring   Although not generally well known in small business circles, factoring is very commonly utilized in certain industries, such as the garment business. A factor is a financial source which purchases the accounts receivable from businesses at a discount to the face value of the receivables. As distinct from borrowing against the accounts receivable, factoring is an actual purchase of the accounts receivable, rather than a loan against them. The money-raising entrepreneur usually can obtain between 70% and 85% of the value of his high-quality accounts receivable. Factor financing is available through specialist companies as well as through chartered banks which provide factoring services through their connection with factoring firms.

k. Leasing   Leasing an asset, whether it is a car, a computer, or a piece of real estate such as an office or warehouse, is a way of obtaining the use of an asset to help generate income without the need to invest capital in the asset being utilized. By signing a lease agreement you create a legal obligation to pay the leasing company, normally a set monthly rate for a fixed term, while at the same time acquiring an asset to use in your business. Leasing is an especially interesting way to help finance the start or growth of a business when there is a high capital cost required to purchase some necessary equipment or property, yet the company has inadequate capital to make the purchase. The attractiveness of leasing, particularly equipment leasing, also depends on current income tax laws, as well as on a number of other considerations, so it is wise to obtain professional advice before committing yourself to a leasing agreement.

l. Government Assistance   There are a large number of both federal and provincial financial assistance programs designed especially to assist emerging companies across Canada. These programs come in many shapes and sizes and include loans, loan guarantees, forgivable loans, export development loans and grants, cost-sharing programs, cash grants and subsidies. For more specific information, refer further to the section on "Government Financing Programs" in Chapter Five.

4. Methods of Equity Financing a Business

As stated above, equity represents the ownership of the business. An investor receives shares in the company for the money that he invests. Like debt, equity can be created in a number of different forms, some of them very specialized and sophisticated. In this section, we will describe the most commonly used forms of equity in normal business practice.

a. Common Shares   Common shares are sometimes known as "ordinary shares" and carry with them the right to vote at shareholder meetings of the company. Whoever owns more than 50% of the common shares of the company is deemed to be the person who "controls" the company because that person will determine the voting at ordinary shareholder meetings including who is elected to the company's board of directors. Thus, it is not necessary to own 100% of the shares of a company to effectively control its activities. However, there is both federal and provincial legislation dealing with the rights of minority shareholders. Once you bring other investors/owners/shareholders into your company, you will become accountable to them in certain ways. These include the fact that they must be given proper notice of shareholder meetings. They may be able to prevent you from taking certain specific actions which legally require a larger majority vote to pass, such as 66-2/3% or 75% of the votes, if you do not control a sufficient number of the shares to carry the vote. Before seeking to sell shares in your company, you should always obtain legal advice in your province to understand exactly what the ramifications of your actions are, especially as discussed above in Chapter Three.

b. Preferred Shares   As the name indicates, the holder of this form of equity in the company is entitled to a preference of some kind. It is a frequent occurrence to create a preferred share that does not carry any voting privileges but pays a fixed dividend to the holder, for example 10% per annum, and has a prior claim to the assets of the company on a winding up ahead of the common shares. Usually, all of the holders of the preferred shares as a group have a prior claim, ahead of the common shareholders, on the assets of the company in the event that the company becomes insolvent. In such a case, with the qualities just mentioned, this share would be called a "non-voting, 10% preferred share."

This type of share is useful in helping an entrepreneur satisfy an investor's SLIP Test. It appears to offer a form of security, being preferred as to the assets of the company on a winding up (although in reality there is rarely any value left for any shareholders upon the insolvency of most private companies), it offers income in the form of a fixed dividend (although this too can be illusory because the terms of the preferred share can be written in such a way that if the company does not have earnings sufficient to pay the annual fixed dividend, then it does not need to pay it and nothing accrues as a continuing liability of the company as a result of the failure to pay the dividend) and it offers a form of potential upside as the company increases in value through growth.

Convertible preferred shares. Because preferred shares generally have certain restrictions attached to them, they can, in fact, be created in such a manner that they become convertible into voting, common shares, at the option of the shareholder, under certain, specific circumstances. In that case, in the example discussed above, the share would be called a "non-voting, convertible, 10% preferred share."

c. Options and Warrants   An option is a right to purchase shares in a company before a future date, in a fixed quantity at a determinable price. The basic purpose of options is to function as an incentive reward for contributing to the success of the company. An example would be for a company to grant to a key employee an option to purchase 10,000 common shares of the company at a price of $2.00 per share any time over the five-year period following the date of granting the option. If, during that five-year period, the shares of the company increase in value to $10.00 per share, the employee has the opportunity to make a gain of $8.00 per share, or $80,000 in total by exercising the option and then selling the shares. Companies often hope to convert the sometimes detached attitude of "mere" employees or consultants to that of being committed "stakeholders" in the company (that is, having a vested "stake" in the success of the company) by granting them options to purchase stock in the company.

There are laws and policies dealing with the issuance of options in both public and private companies. Canadian stock exchanges generally restrict access to stock options in public companies for directors, officers, employees and consultants to an aggregate total equivalent to 10% of the total number of shares actually issued in the company. For example, if a public company had 5,000,000 shares issued, it would be permitted to grant a total of 10% or 500,000 options to directors, officers, employees and consultants. That particular restriction does not apply to private companies. It should be noted that options do not carry any voting or other rights until the options are exercised and shares are purchased. Then, it is the shares which confer voting and other rights on the shareholder, not the options.

Warrants are simply options by another name. Custom has created the practice of referring to options which are issued to people other than directors, officers, employees and consultants by the name of "warrants." They confer the same rights and operate in the same way as options. They are options. In public companies, the warrants can become listed for trading on a stock exchange independently of the shares to which they relate, thus creating an actual and separate market for the warrants themselves.

Warrants are sometimes used by money-raising entrepreneurs as an added inducement to someone to invest in the company. They are an extra arrow in your fund-raising quiver. In negotiations, you may sense that the financial source is very interested in your project, however you feel that you need to "sweeten the deal" somehow. This is where offering the prospective investor some warrants may be enough to close the deal. For example, suppose you propose to an investor that he purchase 50,000 shares in your company at a price of $2.00 per share. He is interested but noncommittal. You then offer him the "sweetener." You offer to grant him "as a signing bonus" one warrant for every four shares that he purchases in your company. On that basis, if he purchases 50,000 shares as you propose, he will be granted 12,500 warrants to purchase stock in the company. Because you are able to create the terms of a warrant just as you do on an option, you offer to make the terms of the warrant such that for each warrant that he holds, he can purchase one additional share in the company at a price of $2.50 each any time in the next five years. Thus, if the shares increase in value to $10.00 per share during that period, the investor would have the opportunity to make an additional gain of $7.50 per share on the 12,500 shares purchased by exercising the warrants. This would yield an additional gain of $7.50 $\times$ 12,500 = $93,750. In the hands of a skillful money-raiser, warrants can be a powerful tool with respect to inducing a prospective investor to act.

5. Mixed Debt and Equity

In commercial transactions today, both investors and money-raising entrepreneurs alike demand the maximum flexibility possible in the types of financing vehicle utilized. As raising money is primarily a marketing exercise, it is essential to strive to give the investor the form of investment that he prefers. One very popular type of financial instrument is designed to give the investor the security, liquidity and income of being a secured creditor, with the potential upside of being a shareholder. The financial instrument designed to achieve this is called a "convertible debenture."

Convertible Debenture. A debenture is like a bond, such as those issued by major corporations or even the Government of Canada. It is essentially a promise to pay the owner of the bond or debenture the dollar amount of the instrument at a set time along with interest at a determinable rate. The security aspect comes from the fact that the debenture is registered at the appropriate government registry office as an encumbrance on the assets of the company. While the company is free to deal in its assets and inventory in the normal course of business, in the event of the insolvency of the company the holders of the debenture will have a claim against the assets of the company. This claim will rank ahead of all of the unsecured creditors and the shareholders of the company, although it may rank behind certain other secured and preferred creditors.

On the more positive side, in the event that the company is successful in its business, the terms of the debenture provide that instead of receiving his money back, the lender may elect to convert the debt into equity in the company (hence the name "convertible" debenture) by purchasing shares in the company at a pre-agreed price. This gives the lender/investor the ability to participate in the upside success of the company should that be the case, yet at the same time giving him a measure of protection in the form of the debenture security. In reality, the protection is more illusory than real because there is usually very little of value left in the insolvency of most small companies, especially after the primary secured creditor, the bank, has realized on its security ahead of the holders of the convertible debenture. However, as a marketing exercise, selling a convertible debenture is often easier than basic shares because of the appearance of security and income.

As the foregoing discussion under the section "The Debt-Equity Decision" clearly indicates, there are a large number of financing options open to the money-raiser as well as a number of advantages and disadvantages to each form of financing. As we have tried to emphasize, your own unique business situation, with the skills and resources available to you, will determine which forms of financing are most suitable for you and your project. However, one thing is certain: for the average investor or financing source, there is one cardinal rule to keep in mind — "simpler is better." Long experience has proven to us that the likelihood of a financing source putting money into your company is generally in inverse proportion to the complexity of the transaction. Keep it as simple as possible.

B. VALUING YOUR BUSINESS

This section is of the essence in answering the question, "What do I need to give up to the investor in return for the investment funds that he will put into my business?" Now that you have some appreciation of the varieties of types of financing in your business that you can grant to an investor, in terms of the form of the debt or equity, you must determine what is the value or worth of your business if you proceed to seek an infusion of equity for your company.

A valuation of your business will be a starting point to help enable you to understand what portion or percentage of the company should be given to an investor for an equity investment in the company. For example, if a financing source proposed to invest $100,000 as equity in your company, how much of the company would you offer him? Would you suggest that he be sold 5% of the shares in the company for his $100,000, or 49%, or the whole thing? What is your justification for holding onto the balance of the shares? The process of placing a dollar value on your business begins to introduce a quasi-objective element which can lead to common ground between the investor and the money-raiser in terms of their views on what the business is actually worth.

1. Entrepreneurial Approach to Business Valuation

An entrepreneur can creatively generate value out of many sources beyond the narrow accounting definitions of asset, or net worth. Assets are described by accountants as something owned by the business, liabilities are something owed by the business and net asset value is the value may be described as the total value of the assets of the business less all liabilities. This is far too narrow an approach to valuation for a money-raising entrepreneur, as most entrepreneurs do not have sufficient assets in the traditional sense to support financing based on assets alone. (In fact, so conservative is this approach that the commercial bank lending system of the chartered banks is actually known as "asset-based financing.")

Entrepreneurial financing is based on the understanding that anything that gives a business value, or the perception of value, is an asset and anything that detracts from value, or the perception of value, is a liability. Your winning formula for building a successful business may not be visible as an asset on the balance sheet at all. For example, commercial "know-how" is not a balance sheet item, and is likely not bankable. Yet it may be all that you need to convince a private investor or a venture capitalist that you have a success system that really works.

Entrepreneurial assets by their very nature are intangible but real. In day-to-day life, some of the elements of life that are of most value to us as human beings are totally intangible yet extremely real to us. These include such intangibles as the love we have for our children, the loyalty we have for our country, and the commitment that we have to look after our family. In a comparable manner, non-balance sheet assets or advantages can translate into success and profits for your business. Entrepreneurial assets include the following:

a. A Contract, or a Right   If, for example, the Sony Corporation of Japan granted you by contract the exclusive right to distribute all of its electronic products in Canada, do you think that you could interest anyone in helping you finance a distribution business? Do you think that the exclusive right to distribute Sony's fine products would have value for you? We think so too! Using the same principle, if you acquire a contractual right which represents a business opportunity, you may well be able to raise money from equity investors to pursue the opportunity. At the same time, it may not be an asset with defined worth, not usable as collateral for a bank loan. However, once you have established the success of your business, once you have demonstrated that your systems work and generate profits, it may then be possible for them to support revenue forecasts which in turn will qualify you for additional financing if required.

b. Management   "Management," representing the key executive talent of a company, rates very high on the list of entrepreneurial assets. Yet it does not appear on a balance sheet as an asset of a company. Most sophisticated investors realize that the real security of their investment, and the likelihood of their making profits, is ultimately solely dependent on the skills and integrity of management. Many venture capitalists base almost their entire decision to invest in a company on the quality of its management. Exceptional entrepreneurs can make money in any industry at almost any time. Yet unskilled businesspeople can lose money in what should be a thriving business. You can sell your strengths and those of your colleagues as the assets upon which investors should put money into your business.

c. Know-How (Industrial Technique or Process)   In many cases, it is superior know-how that gives a tremendous competitive advantage to an entrepreneur. It may be knowledge of a methodology, it may be a technique of some kind, or a process, which is something quite separate and apart from the physical components of a manufactured product. For example, glass blowing is as much an art as a science. How do you measure the value of that know-how? If an entrepreneur can convince the money source that the know-how will translate into profits, then he stands a good chance of raising money on the strength of the know-how. It is not necessary that the methodology be patented. In fact, in some cases it has been an advantage not to be patented if the competitors cannot duplicate your processes. Many trade secrets are of this nature as well.

In summary, entrepreneurial financing is based on the understanding that anything that gives a business value, *or the perception of value*, is an asset and anything that detracts from value, *or the perception of value*, is a liability. In addition to the three items listed above, it also includes such elements as relationships with individuals which can be turned to advantage, it includes having a dominant position in a particular market (be it as small as a neighbourhood or a town), as well as anything that gives your business an edge over its competitors.

2. Classic Approaches to Business Valuation

In stark contrast to the entrepreneurial approach are the traditional or classic approaches to business valuation. By understanding this section you will understand how most financing sources will initially approach the challenge of assessing the value or worth of your company. The traditional approaches to valuing your assets and your company are as follows:

a. Liquidation Value   This is the value which a company's assets would fetch on a sale of those assets if the company were in liquidation. That is to say, if the company had ceased business and the assets were being sold or "liquidated." This is sometimes also referred to as "break-up value." It is basically the lowest valuation that a business would acquire and provides a bottom-level value of interest to fixed-asset lenders such as banks and credit unions, as well as to furnish a worst-case scenario of valuation for an investor. There are two main approaches to liquidation value: that of the "forced sale" and that of the "orderly sale." The names speak for themselves and therefore a forced sale would always result in a lower valuation.

b. Book Value   This is the value at which a company's assets are shown on the "books" of the company; that is, on the balance sheet. This number is likely closest to market value for a start-up or new company because the assets have not yet been depreciated to a significant extent on the books of the company. Like liquidation value, this is a very conservative valuation technique and allows no provision for any added value as may be attained by the entrepreneurial approach.

c. Fair Market Value   This is the value which the company would receive if it were sold by a willing seller to a willing buyer as a going concern in the marketplace. There is a large amount of practice and custom developed as to the methodology of this approach which goes far beyond the scope of this book. It is a study, and indeed, an occupation, unto itself.

Price/Earnings Ratio. Important in determining fair market value is the concept of the "price/earnings ratio," or "P/E". This is the ratio of the selling price of the company to its net after-tax earnings. For example, if a company had been sold by its owner to a willing buyer for $600,000 and its net after-tax earnings for the prior year had been $200,000, its P/E or price/earnings ratio would be $600,000 / $200,000 = 3/1. Long-established business practice in Canada and the United States has allowed the accumulation of information on the typical P/E for virtually every industry. We know, for example, the average P/E for the sale of a metropolitan men's clothing store versus a rural drugstore. We know the difference in P/E for a medium-size oil company versus a medium-size software manufacturing company.

Consequently, when you are raising money, you need to keep three price/earnings ratios firmly in mind:

1. The P/E for your kind of company and industry generally. This furnishes a base-line of reasonableness, an objective standard by which you can defend your asking price. As well, you know that a sophisticated purchaser will be comparing your asking price with this figure in order to determine the fairness of your request.

2. The actual P/E based on your current business operations. This is where you are selling the "history" of your business.

3. The future P/E calculated from your projections of future earnings based on raising the money that you are seeking. This is where you are selling the "mystery" of your business; that is, the unverifiable, unknown, fruition of your dreams of the future. It is important to keep projected future earnings in line with what is known and published about the profit margins for your type of company.

These figures are very useful to the money-raising entrepreneur in a number of different ways. For example:

1. If you presently have earnings in your business, industry price/earnings ratios will tell you what you could probably sell your company for, within a range of accepted price/earning ratios, say between a P/E of 3/1 and 5/1. Thus, if you earned $50,000 in your company last year as after-tax profits, this approach would suggest that you may be able to sell your company for between $150,000 (= 3 × $50,000) and $250,000 (= 5 × $50,000).

2. Therefore, continuing with the previous example, you will know roughly how much of the company you need to give up if you want to raise $75,000 in equity for expansion purposes. If you could sell the entire business for between

$150,000 and $250,000, then a $75,000 equity investment would arguably buy the equity investor from a maximum of 50% of the business ($75,000 / $150,000 = 1/2) down to 30% of the business ($75,000 / $250,000 = 3/10). So, negotiating for the money-raiser, we could see that on purely current figures, the fair market approach based on industry figures would indicate that a $75,000 investment would purchase from 30% to 50% of the business.

3. However, we must take into consideration the effect of the $75,000 on the business. Let us assume that your financial projections indicate that it will double your profitability within one year, raising it from $50,000 to $100,000 per annum. With a price/earnings ratio of from 3/1 to 5/1, the selling price for your entire company based on future earnings should then be between $300,000 (= 3 × $100,000) and $500,000 (= 5 × $100,000). Then ask yourself again, how much of the company should you give up for the $75,000?

If you could sell the entire business for between $300,000 and $500,000, then a $75,000 equity investment would arguably buy the equity investor from a maximum of 25% of the business ($75,000 / $300,000 = 1/4) down to 15% of the business ($75,000 / $500,000 = 1.5/10). You can then see, that as the money-raising entrepreneur you will be arguing that the $75,000 investment should purchase from 15% to a maximum of 25% of the company. You are moving comfortably away from the 50% for which the investor would be negotiating.

It is important to remember that the investor will always argue for the lower P/E, as he will then receive more of the company for his investment. The money-raising entrepreneur will always argue for the highest P/E possible, as the higher the P/E the less of the company he parts with. Somewhere in between is likely where the deal will be struck, depending on how the money-raiser's needs and the investor's degree of interest.

One of the great attractions to taking a company public is the very high price/earnings ratio that the public generally pays for the stock. For example, let's assume the average P/E for industrial stocks on the Toronto Stock Exchange is approximately 14/1. If a stock is considered "hot," often arising because it is an exciting company in a glamour industry, the P/E can run as high as 50/1, or even 100/1. Apple Computers, for years, held an extremely high P/E such as that. Sometimes the P/E ratio of a public company is actually infinite, as when the company has a $30 stock and no earnings, due to the excitement and promotion surrounding a stock based on anticipated future earnings. However, as a conservative rule of thumb, companies can obtain at least twice as high a P/E from a public financing as they would from a private financing and frequently much more than that.

d. Fair Value   Although this sounds the same as "fair market value," it is not. It is a concept that has arisen in jurisprudence, particularly as it relates to a minority shareholder's right to be bought out of his interest in the company at a "fair value" for his stock under certain specific circumstances. The courts have settled on a number of criteria to establish fair value for a minority shareholder's stock, known as "fair value formulae." This issue can particularly arise on a proposed takeover or merger of a company. We bring it to your attention, so that you are at least aware that the concept exists should you ever become a minority shareholder in a company. It becomes particularly relevant when the company is subject to a takeover or merger with which you dissent.

C. FINANCIAL RETURN TO THE INVESTOR

Another way to approach the issue of what you must give for the money that you get for your business is to look at it from the investor's perspective and determine what rate of return he wants or needs to make on his investment. If he wants a venture capital 40% annual return over three years on his equity, then we can calculate how much of the company he will need to own based on the projected earnings of the company.

If, for example, the company projects after-tax profits of $350,000 in three years, and if the investor wishes to invest $400,000, how much of the company must he have to earn his 40% annual return? We will assume that research indicates that the P/E ratio in that industry averages 6/1 to 8/1. In that case, the projected valuation of the company in three years would be:

$350,000 $\times$ 6 to 8 = $2,100,000 to $2,800,000

We can see that a simple calculation of the required 40% annualized return on a $400,000 investment compounded over three years yields the following:

Year 1: $400,000 $\times$ 40% = $160,000 return
Year 2: $560,000 $\times$ 40% = $224,000 return
Year 3: $784,000 $\times$ 40% = $314,000 return
Total 3-year return: $698,000
Total required future value in 3 years: = $698,000 return plus original $400,000 investment = $1,098,000.

Accordingly, in order to achieve that value in three years, the investor will have to own the following percentage of the company:

Using a P/E of 6/1 = $1,098,000 / $2,100,000 = 52.3%
Using a P/E of 8/1 = $1,098,000 / $2,800,000 = 39.2%

The investor can clearly see that if he accepts the projected future earnings of the company, depending on whether he uses a P/E of 6/1 or 8/1, he will need to own between 39.2% and 52.3% of the company in order to achieve his required 40% annualized return. The question then comes back to you: as the money-raising entrepreneur, would you be willing to give up from 39.2% to 52.3% of your company to obtain a $400,000 investment? The question is particularly difficult in this example, as it involves the potential loss of control of the company. What *are* you willing to give in order to get what you want?

5. Which Money Sources to Approach

Once you have determined how much money you need to raise, how the money will be used, when the money is needed, and what you are prepared to give up to get the money, the final question becomes, "Where do I go to find the money that I need?" There is no financial source that provides all forms of financing. Some are highly conservative asset lenders, such as the chartered banks in the main, while others are risk-oriented venture investors who seek an annualized rate of return of 40% or more and are willing to accept significant risk to obtain it. Knowing where to obtain specific types of funding is extremely important to the money-raiser as it will save you significant time in your search and will increase your chances of success by requesting funding from appropriate sources.

A. THE FINANCIAL MARKETPLACE

Like most markets today, the financial marketplace is filled with specialty functions. As we emphasized in the Introduction to this book, the financial world is in constant fluid change and sources of financing reflect this. Canadian chartered banks now own investment dealers, trust companies now compete for term loans, and the walls between financial functions have dissolved to a large degree. However, while there is overlap in functioning between certain types of financial institutions now, such as amongst banks, trust companies, life insurance companies and credit unions, there are still certain distinctions in the availability of the various forms of financing from particular types of institutions.

The chart opposite provides you with a general guide as to which types of financing find expression in which of the several forms of financing, which in turn are obtained from which of the many sources of financing.

A full discussion of the major sources of financing is to be found in Chapter Five, entitled "Identifying Sources of Entrepreneurial Financing in Canada." Also refer to the "Sources of Financing Checklist" in Appendix B and "Sources of Further Information."

4.4 PUTTING IT ALL TOGETHER OR MAKING THE DEAL

You have now determined how much you are going to ask from your prospective investors and what you are prepared to give up in order to get it. You have answered the two fundamental financing questions:

1. "How much money do I need to raise for my business?"
2. "What am I willing to give for the money that I get?"

The next step is to decide which financing sources to approach and then to present them with your proposal in such a way as to maximize your chances for obtaining an investment.

The Decision as to Form of Financing

You are faced with a decision at this point, and it is whether to create a defined and fixed form of investment, such as common shares in a private company with a fixed price and representing a fixed portion of the ownership of the company, or do you move ahead with no fixed terms in mind prepared to negotiate a deal with the funding source? The answer to this lies in where you are most likely to first receive funding. In other words, who are the potential investors most likely to back you financially at this point in time?

TYPES OF FINANCING	FORMS OF FINANCING	SOURCES OF FINANCING

Equity	-Founders' Equity
	-Angels
	-Private Placement
	-Venture Capital
	-Public Offering
	-Earned Surplus
		-Founders
		-Private Individuals
		-Professional Venture
		    Capital Companies
		-Merchant Banks
		-Securities Firms
		-Retained Earnings of
		    the Business

Fixed Assets	-Equipment Loans
	-Term Loans
	-Mortgages
	-Leasing
		-Term Lenders
		-Chartered Banks
		-Leasing Companies
		-Federal Business
		    Development Bank
		-Federal and Provincial
		    Governments

Current Assets	-Demand Loans
	-Operating Loans
	    for Inventories and
	    Accounts Receivable
	-Factoring
	-Floor Planning
	-Warehouse Receipts
		-Term Lenders
		-Chartered Banks
		-Credit Unions
		-Customers
		-Suppliers
		-Factors
		-Commercial Finance
		    Companies

Accounts Payable	-Trade Credit	-Suppliers -Government Programs

Additional	-Personal Loans
	-Employees
	-Credit Cards
	-Life Insurance Policy
	-Franchising
	-Multi-Level Marketing
		-Individuals
		-Credit Card Companies
		-Life Insurance
		    Companies (to policy
		    holders)
		-Franchising Companies
		-Multi-Level Marketing
		    Companies

A. THE "FIXED TERMS" PROPOSAL

For most people without many significant contacts in the financial community, it is easiest to raise money from the people who know you, like you and are interested in you, as opposed to strangers who have no relationship with you. We call individuals who know you, your "warm market" and individuals who do not, your "cold market." When approaching a number of smaller investors, it is much more likely to lead to success, and it is a much quicker process, if you fix the terms of the proposed investment in advance.

With a fixed terms proposal, you prepare the terms of the proposed investment before presenting it to investors, usually by working with your lawyer and accountant. See our comments on this process in Chapter Three. As an example, let us assume that you wish to raise $100,000 for your business. In consultation with your professional advisors, you have decided to sell common shares in your company at a price of $0.50 per share, so that you will need to sell 200,000 shares at that price. At this point, you have already unilaterally settled on all of the terms of the investment except for how much each person will invest and when will he do it. Your next steps are then actually making the presentation and selling the investment to the financial source with the only negotiating being as to:

a. whether or not he will invest at all,

b. for how much money, and

c. when will he do it.

We will discuss the selling process extensively in Chapter Six, entitled "Marketing and Selling Your Deal."

B. THE "OPEN TERMS" PROPOSAL

This approach takes more sophistication or street smarts on the part of the money-raising entrepreneur, or at least on the part of his professional advisors, because every single term of the investment is open to being negotiated. This approach is commonly used when the amount of the investment is very large in the eyes of the money-raiser.

The six major stages of this process are as follows:

1. Be very clear as to your own "bottom line" position prior to commencing negotiations.

That is, know which terms are vital and which are expendable. If you are feeling so desperate and needy with respect to raising money that you will sign virtually any deal so long as you "get the money," we have three words of advice: *"Don't do it!"* While all successful negotiations require flexibility and compromise, if you "give away the ship" you will bitterly regret it later and probably develop resentment and antagonism toward the project and to your investors. This inevitably leads to serious problems and frequently the destruction of the project, or the failure of the business. You must be able to hold your head up and feel satisfied with the deal. In today's terminology, it must be a "win-win" deal. It's not a win for you if you feel resentful about the terms even if you obtained an investment.

2. Listen carefully and learn the investor's needs.

Firstly, by understanding his interests and requirements you can then address them, rather than speaking at length attempting to satisfy issues that are not materially important to him. This will allow you to directly satisfy his concerns, such as the four key elements of the SLIP Test, and will enable you to move the entire process along more quickly, thus saving everyone time. Secondly, this will enable you to better establish rapport with the prospective investor because you demonstrate that you are intelligent enough to pay attention to the needs of the financial source. In fact, it sometimes happens that you will realize in the negotiations that your goals and his needs are quite incompatible. If you can have the integrity to raise this and be prepared to lose the deal, while you may not bring the investor in this time, you will have earned his respect and leave the door open for future investing in a project more suitable for that particular investor.

3. Negotiate with an attitude of solving issues, rather than trying to win every point.

Be creative and look for ways of merging the interests and needs of both sides, rather than trying to make your fixed position dominate. In any case, unless you have that one-in-a-million totally unique business opportunity whereby the world is beating a path to your door; for example, if you have discovered the cure for cancer, the financing source is in a very strong position. You've likely heard of the Golden Rule of Business: "He Who Has the Gold Makes the Rules." This emphasizes the point that you need to be flexible and look for ways of satisfying the requirements of the investor, without compromising yourself beyond the line that you have drawn pursuant to the first point above.

4. Prepare a "term sheet" to summarize the agreed-upon deal.

At the point in the negotiations where you have reached agreement as to the terms of the investment in your company, summarize them in point form. It is most effective if you have each side sign the term sheet. This then is "the deal." Although it may not be legally binding on the investor, it is morally persuasive. It is much more difficult to deny the deal, or to change the terms, when they are in black and white and signed by each party, including the investor himself. Two examples of term sheets are found in Appendix A.

5. Prepare and sign the investment contract.

This is the legally binding agreement which documents the investment transaction and which sets out the rights and responsibilities of each party to the deal. You should understand the major elements of an investment agreement so that you will cover them effectively in negotiations and so that you will understand what your lawyer is talking about when he discusses them with you.

The representations, terms and conditions contained in an investment contract may be divided into seven major functional areas. These are:

a. Closing Preconditions. These are requirements that must be satisfied before the transaction can legally be completed. It is typical that an investor may impose certain preconditions to closing on a company. Given that the investment monies will not be forthcoming until the deal is closed, and there will be no close until the preconditions are satisfied, it acts as a powerful stimulant to the company to put its house in order as required under these preconditions. These frequently deal with "house cleaning" issues, such as that the company be in good standing with the provincial government company registry, or that audited financial statements, not materially different than the unaudited ones previously given to the investor, be completed and given to the investor on or before close.

next

b. Representations and Warranties. These are statements made by the parties which are legally binding upon them, and in the context of an investment contract, the most critical ones describe the condition of the company issuing the shares. For example, the company may represent that it has the exclusive marketing rights for a certain product in a certain area, or it may represent that the financial condition of the company is as represented in the company's most recent financial statements.

c. Investment Description. In an investment contract, this provision goes to the very heart of the deal. It describes the essential terms of the investment, such as how much money, paid to whom, paid when, in return for what type of securities in the company, how many and at what price.

d. Affirmative Covenants. These are the legally binding promises that the company makes with respect to what it will do in the conduct of its affairs. The investor usually requires a number of specific promises from the company with respect to issues that are important to him. For example, he may require that the company agree to spend the money that he invested in a very specific way and that the company's accountant prepare a monthly summary of company expenditures and provide it to him by the middle of the following month.

e. Negative Covenants. These are also legally binding promises that the company makes with respect to what it will not do, or refrain from doing, in the conduct of its affairs. For example, the investor may require that the company agrees not to expand its operations geographically for at least two years so as to consolidate present operations, or that it not make expenditures of any nature in excess of $25,000 without his written approval, or that management fees and salaries shall not exceed certain amounts.

f. Conditions of Default. These are provisions which describe when there has been a breach of the contract. There are generally different ramifications for different types of breach. In addition, there is usually a provision providing for the offending party to correct a breach within a specified time, failing which the offended party can pursue its remedies.

g. Remedies. These refer to the remedial actions that an injured party to an agreement may take in the event that a breach of one or more of the contractual terms has occurred. In the context of this agreement, since the investor's main obligation is to put up the money, a default is most likely a result of something done or not done by the company. Therefore, it is most likely to be the investor who will be looking for a remedy. The exception would be the case where the investor fails to make his investment as agreed.

These seven key elements of an investment contract give you a very brief sketch of the functions of such a document. The specific terms of your particular deal will provide the substance of the contract, particularly as you make affirmative and negative covenants that relate to the unique circumstances of your company, the investor and the transaction.

6. Obtain the Funds ("Get the Money"). Do not be cavalier about this point by assuming that once the term sheet, or even the contract itself, is signed the money will be forthcoming. Sometimes it isn't. Stranger things have happened. In the investment agreement, the signing of the documents, the issuance of share certificates and the payment for the shares all usually occur at a specified time called "the close."

It is incumbent upon you, or if you have a lawyer it is his role, to ensure that the investor has a bank draft or certified cheque or lawyer's trust cheque on hand at the close. It is very effective if you can arrange for the investor to deposit the purchase money in his lawyer's trust account sometime prior to close, to be released to you upon satisfaction of certain conditions, namely your providing through your lawyer all of the required documents including the executed share certificates transferring ownership of part of the company to the investor. You may be relieved to know that unless the purchaser has paid for them the share certificates cannot be issued. You need not worry about a situation where the investor has obtained ownership of stock without paying. The issue that we are addressing is the psychological and emotional commitment of the investor to complete the investment transaction. We want you to get the money.

4.5 ROUNDS OF BUSINESS FINANCING

It is common for most successful companies to engage in a number of different financings over the course of time as their business develops and as their financial needs change. Each successive and different stage of financing is called a "round" of financing. It is important for you to know this because whatever form of financing you choose today, it should be flexible enough to accommodate future rounds. Knowing the distinction between the different rounds of financing is also of practical use because some financial sources will not touch financing at a certain stage. For example, some venture capital firms, despite the name, never provide seed capital and never fund start-ups. However, there is no universal agreement on the criteria for these categories. For example, what is an acceptable "second round" financing to one firm may still be considered to be an ineligible "start-up" to another. A general summary of the successive rounds of business financing is as follows:

"Seed Capital" Financing

This is the very first money that is invested in a project, and is basically for the purpose of proving a concept. It is intended by the investors that this money be the financial "seed," like an acorn, from which a successful company, like a healthy tree, will grow. Seed capital is usually a limited amount of funding which is utilized to undertake the most preliminary of the required work, such as to make an initial prototype, or conduct preliminary market research, or to otherwise prove a concept.

"Start-Up" Financing

This money generally takes a company from the seed capital stage to the point where it is ready to commence business. This is money that is utilized to undertake the initial marketing, complete all necessary product development, put together a management team and have the company in a state of beginning operations pursuant to its business plan. Companies at this stage have not yet been commercially delivering product.

"First Stage" Financing

This funding is to provide capital to the company, after its expenditure of the prior capital obtained from the seed and start-up rounds, for the purpose of moving the company into full operations. It would normally be considered to be lower risk than the previous two stages because production is now ready or actually underway, sales are being made and the management team is functioning together.

"Second Stage" Financing

This may be considered to be the first stage of true expansion financing. It is intended to provide necessary working capital for a growing company which needs more capital for expansion than can yet be generated from revenues. The company may not yet be profitable but it has increasing inventories and accounts receivable.

"Mezzanine" or "Third Stage" Financing

This financing is intended to fund a major expansion of a growing company which at this stage is either profitable or at least breaking even. The money may be used to fund such items as product improvement, facilities expansion, an increase in marketing efforts or just for working capital to allow the company to seize opportunities when they arise. It is generally in the form of term debt that has some form of equity participation as an inducement (an "equity kicker"), such as might be seen in a convertible debenture. It is often used when secured asset lending from a traditional form of banking institution is not available.

"Bridge" or "Fourth Stage" Financing

This is funding for the purpose of enabling a company to pursue its plans pending receipt of major funding, such as from a public offering, which it is in the process of undertaking. This is intended as short-term debt financing and is probably in the form of participating debt which has some sort of bonus, for example, an equity kicker in the form of warrants. It is expected that the bridge financing will be paid out from the proceeds of the anticipated major funding, such as from the proceeds of a public offering.

"Buy-Out" Financing

This occurs when a major shareholder wants to sell a significant portion of his shares in the company, or when the controlling shareholders wish to liquidate their holdings completely by selling all of their holdings in the company. A "leveraged buy-out" refers to the situation where either inside management of the company, or an outside investment group, purchases the entire company, or a portion of it, by borrowing the money to fund the buy-out. The "leverage" refers to the power exercised by the purchasers as a result of being able to borrow the money, rather than having to put up their own capital. The funding is frequently paid-off, in whole or in part, by selling some of the assets acquired through the purchase.

Although most successful mature companies have experienced a number of rounds of financing, there is no reason to expect that every company will experience all of the stages. Most companies will not even last long enough to do so. However, there is at least the comfort of knowing that you do not have to raise all of the money that you will ever need all at once.

4.6 MINIMUM SUBSCRIPTION AMOUNT

As a final very important concept in structuring your deal, you need to appreciate the concept of a "minimum subscription amount." The concept is used in two very different ways, one relating to the company and the other relating to the individual investor. The first usage in particular may mean the difference between success and failure in your money-raising program.

Corporate Minimum Subscription Amount

This is a specified sum of money which is the aggregate minimum amount being sought by a company pursuant to a money-raising program which, if not raised within a certain time period, will be fully refunded to the investors. For example, if a company commences a money-raising program on January 2nd seeking $750,000 for its expansion that year, it may set a minimum subscription amount of $450,000 which must be raised by May 1st, an arbitrary date set by the company itself. The significance of the minimum subscription amount is that the company has stated and agreed with the investment subscribers that unless the company reaches that minimum amount by the date which it set for itself, it will not use any of the funds raised and will return them to the investors. Let us say, in the example given, that if it is only able to raise $400,000 by the 1st of May, then it is obliged to refund the full $400,000 back to the investors.

The purpose of setting a corporate minimum subscription amount is generally to ensure the investors that sufficient monies will be raised to achieve a stated corporate purpose. This purpose would be part of the intended "use of proceeds" of the entire money-raising program. It is the amount which has been deemed by management to be the minimum amount necessary to successfully carry out some defined portion of the company's business plan.

Personal Minimum Subscription Amount

This is the minimum amount which any individual investor will be allowed to invest in the company. If he does not invest at least that minimum subscription amount, he will not be permitted to invest at all. For example, a company seeking to raise $2,000,000 in total and relying on the $97,000 investment exemption to the prospectus requirements in a particular province, may state that no investment subscription less than $100,000 will be accepted. Thus, unless a prospective investor is able and prepared to contribute at least the $100,000 minimum subscription amount, he will not be permitted to participate in the deal.

The purpose of setting a personal minimum subscription amount is normally to ensure compliance with the various available exemptions to the prospectus requirement as discussed in Chapter Three, "Understanding the Law and Money-Raising," while at the same time raising the amount of money that you are seeking. One example of this occurs in the paragraph above. Another example would be the case where you want to raise $1,500,000 to start a business. You determine by consulting a securities lawyer that in your province you could obtain investments from a total of 100 people by stacking together the available exemptions, such as private company exemption, close friends, relatives and business associates and the seed capital exemption. You can see that if you allowed people to put in any little amount that they wanted, you could conceivably have 100 people invest an average of $1,000 each (or less), for a total of $100,000 invested (or less). You are unfortunately a long way from $1,500,000 at that point and you have exhausted your available exemptions under securities laws. Your alternatives at that point are all very expensive and time consuming. Therefore, you want to ensure that your individual minimum subscription amount is large enough so that if people only invest the minimum, you will still be able to comply with the available securities law exemptions to the prospectus requirement. In the example being discussed, if you take the total amount that you want to raise, $1,500,000, and divide that among the 100 allowable investors, you arrive at an average subscription amount of $15,000 each. That in turn will affect your selling strategy, and in particular who you will and won't approach for an investment.

Important Tip: As a money-raising entrepreneur, you hamper your ability to move ahead if you set a corporate minimum subscription amount. We believe that you significantly improve your chances of launching a new business or expanding an existing one if you do not use one. The reason is that you can use the first investor's investment as working capital while you work full-time doing everything that it takes to forward your business. In other words, by not having a minimum subscription amount, you immediately have access to the investment funds which you have raised. This can be essential if you have no other source of income. You could support yourself from the initial investment funds and be able to afford to devote all of your efforts to moving your project ahead. If you have a minimum subscription amount, you are restricted because you will have to rely on other sources of funds to live on and move the project ahead at the same time that you are raising investment monies for your project.

With a corporate minimum subscription amount, the subscription funds are normally paid into a lawyer's trust account and are not accessible to you pending the time that you are successful in raising the required minimum amount. If there is no corporate minimum subscription amount, the subscription funds are paid to the company, and then the company can use them for corporate purposes, which could include paying you a salary while you are launching or growing the company.

Particularly for a start-up, it is a much, much tougher battle to raise the money and move the company ahead if you have a corporate minimum subscription amount. There is generally no legal requirement for one; it is mainly a marketing issue. The question is whether investors will invest without one. We have found that with private investors such as friends, families and "angels" (see section 5.3), the answer is generally yes, they will invest without a corporate minimum subscription amount.

With respect to a personal minimum subscription amount, there may be no need to set one if the amount of money which you seek to raise is relatively small (say, for example, $300,000 or less) and if there are a sufficiently large number of exemptions available to you (say, for example, 100 investors are allowable). Refer to the "Shareholder List" checklist in Appendix B.

By proceeding without either a corporate or a personal minimum subscription amount, you will be able to immediately utilize the money you raise to move your project ahead. If you elect to proceed in this manner, it is extremely important that you be familiar with the contents of Chapter Three, as well as to consult with an experienced securities lawyer to be absolutely certain of the disclosure requirements in your province and to be certain as to the exact criteria of each of the prospectus exemptions.

4.7 CONCLUSION

In arriving at this stage, you have already made very substantial progress on your money-raising program. You have now accomplished the following:

A. Created an enrolling vision for your business;
B. Analyzed the feasibility of your project;
C. Prepared your business plan;
D. Prepared draft financial projections for the enterprise;
E. Briefed yourself on the main points of the law and money raising;
F. Learned the basic elements of structuring an investment;
G. Learned the four key factors every investor needs satisfied;
H. Decided what you are willing to give in return for the investment that you receive;
I. Learned the major sources of both debt and equity capital.

However, we should forewarn you that no stage is ever really completely finished. Your knowledge needs to be kept current with changing business practice and you will continue to learn more as your business develops in the future. You will continue to revise your business plan as long as you are growing the business. Likewise, your cash flow projections will change and financing methods and sources change.

As you can readily appreciate by now, successfully creating a financing deal which works for all parties is as much of an art as it is a science. Although there is no fixed form, there are identifiable building blocks. You are strongly advised to use legal counsel well experienced in commercial negotiations right from the beginning. A seasoned lawyer who understands contracts and business financing, and who has been through dozens of investment negotiations before yours, is worth much more to you than his fees. He may be the strongest resource that you can bring to the process of negotiating and structuring the financing for your company. Don't wait too late in the process to retain knowledgeable counsel. Having an experienced financing professional right from the beginning of the often complex financing process can also give you greater confidence (it's like having someone strong fighting on your side with you) and a sense that realizing your dream is truly possible after all.

CHAPTER FIVE

IDENTIFYING SOURCES OF ENTREPRENEURIAL FINANCING IN CANADA

A jug fills, drop by drop.
Buddha

5.1 INTRODUCTION

It is now time to more precisely identify those financial sources, whether of debt or equity, which are most appropriate for your business. In this chapter we are going to discuss the main sources of entrepreneurial financing in Canada for people in start-up, early stage and emerging companies.

Within each category of financing that we will examine, there has been a history of concrete results in the provision of significant amounts of capital in various forms to Canadian entrepreneurs at various stages in the development of a commercial enterprise. Sources of financing are not all equally receptive, or appropriate, to each stage of business financing. For example, Canada's chartered banks are not normally sources of risk capital, yet they are important sources of term financing for successful entrepreneurs. Private investors, such as family and friends, or "angels," are frequent sources of risk capital and not usually of secured long-term debt. Remember also that within each category there are many different individual sources with their own investment policies and targets. A turndown by one prospect does not mean there will be a turndown by all. Some of the greatest entrepreneurs in the history of North American business were once fired from their jobs, or turned down for financing time and time again, and sometimes both, until they finally reached their stride.

The sources of financing which we will examine in this chapter are as follows:

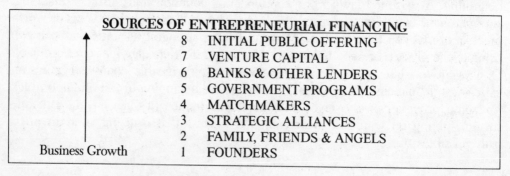

SOURCES OF ENTREPRENEURIAL FINANCING	
8	INITIAL PUBLIC OFFERING
7	VENTURE CAPITAL
6	BANKS & OTHER LENDERS
5	GOVERNMENT PROGRAMS
4	MATCHMAKERS
3	STRATEGIC ALLIANCES
2	FAMILY, FRIENDS & ANGELS
1	FOUNDERS

Business Growth

Also bear in mind that in your choice of financing sources there is more at stake than just the immediate money that you are presently seeking. Ask yourself, "How can this financial source help me in other ways to grow my business?" A successful business is built on relationships of many kinds. You need to build a network of support, ranging from experts in your field upon whom you can call for assistance when you need it, to reliable suppliers, to knowledgeable professional advisors, to the all-important loyal customer. When considering alternative ways to finance your business, always consider the various ways that the source can help you beyond the immediate cash. Can he open doors in the world of business or finance for you that you cannot do yourself? Can he introduce new business opportunities? Always take a broad perspective about your business, ascertaining where each component, such as a financing source, fits into the whole picture of your enterprise.

5.2 FOUNDER'S FINANCING, OR "BOOTSTRAP FINANCING"

Acting either alone or with co-founders, the founder of the enterprise is usually the first source of financing. This is sometimes called "bootstrap financing" because the founder pulls his venture together by his own bootstraps. He normally contributes to a proposed business in one or more of three different ways:

- **Equity,** which is capital and not normally repaid until the founder sells his interest in the business.
- **Debt,** which is a loan to the enterprise and is expected to be repaid within a foreseeable period.
- **"Sweat equity,"** which consists of all of the labour and organizational work that a founder contributes in order to launch a business. This is sometimes referred to as the "entrepreneurial perspiration" by which value is built from ideas and dreams.

The true nature of founder's financing was revealed by one entrepreneur who called it "finesse financing." You finesse your way to providing your own basic stake in the business in any way that you possibly can. For example, your equity contributions can be in many forms other than simply cash as long as it they have value. Non-cash forms of value that you can contribute include:

- **Assets** of all description: such as computers, printers, office supplies and furniture.
- **Rights under a contract:** such as marketing rights for a defined territory such as all or part of Canada, or manufacturing rights, or a distributorship or franchise.
- **Business relationships:** you may have pre-existing relationships of trust with suppliers who know you from your previous employment or other interaction. As a result, they may well provide inventory or services on very favourable terms.
- **Patents, copyrights, trademarks and industrial know-how** can be very real assets of a fledgling enterprise. So much so, that it is often possible to obtain very substantial outside financing based solely on a potentially profitable technology or process.

Tip: One powerful technique for money-raising is to obtain a third-party independent appraisal by a professional appraisal firm on the market value of your technology or know-how. This value can be the basis of your maintaining a very large ownership position in your company as you raise other money for your business, because your company issues shares to you based on the value of the appraisal as the worth of your contribution. For example, if a third-party appraisal estimates that the market value of your technical know-how is $500,000, you could use that as the basis of valuing your contribution to the company.

- **The reputation and effort of the founder** is in many cases the greatest asset that the new enterprise has and is often the basis of the founder's share of the ownership of the business. His business reputation is worth exactly as much as the entrepreneur can convince people with cash that it is worth. For example, if the business requires $50,000 in real cash to get started, a founder may make a deal with an investor to put up the entire $50,000 in return for 49% of the shares in the business (or any other percentage that is negotiated) while the founder is granted 51% for his knowledge, experience and effort. They will then agree as to how each of them is to be remunerated from the profits of the business and should also agree in advance as to how they will deal with the requirement to inject additional capital into the company should the need arise. As we have stressed throughout the book, virtually everything having to do with the structure and financing of a business enterprise is negotiable. However, once a deal is struck, to best ensure certainty and to protect the interests of everyone involved, the result of the negotiations should always be recorded by way of a contract signed by all of the parties.

When the founder intends to finance the business from his own personal financial reserves, such as putting a second mortgage on the family home, or collapsing an RRSP to gain access to the funds, we strongly recommend that the founder, along with his or her spouse, discuss the business prospects with trusted people who are knowledgeable about the industry. There is nothing so desperately debilitating to family life than to be in fear for your financial future. It is tragic how many marriages and families have broken up due to the increased pressures and strains imposed by financial loss. *A business founder absolutely must have his spouse's fully informed support before risking any of the family's essential assets.* They both must fully understand the likelihood and implications of losing everything invested. Only if the spouse agrees to risk the basic family assets should the entrepreneur proceed with that form of financing, because only then will there be a reasonable chance of the relationship staying intact through a financial crisis and loss. In addition, if you do decide to proceed, you are strongly urged to consult with a lawyer to help you organize your affairs to minimize the downside risk to your family. It is important to obtain this candid and objective advice *before* you commit your personal or family assets, or give personal guarantees or request personal guarantees of family members. *One cannot overstate how important it is to preserve and protect basic family assets to the fullest extent possible.* This will provide a sanctuary from the vicissitudes of the business world and minimize the impact of a business reversal.

5.3 PRIVATE INVESTORS, OR "INFORMAL VENTURE CAPITAL"

The largest source of start-up and early-stage financing for Canada's entrepreneurs lies in the private contribution of capital by family, friends and "angels." Aptly named, the word "angel" has come to be well recognized in the financial community as referring to an individual investor who puts risk capital into start-up and early-stage companies. In recent years, several studies by social scientists in Canada and the United States have shown that *private investors are the single largest source of capital for new and emerging companies*. Studies have also shown that more money is raised from private investors for start-ups and early-stage companies combined than is raised from either the founding entrepreneurs themselves or professional venture capital.

"Lovemoney" or "Family & Friends Financing"

"Lovemoney" is another apt description. It refers to the risk capital contributed to a start-up or early-stage company by those who are closest to the entrepreneur, his family and friends. It is also referred to as "F & F" financing from the words "family and friends." These are the people who are closest to the entrepreneur in all the world. These are the people whose most natural inclination is to want to help the entrepreneur be happy and successful. With respect to these special people in your life, we are going to offer you some hard-won advice that has come from our own and many other entrepreneurs' real-world experience.

We strongly urge you to consider all of the implications for you and your family and friends before approaching them for investment monies. We have seen over and over again that no one ever looks at you the same way again once you have lost money for those who financed your business. It is a cruel fact of life that relationships are almost always damaged when money is lost. Even when the prospective investor has confirmed in advance that he can afford to lose the money, and is willing to take the risk of doing so, when it actually happens it is quite another thing. At the worst, it will destroy your relationship with that person; at the least, you will definitely lose credibility or stature in the eyes of the person whose money you lost.

With all of the slings and arrows of outrageous fortune that life throws at each of us, our family and friends are the safe refuge with whom we can seek comfort, solace and sanity. Their value to us goes infinitely beyond calculation in dollars and cents. Thus, we say, go slowly and thoughtfully before bringing your family and closest friends into a business deal with you. How will you feel if you let them down? How will you feel if they never look at you with quite the same degree of trust and respect again? While people can forgive, few will ever forget. Parents are generally the most forgiving of financial loss, while friends tend to be the least.

Given that more than 50% of the start-ups and early-stage companies in Canada will likely be financed originally just by family and friends, we know that there will be many readers of this book who will, amazing but true, choose to ignore our sage words of warning on this topic. So, for those of you who will press ahead to enroll family and friends in your new business, we provide the following recommendations.

A. USE YOUR BUSINESS PLAN

Before they invest, show each of the F & F prospects your business plan. Have them review all elements, particularly Risk Factors. If, after reviewing your business plan, they decide that there are problems with the project, that they don't think the business is viable, then you may learn something. If these people won't fund the project, it may well not be worth financing. Do not hesitate to have them show the business plan to an outside consultant. If he approves of the project, that will help preserve your relationship in the event of failure. You can both say, "Hey, even the expert consultant liked the deal!" On the other hand, if he recommends against it, you should listen to his reasoning and try to learn something. You may receive some valuable free coaching.

B. USE A SHAREHOLDERS' AGREEMENT

In the case where there will only be a small number of investors in the company, make use of a shareholders' agreement. By small we mean an intimate, manageable number of people for you. It will vary according to circumstances, but is likely under ten people. A carefully written agreement that sets out the possible upside and downside, the risks and benefits, the rights and remedies, is essential to attempting to preserve good relationships with your investors when things go bad, or at least are off target, as they frequently are. It is very important to carefully spell out the consequences of the happening of certain events. Such as, if the business becomes insolvent, what happens to the assets? Or, if the business is still alive but not growing according to projection, and you advise that more money must be contributed by each of the investors to make it grow. What happens if some of the investors will not contribute any more? Under what circumstances can an investor get his money back? A properly written shareholders' agreement will deal with all of the critical issues such as these.

C. REPORT TO YOUR INVESTORS VERY REGULARLY

You now have some of their money. They want to know how it's doing. Since these investors are your family and friends, you do not want or need to have lurking silently behind every conversation with these people, their unspoken question, "What's happening to my money?" Tell them, and often. We recommend a brief reporting letter once a month to your F & F investors. No less than once every two months. A brief letter summarizing the functional areas of the company, its progress and problems, will suffice.

Tip: From long experience, we have found that investors are much happier and satisfied if they are advised of problems as they develop, rather than getting some very bad news at the last minute. We recognize that this is against the inclination of many, if not most, entrepreneurs who optimistically believe, or at least hope, that the solution is just around the corner. Ongoing disclosure is the most effective practice. Most investors can accept your failure and their financial loss if they know that you have kept them fully informed throughout and that you have done your very best to make the project work. In addition, if the investors are aware of major problems as they develop, each of them likely has a wide sphere of influence and acquaintances, so he may be able to find assistance for you somehow. It's clear that people cannot offer support if they are kept in the dark as to what is going on.

"Angels"

"Angel" is the very appropriate name which is used in the financial community to describe an individual who puts up money as a private investor in someone else's business. The term "angel" is generally applied to an investor who is not a family member or friend of the entrepreneur, so as to distinguish him from providers of lovemoney. Usage is not consistent in this regard, however, and some financial writers use angel to apply to all informal investors including those in the family and friends category.

Angels have been described elsewhere as investors who are willing to take an unusual risk for an unusual rate of return. This is consistent with our Great White Shark theory of investment. These are the people who are willing to sacrifice to a significant degree security, liquidity and interest in order to achieve a very significant potential upside return. Angels go in where chartered banks will never tread.

A. WHO ARE THE ANGELS?

Angels are any affluent members of your community, and those across the country, who are ready, willing and able to invest some of their own money into other people's ventures. They are financially comfortable individuals, such as successful businesspeople and executives; doctors, dentists, lawyers, accountants and other professional people; self-employed tradespeople such as plumbers and electricians; successful commission salespeople; government administrators and others. They are frequently not the very wealthiest people in your province, or owners of very successful businesses, as these people often have significant investments of their own with professional investment advisors.

Angels are generally who you would think of as being successful middle-class and upper-middle-class people. Some of the best prospects to be angels are frequently people who are not themselves in business, yet nonetheless enjoy an above-average income. Many such people have a sense that they are missing out on profitable private business and investment opportunities because they are not directly engaged in business. This category particularly includes people involved in the professions, particularly medical and technical, management people in large corporations, educators and middle to higher-level government employees.

B. WHERE ARE THE ANGELS?

As financially comfortable members of your community, angels may be found almost everywhere in Canada. Initially, you need look no further than your own city or municipality. You will know, or know the names of, many prospective angels. See our comments on how to pursue them in Chapter Six, "Marketing and Selling Your Deal."

C. WHAT KIND OF INVESTMENTS DO ANGELS WANT?

Most angels do not have a well-formulated private investment strategy. This will generally work in your favour. As private individuals who earn their living in some way other than the financial business, angels tend to simply respond to the individuals who approach them on a case-by-case basis. It is thus your responsibility to enroll the angel in becoming part of your dream. Remember what we have said before in Chapter One: *The essence of raising capital is to enroll the prospective investor in your vision of the outstanding success that you will make of your business with an injection of his capital for your mutual profit.*

In every instance, you must satisfy the four elements of the SLIP Test as described in Chapter Four:

1. Security;
2. Liquidity;
3. Income;
4. Potential upside.

As we discussed at length in that chapter, the potential upside is the key element in the SLIP Test. This needs to be enticing, or at minimum, very attractive. However, the financial return is not always the only, or sometimes even the most important, reason for an angel to invest with you (and that is certainly the case with family and friends). Many people will invest with you for reasons that are important to them, but are not strictly monetary in the conventional sense. Some of these reasons include:

1. Participation in Something Exciting

Many hobbyists or afficionados of a sport or pastime will invest in a young venture because it excites them; they feel emotionally stimulated by participating in the deal. As a real example, almost all of the largest Canadian helicopter skiing operations, which have become the preeminent heliskiing operators in the world, were funded initially by the private subscription of avid powder skiers. Initially, hundreds of thousands of dollars and eventually millions of dollars of investment monies were raised privately from business and professional people who were absolutely wild about powder skiing. By being in a small way an "owner" of the heliskiing business, these "powder hounds" fulfilled some of their longing for excitement and adventure in a sport that they adore.

2. Opportunity to Help

Many people will invest in order to help the struggling entrepreneur when they are either interested in the entrepreneur, or more likely, the field of endeavour itself. In the heliskiing example, many of the early investors genuinely were interested in seeing the sport of heliskiing literally "take off" in Canada and were motivated to help the mountain guides who founded the businesses turn their dreams into reality. This motivation could be harnessed in many other industries and fields of action. For example, medicine and the environment are two areas where many professional people would obtain a sense of satisfaction in helping a young company grow and become successful when that company is developing a product that could contribute to a better world.

3. Get a Job or Perform a Service

Sometimes people with substantial savings will invest in a business on condition that they be retained to perform consulting services for the company or even be hired as an employee by the company. Or, on a variation of this, sometimes lawyers, accountants and consultants in other areas will perform their professional services in exchange for stock in the company. This is as good as cash for the company when these services are ones which would have to be obtained and paid for in any case.

4. Opportunity to Learn

There have been many instances where someone will invest in a company to become acquainted with a new technology, or to learn something about an area that is of interest to him. This may be a rancher who invests in someone's dairy technology, or a doctor who invests in a private clinic. They may feel that there could develop a financial opportunity or advantage out of learning about the business that they have invested in.

One note of caution: Prospective investors, like everyone else, always have strong personal interests and preferences with respect to what interests them most in the world. This can work both for and against you, and you should be as fully informed as you can be about any particular person's background and interests before meeting with him. For example, if you have created a new piece of hardware for sailboats, it would seem to make sense to target affluent individuals who love sailing and the marine environment to show your project to first. Theoretically, they will understand the product and have an emotional interest in the subject. On the other hand, we have seen that strategy fail completely when the product or service is so revolutionary in the field that people currently involved in the industry are highly sceptical. In that instance, if you have such a reaction from the first few people in the industry that you show it to, you may switch gears and refrain from showing it to people who know something about that industry. Instead, you show it to people who have no preconceived notions or experience with this type of product or service. Your strategy would then become one of approaching angels not associated with that particular industry in any way and who have no pre-existing bias which would work against your proposal.

D. HOW MUCH WILL ANGELS INVEST?

So that you have at least some guideline as to what has worked for other people, we have found that from our own experience the average investment size of a middle-class or upper-middle-class investor in Canada is from $15,000 to $20,000. That figure has been obtained from real projects with no minimum subscription amounts of either kind.

To calculate this, we have reviewed a number of actual, successful money-raising programs in Canada, mainly for technology-related projects, where the private placement offerings ranged from $1,000,000 to $3,000,000 in size. The size of each individual investor's participation ranged from a low of $1,000 to a high of $300,000. In these projects, involving a total of approximately 500 investors altogether, a handful of those people invested $100,000 or more, and approximately fifty invested $50,000. The balance were less, with several below $5,000. The average investment was approximately $17,500. In these successful private money-raising programs, which were in each case sold by the entrepreneurs themselves, the investors covered a wide socio-economic spectrum, from civil servants to tradespeople, from self-made millionaires to heart surgeons.

If you are looking for $100,000 for your business, you may hit it lucky and do it with one angel. On the other hand, it may require you to find ten people at $10,000 each, or a combination of one person at $20,000, three at $15,000 and seven at $5,000 each, or one of any number of possible permutations. The parameters that you must remember are the securities law rules with respect to how many investors you can sell to without a prospectus. This is discussed extensively in Chapter Three.

The size of the average investment will climb as you focus your prospecting on increasingly higher economic groups; in other words, on wealthier folks. Many Canadian private placements have restricted themselves to minimum investments of $100,000. However, this is a very specialized market and should normally only be attempted with the help of a very sophisticated professional investment advisor.

We believe that for the typical middle-class Canadian entrepreneur with an average range of contacts through family, friends and business associates, if you make your plans based on raising an average amount of $15,000 to $20,000 per investor, you will not go too far wrong. If you have a good project, you are bound to get lucky and some investors will likely go for significantly more than $15,000 or $20,000. That would allow you to bring in more very small investors in order to complete the financing, all the while staying within the permitted number of exemptions under provincial securities laws.

Important Tip: In looking for your investors, don't waste your time trying to hit a home run, go for base hits. In other words, do not restrict your searching for that one big investor who can do your whole deal. You are much more likely to find several people who are all willing to invest a little, rather than one person who will do the whole thing. That is why it is useful not to have an individual minimum subscription amount.

Angels will invest as much as they can afford to, and sometimes more, if they like your proposal well enough. There is no special formula as to how much they will invest. The amount varies with the size of their bank account and the psychology of the investor. However, our experience indicates that planning to raise an average of $15,000 to $20,000 per angel investor is both conservative and attainable for an ordinary middle-class person with an ordinary range of contacts starting or growing a business. How much can you raise? Again, venturing way out on a limb, we believe that the same hypothetical "ordinary entrepreneur" (we appreciate that this is a hypothetical creature indeed, and probably an oxymoron as well) utilizing the coaching in this book and following all of the instructions, can likely raise at least $250,000 for any viable and financially attractive project, and often a great deal more.

5.4. STRATEGIC ALLIANCES, OR "CORPORATE PARTNERING"

Introduction

The purpose of this section is to point out to you that there may be a way of accomplishing your goals without further diluting equity, or accumulating debt, in your company. The method is in making a commercial agreement with an existing company, probably significantly larger than your own, either domestic or international, currently involved in some aspect of its business which interacts with your needs and interests. This type of contractual arrangement comes in many forms and goes by many names, such as strategic alliance, strategic partnering, corporate partnering, business collaboration or joint venture. In the final analysis, no matter what the name, each company has decided that the other has something that it wants, and it chooses to enter into some kind of cooperative arrangement to combine resources rather than each pursuing these particular aims independently.

Three broad goals that can be achieved through forming strategic alliances are as follows:

- Develop alternative ways of financing product development, production and marketing;
- Facilitate more rapid expansion of new-technology applications and penetrate distant markets; and
- Build a stronger competitive position through establishing relationships with other companies.

Strategic alliances are not only being pursued by small companies with few resources, but by major transnational corporations with sales in the billions. For example, fierce long-time rivals in the personal computer business, IBM and Apple, have made an agreement to combine resources and cooperatively develop their next whole new generation of personal computers as a joint venture. What is interesting about their agreement, is that they will continue to compete tooth and nail on the sales and marketing side as separate companies pursuing market share, yet they have recognized the benefits of sharing research and development costs.

Closer to home, arch rivals like the Bay and Eaton's, which pride themselves on their independence, have for years been cooperating in the development of new regional shopping centres across the country where they both become anchor tenants of the same shopping centres. After competing against each other for generations right across Canada, they came to realize that there were many advantages to cooperating, such as increasing the ability to attract shoppers by the strength of their combined drawing power. Today, they are competing and cooperating at the same time. This is true for rivals in virtually every industry. Newspapers daily announce new alliances among rivals and non-rivals alike, whether it be international airlines, car manufacturers, consumer products, law firms, management consultants, or any other industry segment. It is clear that the old concept of a commercial competitor as being a business enemy under all circumstances is no longer viable, with the high costs and great complexity of much of today's business life.

Types of Business Collaborations

There is a number of ways that you can create a relationship with another organization which could be beneficial to you both. For example, if a small firm has a concept, prototype or product of interest to larger companies, these are often willing to enter into research, development, licensing, manufacturing, marketing or distribution agreements with the smaller companies. Another approach is to divide the world into territories for a product, and sell rights to individual countries or areas. One individual we know sold the rights for his patented technology to an Asian group which is now manufacturing and distributing his product throughout the Far East. The Canadian inventor is pursuing market development on his own in Canada and the United States with the money, almost $1,500,000, which he obtained in one lump-sum payment by selling the Asian rights.

The number of possible business arrangements that it is possible to create is only limited by your imagination, and that of the other party and your professional advisors. Such alliances include joint venture; research and development agreement; production agreement; and marketing agreement.

A. JOINT VENTURE

This is a generic phrase used to cover a multitude of possible business combinations whereby a new and independent business is created by two or more different companies. One interesting example of this is in the legal profession. A number of independent Canadian law firms have combined forces and formed joint ventures — that is, new firms with new names — to provide mainly Canada-related legal services in Asian capitals such as Hong Kong and Taipei. In this way, they reduce the substantial set-up and operating costs involved and, in some cases, even combine their strengths in the marketing of legal services.

B. RESEARCH AND DEVELOPMENT AGREEMENT

This is an arrangement with respect to research and development which allows companies to spread the risks and the costs associated with R & D. It is often the case that an individual inventor working alone, or an energized and motivated team in a very small company, is responsible for creative breakthroughs of all kinds. It is also the case that this often requires significant capital to pursue. This is where finding a bigger brother to provide the resources necessary to pursue the R & D can make all the difference. This can mean the larger company providing any number of benefits, from access to labs and research facilities, to the loan of trained staff, to contributing raw materials, to putting up cash. A detailed agreement would have to be drawn up by the lawyers for the parties in order to ensure that the manner of exploitation of the development was absolutely clear. This would include such matters as the responsibility and manner of carrying out the production of the product, the financing and execution of the marketing, and the sharing of the returns.

C. PRODUCTION AGREEMENT

This is an arrangement with respect to production or manufacturing which allows companies to cooperate to produce something. For example, a small company contracts with a larger company with manufacturing facilities to produce goods for the small company. Another example would be where two or more roughly equivalent-sized businesses combine resources to produce a product for market. After having been exposed to a lifetime of aggressive television commercials by all of the large gasoline marketing companies in Canada extolling the virtues of their specific brand, it is often a moment of disquieting enlightenment when a first-year college marketing student learns that many of those different brands of gasoline from different companies often come out of the same refinery. It's exactly the same stuff!

D. MARKETING AGREEMENT

This is an arrangement with respect to sales and marketing which allows companies to expand into markets where they have neither the staff, the know-how, the money, nor the resources generally, to be able to effectively penetrate the desired markets. One example is furnished with respect to Japan. Several small Canadian companies have utilized the marketing services of one of Japan's very large international trading companies in order to harness the local expertise and resources to penetrate that immense market. Perhaps your product is also complementary to that of a larger company's product line. Another example is that of a small Canadian software developer which entered into a marketing agreement with a larger American software company with an international distribution network in order to accelerate the sales growth of the Canadian company. If the smaller company had waited for years to enter the international market on its own, as was the practice in former times, its larger competitors would almost surely already have penetrated the international markets and seized the technical advantage away from the smaller company.

Advantages and Benefits of a Strategic Alliance

Some of the potentially positive aspects of a strategic partnering arrangement include the following:

A. Raise Financing. A large strategic partner may be willing to assist you in numerous possible ways, directly or indirectly, to finance the development, production or marketing of a product that is of interest to the larger company.

B. Increase Probability of Business Success. One or more strategic partners can help decrease the financial and technical risk and increase the likelihood that a project will succeed, whether from the needs of project cost, development, manufacturing or marketing.

C. Make Larger Projects Possible. With the help of a sophisticated and wealthier partner, the creative vision of a smaller company can be made real through access to far greater technical and financial resources.

D. Achieve Access to New Markets and Improved Market Intelligence. An alliance with a company already successfully selling to a particular market can achieve a breakthrough that would not otherwise be possible for a small company, particularly overseas markets. In addition, a partner already familiar with that market can advise on whether, and how, any specific product or service of yours would gain acceptance in that market.

E. Avoid Expensive Duplication and Save Money. When companies cooperate in aspects of their business, whether development, production or marketing, they save the costs of duplication of effort that would otherwise be required. Even if they compete in large parts of their business, they can cooperate in others. The IBM-Apple or Eaton's-Bay relationships illustrate that.

F. Attain Economies of Scale. By combining resources and even integrating some of their operations with their partners, companies can achieve lower unit costs to a level comparable with much larger competitors. This may also allow the partners to acquire new technology, equipment or know-how which they could not individually afford.

G. Boost Credibility of a Small Firm. An association with an established, respected larger firm will bestow instant credibility on a small firm. This will help overcome many potential objections to buying products from a new firm, such as they will not be able to adequately service the product, or they will not survive long enough to honour warranties and provide follow-up products.

While these outline some of the more obvious advantages of forging an alliance with one or more corporate partners, there are many disadvantages as well. Each situation that you face will have to be evaluated on its own merits. Do not assume that in every case the advantages will outweigh the drawbacks. That is not necessarily so.

Disadvantages and Drawbacks of a Strategic Alliance

Some of the potentially negative aspects of a corporate partnering arrangement include the following:

A. It Can Be Expensive to Set Up and Administer. A joint venture of economic significance to your firm will take a considerable amount of time and money to research, negotiate, structure, implement and manage. It must be carefully set up with its own business plan, goals, management and budgets.

B. Excessive Use of Senior Management's Time. Particularly for a small firm with thin executive talent, the time taken away from the normal day-to-day running and building of the business will be considerable. A large amount of time must be devoted to successfully establishing any significant joint venture business relationship. Each firm entering into the search for a joint venture partner must be prepared to have senior management preoccupied with that project for a considerable amount of time.

C. Friction and Misunderstanding between Corporate Cultures. This is usual even between companies in the same industry from the same country speaking the same language. When you make an alliance with people halfway across the world from a different cultural background with a different native language, you know in advance that there are going to be misunderstandings. The harm that can be done to your company in this regard should not be underestimated. We have seen some small Canadian companies put in desperate financial condition by relying on production from overseas partners in less-developed countries, when despite clear engineering specifications and to the Canadians what were clear operating guidelines, the products produced were consistently substandard and unacceptable. This caused tremendous problems for the companies and their own customers. Large Canadian corporations have the financial strength to take the time to overcome such problems with offshore partners; frequently small companies do not.

D. Loss of Proprietary Technology and Trade Secrets. Smaller Canadian companies with limited financial resources must be extremely cautious before disclosing their trade secrets and proprietary technology, particularly to companies based outside of North America, Western Europe, Australia and New Zealand. Many experienced commercial lawyers involved with technology transfer from Canada offshore, to Asia in particular, have a highly sobering operating principle: Offshore Technology Transfer Agreements = Technology Rape.

If your offshore partner steals, takes, appropriates, confiscates, copies or otherwise rips-off your proprietary technology anywhere in Asia and in much of the rest of the world, you will be almost powerless to recover it, defend your position, or obtain satisfaction. It will be too expensive, too long, too difficult and too late. Accordingly, any agreement dealing with access to your technology must be extremely carefully thought through. **Tip:** Many small Canadian companies have discovered the best solution is simply to sell their technology outright and not attempt any ongoing relationship that requires monitoring, such as royalty payments based on foreign sales.

FOUR IMPORTANT CAUTIONS

1. Protect your company from the beginning with a Confidentiality/Non-Disclosure Agreement. You must also understand, that for all practical purposes, this agreement is completely unenforceable by you in most parts of the world. Therefore, do not rely on it.

2. Do not send key technical data, drawings, etc. even with a Confidentiality/Non-Disclosure Agreement in place because you don't have the resources to defend yourself in most overseas jurisdictions. It is difficult enough here as it is.

3. Do not enter into extended payment schedules with overseas distributors, such as royalty agreements, whereby you will be paid for your know-how and technology over time.

4. Before entering into a joint venture agreement with an offshore partner, do a very thorough due diligence investigation and satisfy yourself in every possible way as to the honour and integrity of your proposed partner in addition to his commercial acumen. In addition, seek advice from legal counsel experienced in doing business with companies from the country in question.

How to Find the Right Strategic Ally

The key question to ask yourself here is, "Who could have an economic interest in what I am doing?" or, "What kind of business or organization could see a way of making money from what I am involved with?" If you can figure out who could potentially make a profit from, or otherwise have an interest in, what you are creating/developing/building/making/offering/serving, then you have a potential ally with whom to combine resources, or if is what you seek, to contribute new capital to your company.

Start with your own contacts in your own industry, then expand by doing research to discover which companies are engaged in the industry, the activity and the location which interests you. The federal and provincial governments, along with the trade commissions and consulates of foreign countries, have staff dedicated to helping you identify potential business partners in all spheres of industry and commerce. There are also numerous private consulting firms purporting to have valuable connections and expertise in the area of forming strategic business alliances, particularly with offshore companies. These private firms should be considered with a respectful scepticism and a "show me" approach. Before engaging a private firm to make contacts, you should obtain a list of satisfied clients for whom the company has successfully produced results and then actually contact some of the clients and determine how the consultant performed. In addition, you should make any financial arrangements with such a consulting firm contingent on performance; that is, upon your entering into an agreement with a strategic partner through their efforts. It should go without further saying, but out of caution we will mention it again anyway, that you should do a very thorough investigation of the company with whom you ultimately choose to enter into a strategic alliance before you sign the contract.

Here is a list, in random order, of some of the sources that may help you connect with an appropriate strategic partner:

- your personal network of contacts and those of close associates
- current suppliers to your business
- current customers of your business
- previous business associates of any kind: customers, suppliers, professional colleagues
- trade shows and conventions
- distributors and wholesalers
- yellow pages
- federal and provincial government agencies
- accounting and law firms
- consulting firms, particularly those doing work in the industry
- industry associations and directories
- trade magazines
- banks and banking magazines
- venture capital companies
- foreign trade missions and consulates.

The Strategic Alliance Contract

This contract will be one of the most, if not the most, important contracts that your company will ever enter into. The ramifications flowing from a successful joint venture, as well as the consequences which could result from a disastrous alliance, are so important to your company that this agreement should only be drafted and entered into with the input of all of your key advisors, particularly the heads of marketing, finance and production, under the guidance of an experienced commercial lawyer. This type of commercial arrangement is of sufficient gravity to be able to literally make or break many smaller companies.

A THREE-PART PROCESS

We strongly recommend that you approach the negotiations leading to the signing of a formal joint venture agreement as a three-part process as follows:

1. Initial Investigation, Due Diligence Research and Assessment.
2. Negotiation and Preparation of a Memorandum of Understanding.
3. Execution of the Strategic Alliance Contract.

1. Initial Investigation, Due Diligence Research and Assessment

a. You must be very clear in advance why you are seeking to enter into this arrangement, how you propose to benefit, how your proposed partner will benefit, what you are prepared to contribute, what you expect your partner to contribute, and what the experience and reputation of your partners happen to be. Have they entered into this sort of agreement before? How did they perform? What do their previous partners have to say about the experience?

b. Prepare a planning document which will give you guidelines through the negotiations and help you understand the issues involved that need to be covered as a matter of the functioning of the joint venture and that must be covered in the contract. Some companies go so far at this stage as to prepare a business plan based on the information available to them at this point. You will need a budget and cash flow projections for the investigation, negotiations, implementation of the signed agreement and the operation of the joint venture.

c. You must always keep your corporate objectives clearly in view throughout the processes of investigation and then negotiation. Always be asking whether the direction that the proposed alliance is heading in is really what you want. Some businesspeople have ended up at the conclusion of negotiations with a deal quite different than they had originally intended and really not as congruent with their stated corporate objectives as they need. Many entrepreneurs have thought that it was a sexy idea to have an offshore joint venture, only to run aground on the shoals of reality. Do not fall in love with the idea of having a joint venture relationship with another company just for its own sake. In other words, keep your eyes on the prize!

2. Negotiation and Preparation of a Memorandum of Understanding

You must determine what the business deal is before you settle on the final legally binding contract. When you have worked out a relationship and a deal that as businesspeople you like, feel comfortable with and wish to proceed with, it should be written out in your own words as the building block on which to construct the legally binding contract. This business document is not intended to be legally binding, but it is morally binding in the sense that this is the deal. This document is variously called a memorandum of understanding, or letter of understanding, or heads of agreement, or memorandum of agreement, or memorandum of intention, or various other names. It records your understanding with the other party.

a. Conduct of the Negotiations   While there are many books on negotiating, and that subject is beyond the scope of this book, we would like to make some suggestions that seem to be frequently overlooked and yet are highly effective with respect to the conduct of the negotiations:

i. Ensure that all the members of the negotiating teams have become at least somewhat known to each other, have had an opportunity to familiarize themselves with each other, and understand each person's role in the discussions.

ii. Discuss the philosophy driving each side, what their greater business purpose is, how the joint venture will reflect that and define the vision for the project. Many hard-nosed businesspeople ignore this part of the discussion to their eternal regret. What you may discover is that the two sides have quite different and incompatible agendas. This may be referred to as hidden agenda, yet it may not be devious or in bad faith at all, yet it may put the parties in incompatible positions.

One example might be the case where an aggressive, highly profit-driven, real estate development company enters into a joint venture with a long-established, socially and environmentally conscious land-holding family to develop a large, mixed-use "model community" on the family's vast acreage adjoining a major city. The intention may be that the family mainly contributes the land and the private company mainly contributes expertise and funding. The developer may have as his goal the maximization of his revenue stream through high management fees followed by a quick capital gain by means of an early sale of his interest in the project. The family, however, may view the project as part of their long-term social and environmental contribution to the community. The family may want the project to provide low-cost services to community members, job training and employment opportunities for disadvantaged members of the community, and they may want a long-term stewardship relationship with the land to ensure continuity of the parks and green belts as well as other socially-driven aspirations. If those disparate goals are not soon laid on the table for discussion and decision-making, there will clearly be difficulties down the road as one side attempts to take actions incompatible with the desires and needs of the other.

iii. Identify key issues to be discussed, and prepare an agenda or outline for discussion so that each side will know what the most important issues are and can prepare accordingly.

iv. Set a timetable for the negotiations and a target date to have a final contract signed. Obtain agreement from each side committing the people and resources to the negotiations so that you can have confidence that the negotiations indeed will proceed within a workable time frame. If you do not set dates and obtain commitments, the process may never come to fruition. Many commercial ventures have only a limited window of opportunity and if this is to be seized, the negotiations must be consciously structured to move ahead as required to seize that opportunity.

b. Contents of the Memorandum of Understanding A successful strategic alliance is much more like a marriage than going out for a few dates. This is a long-term relationship that requires everyone to win. If one side feels that it has been "tricked," "screwed," "beaten," "bettered" or "taken advantage of" at the start, then the project will falter and may even be doomed from birth. You need everyone that is involved to be enthused and committed to its success right from the beginning. A joint venture business relationship is like a marriage in another way, in that even with the best will in the world from both parties, it still takes a lot of intentional effort and nurturing to make it work well for each side.

In order to ensure that you and your prospective partner have covered the main topics of importance to each of you in your negotiations, the memorandum of understanding should cover at a minimum the following areas:

i. the purpose of, and your vision for, the project;

ii. the specific objectives of the project;

iii. the size and magnitude of the project;

iv. the role and contributions, including manpower and money, of each party;

v. method of valuation of each party's contribution;

vi. methods and amounts of funding of the project: how much, what kind, when, by whom, for what;

vii. the consequences of default of contributions;

viii. ownership of the project and its constituent parts;

ix. management and control of the project and its different activities, including methods of selecting and changing management, reporting relationships;

x. management and service agreements between the project and related parties;

xi. what committees will be necessary and selection procedure for their members; employee selection, advancement, remuneration and benefits;

xii. government involvement, including necessary regulatory agencies and permits, environmental review, workers, health and safety, and financial assistance;

xiii. accounting policy and practices, financial reporting, budget preparation and management;

xiv. terms of the distribution of profits;

xv. protection of trade secrets and proprietary information and technology;

xvi. conflict resolution procedures, including applicable jurisdiction, and processes of mediation and arbitration;

xvii. provisions for the termination of the agreement: how, for what reasons, and under what circumstances;

xviii. such other provisions as are vital to the interests of either party.

By focusing on these key issues at an early date, you will soon discover whether or not you will be able to come to terms with your proposed strategic partner. It is much better to learn of your incompatibility before you get married, rather than undergo a messy, costly and probably damaging divorce later on. There is also a huge opportunity cost incurred having a liaison with an ultimately unsatisfactory strategic partner, because all of the time that you ultimately spend with that party is time lost when you could have been walking down the aisle with someone with whom you would make a great match.

3. Execution of the Strategic Alliance Contract

By the time you get to the point of drafting the legally binding agreement between you and your strategic partner, if you have worked through the first two stages described above you will be reasonably sure that the deal will come together and on what terms. You will be providing the lawyers with an excellent framework upon which they can flesh out the final form of the agreement.

You should do your utmost to create both an atmosphere between the parties and a written contract which provide for flexibility and the ability to have ongoing business discussions and decision-making which affect the operations of the alliance. Business is fluid and dynamic. As technologies, the market, government regulations, competitors and all other aspects of your operating environment change, you need to be assured that the legal structure which you have created provides for evolution and change in the strategic alliance itself.

The are many approaches to providing for such evolution in a contract, along with mechanisms for dispute resolution which do not necessitate going to the courts. Exit clauses must make provision for a partner to leave the alliance without necessarily destroying the combined joint venture business. These provisions will deal with the disposition of joint venture assets on the departure of one of the parties or the termination of the entire joint venture. The contract should be constructed to reflect the fact that your relationship with your strategic partner is alive, changing and continuously evolving. In other words, the signed agreement should reflect the fact that your joint venture is an ongoing process, rather than a fixed event etched in stone.

5.5 MATCHMAKERS AND OTHER FINANCIAL INTERMEDIARIES

The concept of a matchmaker is simple. A person, company or government agency acts as an intermediary in attempting to match investors who have money to businesses that require money. Both government and the private sector are involved in this activity. The cost for the service varies from no cost to a specified fee, depending on the nature of services involved, the experience of the person offering the service and whether it is the private or public sector. Refer to "Sources of Further Information," Section H, for a list of various matchmaking services.

Basically, there are various forms of matchmaking:

- **Provincial government:** Some provincial governments offer a matchmaking service. The information may be accessed in various ways depending on the agency involved from a data base of other potential investors, to a regular publication of potential financing sources and projects. Check with your provincial government for current information. Contact numbers for various relevant government departments can be found in "Sources of Further Information."

- **Business organizations:** A number of business organizations act as intermediaries in some capacity. For example, the Bank of Nova Scotia has a matchmaking publication. The Canadian Chamber of Commerce also operates a matchmaking service called COIN (Canadian Opportunity Investment Network). See "Sources of Further Information," Section H, for contact numbers.

- **Private networking organizations:** There are several privately operated networking groups that operate in a manner similar to investment clubs. They meet regularly sometimes for breakfast or evening meetings. The purpose is to have prospective investors and those seeking funds meet on informal basis. If there is mutual interest, both sides can follow-up on a result of the initial contact. Refer to the yellow pages of your phone book under "Associations" and "Clubs."

- **Professionals and consultants:** Various lawyers, accountants, business consultants and brokers perform a matchmaking service for a fee, as well as give advice on preparing a business plan or prepare one for you. A candid critique and assessment of your financing request is also given. Refer to the yellow pages of your phone book under "Financing." Also see the Appendix under "Matchmaking Services."

One of the authors of this book, Brian F. Nattrass, has established the National Business Finance Network, Inc. which provides many services, including matchmaking, to both entrepreneurs looking for capital and to investors looking for appropriate investments. For information on how the company may assist you, contact the National Business Finance Network, Inc. at #207–1425 Marine Drive, West Vancouver, B.C. V7T 1B9 Tel: (604) 886-3373 Fax: (604) 886-9605.

5.6 GOVERNMENT FINANCING PROGRAMS

The amount of financial assistance available to small- and medium-sized businesses through various levels of government amounts to billions of dollars a year. All levels of government have assistance programs. This would include federal and provincial governments and Crown corporations as well as a few municipal governments.

There are literally hundreds of different programs available, some that are specific to a certain industry, some that are specific to the type of expenditure involved, and others that are general business stimulation initiatives.

Government financing and assistance programs are available for all stages and needs of a business development, including developing your business management skills, financing your business, researching and developing the product, developing your employee skills, manufacturing your products and marketing your products and services. Generally, government programs do not give you financing for existing debts, for obvious reasons, unless approval is given to consolidate debts and advance additional funds in a unique situation that meets their criteria. In addition, it is not common to receive goverment funding for working capital (ongoing monthly expenses). Of course, there are exceptions to this statement.

Because all levels of government are aware of the vital importance of small and medium-sized business to the economic well being of the country, governments maintain a comprehensive range of direct and indirect financial support programs to simulate and foster entrepreneurial activity and success. Government programs are always in a state of flux. New programs are added and existing ones discontinued or modified.

There are attractive benefits to considering government for financing assistance. In general terms, there are fewer requirements for collateral security compared to the private sector, and the amount of equity you are required to have in the business is less. This means less financial risk to you and, therefore, a reduced need to obtain funds from friends, family or other investors. In addition, the cost of government loans is usually less expensive, and government has equity financing, subsidy, cost-sharing and grant programs that do not have to be repaid. Another benefit is that after you have obtained government financing, you are more credible and attractive to other potential lenders or investors.

A. FORMS OF FINANCIAL ASSISTANCE PROGRAMS

Financial assistance programs take various forms as follows:

- **Loans at reduced interest rates:** These would be loans at rates of interest lower than conventional sources of financing. Loans from the Federal Business Development Bank (FBDB), a federal government Crown corporation, is an example.
- **Loan guarantees:** The government will guarantee that a loan made to you by an approved conventional lender will be repaid. An example would be business improvement loans (BIL). This federal government program is designed to assist small businesses in the purchase, installation, renovation or improvement of equipment, usually fixed equipment. Includes renovation of premises, leasehold improvements, purchase of land, construction and purchase of premises. Funds are advanced by chartered banks, and some trust companies and credit unions. In the event that you go out of business, the government guarantees the lender that it will be reimbursed for the debt outstanding. Another example would be the Export Development Corporation. This federal Crown corporation, among other roles, issues guarantees to banks making export loans or issuing performance and bid guarantees.
- **Forgivable loans:** These are loans that are payable in part or full, in certain situations, unless certain conditions are met or not met, in which event the loan is forgiven (not required to be repaid); for example, the Program for Export Market Development (PEMB) offered through External Affairs and International Trade Canada. This program has various components. One initiative is to assist a Canadian company to export by paying for the company representative to attend trade shows outside Canada. If the company receives export orders within two years of the trip, for example, the money is repaid. If it doesn't, the loan is forgiven.
- **Loans with favourable repayment schedules:** In this situation, the repayment schedule of the loan is structured to be comfortable with the cash flow history of the company. This is common in businesses that are seasonal in nature, or where receivables come in at the end of a project or at various phases in the project. A Federal Business Development Bank (FBDB) loan is an example where this type of flexible repayment arrangement can be negotiated.
- **Grants:** This would consist of money paid by the government directly to the company or organization without any requirement that it needs to be repaid.

Many federal and provincial governments have these types of programs to stimulate job creation or research and development; for example, if you were going to expand your business operation by building a much larger plant or other facility thereby creating more employment. This would have the effect of saving the government money in UIC or welfare payments, and creating a new tax revenue base from the increased business income and from additional employees paying income tax.

- **Cost sharing:** This form of assistance involves the government sharing the cost of the project. The National Research Council through their IRAP (Industrial Research Assistance Program) is an example of a federal government agency involved in cost-sharing programs.

- **Subsidies for wages:** Government partially or completely pays for an employee's wages. Many of these programs are done through Employment and Immigration Canada (CEIC). The purpose is to create new employment.

- **Subsidies for training and education:** There are many government programs to assist in training and education. For example, CEIC has programs which fund up to 75% of the cost of employee skill upgrading (e.g., computer training) or management training for business owners. Another example would be the NEBS (New Exporters to Border States) program conducted through the FBDB and/or provincial governments. Financial assistance up to 75% of the program cost is possible and and easy payment plans are also arranged in many cases. In addition, the federal and provincial governments have prepared excellent booklets and other publications and materials on a wide range of topics. Most of this material is free or available at a nominal cost. Many government departments also have seminar programs to assist you in understanding the application process for funding, selling to government, exporting or developing general business management or marketing skills; for example, Supply and Services Canada, Industry, Science and Technology Canada, and External Affairs and International Trade Canada. These represent just a few of the federal government departments who offer seminar programs. Contact them and ask to be placed on a mailing list for upcoming seminars. Also contact your provincial government departments in your areas of interest. As mentioned before, contact services for the main government departments are located in "Sources of Further Information."

- **Subsidies for consulting services:** The federal and provincial governments have consulting programs that are free or at a reduced or nominal cost. The CASE (Counselling Assistance to Small Enterprise) program administered by the FBDB is an example. Experts in various aspects of business provide a wide range of consulting advice at a subsidized cost. Various provincial and federal government departments provide researching, negotiating and marketing assistance without charge. An example of this would be the various services offered by Industry Science and Technology Canada and External Affairs and International Trade Canada. They assist you in research, marketing and negotiating in many instances, and without charge. In addition, Statistics Canada has an excellent selection of research and other data that can assist you.

- **Insurance coverage:** The federal government and some provincial governments have insurance protection that you can obtain in the event a supplier does not pay you. This relates to exporting to other countries, and minimizes the inherent risk that might otherwise be there.

- **Tax or other concessions:** In this situation, the federal or provincial government departments involved provide tax incentives for people to invest in your business or project. Examples would be the provincial incentive of providing provincial tax credits up to a certain percentage (e.g., 30%) to people who invest in a provincially approved venture capital program (VCC) or employee share owner-ship program (ESOP). Another example would be the federal government im-migrant investor program. In this case, the federal government will grant landed immigrant status to people from other countries who invest a certain amount of money in an approved investment or do so for a certain period of time.

- **Equity financing:** The government, in this situation, would become a minority equity partner in your business by investing a certain amount of money. The FBDB is an example of a federal Crown corporation which has a program with this type of venture financing.

- **Government contracts:** This is an indirect form of government financing your business. Federal and provincial governments and their Crown corporations buy billions of dollars of goods and services each year, and have a mandate to pur-chase from Canadian suppliers first. For information on selling to the federal government, contact Supply and Services Canada. See Appendix for a reference address or the blue pages of your phone book, under "Federal Government." Speak with your provincial government purchasing department to get further information on doing business with them. To contact them, look in the blue pages of your phone book, under your provincial government. Alternatively, to contact your provincial small business department, see the the reference list in the Appendix.

B. STEPS TO FOLLOW TO OBTAIN GOVERNMENT FINANCING

1. Research Sources of Government Funding

There are many sources of information in terms of government (federal and pro-vincial) funding programs. It requires time and persistence, and you want to be thorough to make sure you have current information. The key sources are:

- **Directories of government financial programs.** You can obtain these from the business division of your public library or local business resource centre of your provincial small business department. The main directories, with updating serv-ices, are *Canadian Government Programs and Services* (updated monthly), *Canadian Small Business Financing and Tax Planning Guide* (updated monthly), *Industrial Assistance Programs in Canada* (annual), all three published by CCH Canadian Ltd.; *Guide to Federal Programs and Services* (annual), published by Canada Communications Group; and *Canadian Reference Directory on Business Planning and Funding* (annual) published by Canadian Sources of Funds Index.

- **Provincial government small business resource centres.** Look in the blue pages under provincial government. Refer to the provincial government listings in the Appendix. They can tell you about financing programs and refer to you to other government departments for information on venture capital companies, employee share ownership programs, immigrant investor program, etc. The provincial government small business information services would also be aware of the availability of many of the federal government financing programs in your area of interest.

- **Specific federal/provincial and municipal government departments.** Once you determine your needs, and have done some preliminary research, contact specific government departments in your area of interest for current financing program information. For example, this would include the Federal Business Development Bank; External Affairs and International Trade Canada; Industry, Science and Technology Canada; and Employment and Immigration Canada. The contact information for these government departments is located in "Sources of Further Information" or check in the blue pages of your phone book for a local contact number.

If you have difficulty reaching a government department, contact Reference Canada, located in the blue pages of your phone book. The number is toll-free. You can make inquiries about federal and in many cases, provincial government programs and services.

2. Determine Specific Program Availability

Although a program may in theory be available, in fact it could have been cancelled in the last budget process or possibly all the funds have been used up for that budget year. All government fiscal years run from April 30 to March 31, so there is a fresh infusion of funds in the early part of the fiscal year.

3. Become Knowledgeable on Program Application Procedures

Find out as much as you can about the program. Obtain the program information directly and read it thoroughly, speak to people providing information on the specific program, and those who can assist in the approval process. Determine precisely what the eligibility criteria is. The government employees administering the program are invariably helpful. Their function is to assist you in attaining your funding objectives if at all possible, assuming you meet the eligibility criteria.

Even if you don't meet some of the programs' specific requirements, but meet their general requirements, don't hesitate to pursue the matter further. It could be that an exception would be permitted, or that some other program would be a better fit for you.

4. Find Out the Reasons Why the Program Is in Existence

This is very important to determine. All government programs are designed with specific objectives in mind. In general, the government programs are designed to enhance economic and social objectives in order to develop and ensure a vibrant society, stable and growing economy, and optimal equipment. The programs are designed to obtain these general objectives and meeting other more specific employment. Your proposal should, therefore, conform to attaining the government's objectives in order to be viewed favourably. In other words, what potential benefits will funding to you provide to their program? In providing these benefits, of course, you are attaining your own business financial and planning objectives.

Here are some of the benefits that you could provide to the government to meet their stated program objectives in exchange for funding. Attempt to identify other ones as well

- developing new products
- researching and developing new technology
- replacing imported goods with Canadian-manufactured ones
- increasing the efficiency and productivity of your workforce or business
- creating new employment opportunities
- developing or increasing employee skills
- developing potential export markets
- stimulating employment in an area of slow growth or depressed economy
- conserving natural resources
- protecting the environment
- developing skills or opportunities in specific industries designated by the government as particularly important at that point in time.

5. Design Your Request to Conform to Government Needs

As mentioned, it is important to understand the spirit and intent of the program, and identify the benefits to the program if the government supports you financially. Customize your request to comply with their needs and within the context of the eligibility requirements. The emphasis should be on how you will meet their needs, not how you will benefit from their funding.

On the other hand, it is important to point out that to benefit their program, you do need their money and without it you could not benefit their program. The government also wants to be satisfied that your business has sound management and that the purpose of the funding is realistic and attainable.

6. Get Assistance in Preparing the Proposal

If you have never had experience writing proposals or feel unable to express yourself persuasively in the written word, make sure you obtain professional assistance. There are lawyers, accountants and consultants who are experienced in preparing proposals, and in many cases representing clients in the funding application process. You want to make sure you have everything going for you. If you decide to prepare your own proposal, it is highly recommended that you have it reviewed by more than one professional to obtain candid feedback.

Positive first impressions of your proposal are very important, for obvious reasons, in order to instil confidence in the viability and management of your business. If you have to resubmit the proposal because it was incomplete or poorly prepared, that fact alone could impair the final decision and result in your application being rejected.

Generally, there are more people applying for funds than there are funds available. The screening process for eligibility therefore has to be selective to enable the applicants with the greatest chance of fulfilling the objectives of the program to have access to funding.

7. Look for Additional Funding Programs

In the process of researching your government funding sources, you should see various programs that you could be eligible for. Depending on the needs of your business during the various stages of your business operation, you may decide to apply concurrently or sequentially for more than one program. Don't limit your potential funding opportunities by just restricting your strategic financial planning to just one program.

8. Be Patient and Persistent

Most programs involve a lot of paperwork and approval can be a lengthy process. The more complex the proposal or the more money involved, the longer it will take. Also, be persistent and don't let any initial rejection deter you. Find out why your proposal was rejected and see if you can modify the proposal to comply with government needs. If not, look for other program possibilities.

Remember to look for a range of potential government funding sources on an ongoing basis throughout the life of your business.

5.7 INVESTOR IMMIGRANT PROGRAM

The Canadian federal government recognized a need in Canada for more sources to which businesspeople can access when raising equity capital. The Investor Immigrant Program (a segment of the government's Business Immigration Program) is a result of this initiative.

From the point of view of Canadian businesspeople looking for long-term equity investors, the Investor Immigrant Program offers an interesting opportunity in the right circumstances. There are certain essential requirements:

- You must have a sound business opportunity;
- The opportunity must be identified not less than eighteen months in advance;
- You must have access to a reputable sales network in the foreign country where you intend to market the opportunity; and
- The opportunity must be of sufficient size to justify the costs that are associated with this kind of project.

If these criteria are met, the Investor Immigrant Program may well offer you a source of financing on very advantageous terms. There is a minimum five-year hold period during which the investors' capital cannot be returned. Part of what the investor gets for making his investment comes from the government in the form of a visa to become a permanent resident of Canada, so that the investor is prepared to accept a smaller financial return from the investment than would otherwise be the case. The security of the investment and some certainty of making a modest return is frequently more attractive to such investors than a riskier investment with a larger upside potential.

Qualifying Investors

In order to qualify for the Investor Immigrant Program, an investor must be a person who, through his or her own efforts, has a net worth of at least

$500,000 Canadian, and who makes an equity investment of a minimum of $250,000 ($350,000 in British Columbia, Ontario or Quebec) in a program that has been designated by the federal government. A person who meets these requirements need only obtain twenty-five points (as opposed to the normal seventy-five points) out of a possible 100 points when an assessment is made of that person's suitability to become a permanent resident (landed immigrant) in Canada. In addition, investor immigrant applications are given a high priority in visa processing. Once a visa is issued, the applicant has twelve months within which to take up residence in Canada and, in due course, is entitled to become a Canadian citizen. Some allowance is made for permanent residents who maintain business and connections abroad so as to permit them to keep up those activities, which may well not be easily transferable to Canada. However, Canada is not prepared to become a "flag of convenience" providing a safe haven in time of trouble for persons who otherwise have no intention of settling here; a person who utilizes the Investor Immigrant Program should have the wish and intention to make Canada a permanent home.

Contacting Investors

The single largest difficulty encountered by businesspeople who wish to make use of this program is making contact with prospective investors abroad. This is an area where personal contacts are very valuable. An alternative is to make use of an agent. However, you should be aware of the need to check very carefully into the track record and reputation in the country where selling is to be done of any agent whom you employ. Becoming associated with an agent with a poor reputation abroad can undo all of the careful work and sound planning which you have undertaken in Canada.

Approved Programs

Programs may be either specific projects or investment syndicates (blind pools). The process of approval commences with a review and approval by the provincial government where the project or syndicate is located, following which a further review is conducted by the federal government. Each province has its own guidelines governing the kinds of businesses which it will approve for a program. A good rule of thumb is that a program must generate at least one permanent job for Canadians for each immigrant investor. Residential real estate projects are excluded and commercial real estate projects are limited to those projects which involve adding value to real estate. In some provinces (notably British Columbia), real estate projects are only permitted in certain parts of the province.

Restrictions on Size

The program is not intended to provide an alternative means of access to capital for large businesses. The gross assets of the business in which an investment is made (which includes for this purpose the gross assets of entities "associated" in a broad sense, with a business) cannot exceed $35 million. However, there is no prohibition on an investment fund or syndicate doing business with a large entity on an arm's-length basis.

Lock-up Period and Guarantees

The investment must remain committed for a minimum of five years. The regulations prohibit the granting of a guarantee (directly or indirectly) as to the return of the investment at the expiry of the five-year period. Various methods of doubtful legality have been used to get around this prohibition. An option on the part of an investor fund or syndicate to sell its interest at market price to a third party at the end of the five-year period would not be a guarantee; however, a right on the part of a third party to require that the investor's interest be sold to the third party at a predetermined price would not be acceptable.

Timing

Depending on the location of the Canadian embassy where the investors apply for their visas, there can be considerable delays in processing (two years is not uncommon in Hong Kong). In order to allow access to the investors' funds during this waiting period, the funds may be released subject to a 20% hold-back to provide a cushion for the possibility of investors being refused their visas, or the investors may be asked to sign a specific waiver authorizing the early release of their funds. The investors' funds will be held by a trust company or other depository as escrow agent until the minimum required for the investment is reached (there is a minimum of $1 million and projects frequently need a larger minimum than this in order to be economic). No money is releasable at all until the minimum amount has been placed in escrow by the required minimum number of investors.

Current Developments

A ministerial task force on the Investor Immigrant Program released a discussion paper dated January 16, 1992 proposing various amendments to this program. At the time of writing, it is too early to forecast the extent of the changes which may be made to the program as a result of the experience which has been gained in its operation, but you should be aware that changes can be expected. If you intend to make use of this program, you should contact a lawyer who practices in the area, so as to check on the regulatory regime that is in force when you begin your planning.

5.8 BANKS AND OTHER LENDERS

Approximately 87% of small business in Canada utilize a chartered bank for financing purposes. This does not mean that a small business is using a bank exclusively, but for at least part of its financing needs a bank is utilized. Therefore, it is important that you understand the process involved in the granting of loans. This will assist you in negotiating with the lender. There are specific questions that you should ask when selecting a lender.

Credit-Granting Process

Factors involved in the loan-granting process are your meeting and request for money; the criteria used by the lender for approving funds; an agreement between the borrower and the lender regarding terms and amounts of money; security and other factors; confirmation in writing as to the agreement between the parties; and signing of the necessary security required before the funds are advanced. The following is a discussion of the process.

A. REQUEST BY BORROWER

It is best to set up an initial appointment to discuss the lender's policies without necessarily going into the details of your proposal. During the interview you can discuss in general terms such questions as what type of collateral might be required, limitations that the bank might have on types of business loans that you are considering, the type of reporting information that you may be required to make, and any other information that the bank needs. This will prepare you for the type of information needed in your loan proposal. By this time, it would be prudent to have determined your personal cost-of-living budget (see Example 5 in Appendix A) and projected financial needs for the first three months of the business, assuming it is a small business start-up (see Example 6 in Appendix A). Depending on the amount and purpose of the loan, the loans officer may give you a personal net worth statement to complete (refer to Example 7 in Appendix A) or loan application form to complete (refer to Example 8 in Appendix A for a typical business loan application form).

At the preliminary meeting the prospective lender may ask questions such as:

- How much money do you need?
- For how long do you need it?
- What do you plan to do with the money?
- How do you intend to repay the loan?
- What are the alternative sources of repayment if you have a problem?
- What types of security are you prepared to provide?

After the meeting, you should finalize your business plan and financial plan. Set up another meeting with the lender. Present your business plan and financial proposal along with a one-page outline of the essence of your application for funds. More detail on the preparation of a business plan and financial plan was discussed in Chapter Two.

Give the lender a reasonable time to assess your proposal. Depending on the complexity of the proposal, it may need to be referred to another level within the bank.

B. LENDER'S APPROVAL CRITERIA

Prospective lenders want to know as much as possible about you and your business before making a decision to provide you with financing. The lender will be looking at various criteria, including character, capital, capacity, conditions and collateral. Risks and bank policy are also considered. A brief description of these criteria follows:

- **Character:** The trustworthiness of a potential borrower will be considered. Your track record and integrity in terms of your business and financial history, such as personal credit history and management ability as demonstrated in your business plan, will weigh heavily in the lender's decision. Your level of commitment to the business, other than financial commitment, is another perception that will be considered.

- **Capital:** This refers to the equity or financial investment that you are going to be putting in the business. Factors are taken into account such as the amount of investment, the quality of the assets that are purchased with your investment, the liquidity of the assets (ability to sell quickly for cash), and the overall liability of the firm. If you have a large financial investment in the business, this demonstrates to the lender a high degree of commitment on your part to ensure that the business succeeds. If you have very little invested, then in the eyes of the lender you could have very little to lose.

- **Capacity:** This refers to the capacity of the business to pay back the loan. The lender of course wants to get paid from the cash flow and profits of the business, and not from having to sell the security that you have pledged. The lender is interested in your cash flow projections and the basis on which you have made those projections.

- **Conditions:** The lender takes a look at the various economic conditions nationally and locally that are significant to your type of business. In addition, the trends in your industry are an important factor. Banks compare your ratios with those of similar industries to see how realistic your projections are. In addition, banks monitor various types of industries that have a high failure or loan default rate.

- **Collateral:** Banks will frequently ask the owners of a corporation to sign personal guarantees or request other forms of collateral.

- **Risk:** The bank will look at the relative degree of risk involved in lending you money, and the return that it will get in exchange.

- **Bank policy:** The lender assesses your application within the overall context of the bank policy. For example, the bank might have a policy against lending any money to someone in a speculative real estate development business at a time when the economy is poor and there are numerous foreclosures. The bank may have a policy that there is a four-to-one security-to-loan ratio required for new start-up businesses. If you are able to provide security which is only three times the value of the loan, then you would not technically comply with the bank policy. The bank may have a policy that all directors of the company have to sign guarantees for the loan. If there are three directors and two of them are not prepared to sign personal guarantees, then the loan can be turned down for that reason alone.

C. AGREEMENT ON TERMS AND CONDITIONS

During this phase of the loan-granting process, both parties agree on the amount, type, and structure of the loan, the interest rate that is to be paid for the loan, and the security that is being pledged for it. By this time, depending on the amount of the loan requested, you may already have given the lender the financing proposal outline. See Example 9 in Appendix A. You may also have prepared a business plan for the lender. Alternatively, the lender may only have requested a business loan application and/or personal net worth statement.

There are various factors taken into account in determining the interest rate:

- the cost of funds (prime rate and money market conditions).
- administration costs.
- the degree of risk involved.

Sufficient lead time must be allowed when making a loan application. The length of the process may vary depending on the loan complexity from one day to one month or more from the commencement of the preliminary meeting to the finalization of the loan approval.

D. CONFIRMATION OF LOAN AGREEMENT

This is the final phase of the loan-granting process. The lender may provide you with a bank loan confirmation letter setting out the terms and conditions (see Example 10 in Appendix A), or if the amount is small, the bank may confirm approval to you verbally. After the bank has accepted the loan application, the security documents will have to be signed before the funds are advanced to you. Make sure that you have spoken with your lawyer as well as your accountant before you agree to any final loan security documentation. Remember, you are trying to convince the lender of three important factors:

- That your loan application for funds is for a worthwhile purpose and those funds are sufficient to accomplish your business objectives.
- That you have the credibility, integrity and commitment to make your business a viable one, and the management skills or access to those skills to make it a profitable one.
- That the loan can be repaid out of the normal operational activities of the business on a realistic cash flow basis, and the bank will not have to realize on their security.

Types of Security Requested by Lenders

When providing financing to a small business, lenders require security to ensure that they are repaid. Often the value of the security is considerably more than the amount of the loan. This is because if the lender has to "realize" on the security and convert it into money, only a portion of the value of the asset will be obtained after the sale. As well, costs of hiring a lawyer, accountant, receiver, or trustee may be involved, which could be considerable.

In terms of risk assessment for security requested, your business may be evaluated by three different methods:

- **Going concern value:** This is the most optimistic method, which is an estimate of the business based on its capitalized earnings. This method assumes that the selling price, sufficient to cover the loan, will be obtained if the business is sold as a going concern. This method gives no indication, of course, of the value of the assets if the business is not sold in this manner. Lenders would be interested in a going concern value if they have a debenture on the company.
- **En bloc:** This is an estimate of a price at which the assets could be sold, without removal or alteration, if the business ceased to operate. The en bloc value is

based on the purchase of all the assets, not just some of the assets, and on using the same location for operation.

- **Current liquidation value:** This is the most pessimistic method of evaluating the assets of the business. It is based on the estimate of what price the assets might be expected to realize in a forced sale or winding up of the business. Most lenders use this valuation in appraising the security for a loan, because they operate on the conservative premise that in a business problem situation, they cannot be assured of any higher value.

In Canada, we consider two basic types of property. The first is real estate. All the rest is known as "personal property." This includes goods and chattels, accounts such as accounts receivable, money, securities and intangibles such as trade names, trademarks and other forms of goodwill.

The types of security frequently requested for loans are considerable in number and variety. Mortgages of real estate form one type of security. With the advent of new Personal Property Acts in many jurisdictions in Canada, security for all personal property has become standardized. The old forms of corporate debentures, assignments of book accounts and chattel mortgages have all but disappeared in most provinces, to be replaced with sleek, multi-purpose Security Agreements.

A. GENERAL SECURITY AGREEMENTS

Wherever a borrower owes money or any kind of obligation, it can grant a security interest in any personal property it owns. It is not necessary to set out the obligations in the security agreement. In fact, the obligations may be continual, and may change from time to time. There will be a place to set out the nature of the personal property being secured. These can include Accounts, Equipment, Inventories, Tangible Personal Property (documents of title, securities, chattel paper), Intangibles (contracts, licences, goodwill, patents, trademarks, trade names, industrial designs and intellectual property), and the Proceeds of the sale of any personal property.

This type of document allows the lender to take continuing security over every facet of your business. Consider the case of a manufacturing business. Everything from raw materials to inventory to the proceeds from sales can be secured to the lender under General Security Agreements. In the same manner, a financing company can factor its securities in order to raise more capital.

The security agreement will contain standard terms worth noting. You will covenant to protect the security, insure it, and keep it in good repair. You will also agree to provide the lender with timely finanical information about your business. You will also agree to pay for the cost of preparing and registering the security, and any costs of the lender if it is forced to realize on the security.

The document will describe events of default, in which case the lender will be at liberty to realize on the security. These typically include default in payment of any loan, the death or winding-up or bankruptcy of the borrower, the seizure of security by another creditor, and the impairment or destruction of some or all of the security.

In the event of default, the lender will have rights given to it by the security agreement. It may seize and sell the security, or appoint a receiver of the business of the borrower, all at the cost of the borrower. The receiver may go in and take over and run the business of the borrower, and it may sell off the assets of the business, or sell the business itself as a going concern in order to realize the monies necessary to pay off the debt.

Care should be taken if you are not incorporated. These documents do not distinguish between personal and business assets, and you could be pledging more assets than you intended.

B. SPECIFIC SECURITY AGREEMENTS

These types of agreements are modelled on General Security Agreements; however, they secure only the assets listed. The rights given to the lender are not so wide as the General document. These provide security more like the old chattel mortgages and assignments of book account, whereas the General Security Agreement is more like the old form of document called a debenture.

C. REGISTRATION

While these documents create rights and liabilities between you and the lender, it is necessary for the lenders to protect themselves from third parties who may loan you money on the strength of the same security, or who may buy the security from you. For this reason, every jurisdiction has developed a Personal Property registry system where notice of the security is registered. The registration of this notice "perfects" the security, and provides the lender with the added protection it requires, relative to other lenders who may have the same use of security document granted to them subsequently.

After negotiating with the bank, be certain to request that the bank confirm in writing by means of a loan confirmation letter that it is prepared to advance funds, and under what circumstances, and with what security. (See sample letter in Appendix A.) Take the letter to your accountant and lawyer and discuss the implications of it before agreeing to the terms outlined. You may wish to have your lawyer or accountant go with you when you finalize the bargain. Once you have signed the security documentation, make sure that you obtain copies of it for your lawyer as well as your own files. Never agree to provide security without fully understanding the nature and purpose of the security documentation.

As mentioned, it is critical that you obtain advice from your lawyer and accountant regarding the implications of these various types of security from the legal, accounting and tax viewpoint. Whether you are negotiating with a bank or other lenders, it is important that you agree to a package which is acceptable to you in terms of your risk, personal exposure and leverage.

Maintaining a Relationship with the Lender

Although a bank's head office has basic lending rules and criteria, branch managers tend to have a considerable amount of discretion and flexibility over the loans they approve or reject. In addition, the terms and conditions of the bank loans may vary widely from branch to branch of the same bank, as well as between banks and between credit unions. There can also be a wide range of expertise and experience in evaluating and approving loan applications in certain business areas. A more experienced lender might make a favourable review of your proposal, whereas an inexperienced lender might reject it, or vice versa.

It is important to determine the lending limit of the loans officer you are dealing with. If the manager has a lending limit of, for example, $100,000, and your projected needs will never exceed more than $50,000, you only have to convince that one person on the merits of your application. If, on the other hand, your needs exceed the lending limit, the manager will have to refer your request to a senior manager, or to the head office, for approval. In this latter example, someone would be making a decision on your loan proposal without ever having met you. If the manager has had success in managing the loan accounts, that reflects favourably on his judgement and will assist your loan approval.

In your selection process, you would therefore ideally search for an experienced bank manager with excellent connections and approval authority for a lending limit beyond your needs. You would also want expertise not only to judge the merits of your business application, but also to understand your type of business and industry sector. The lender has discretion on the interest rate, the amount of collateral, and the repayment terms of any loan approved. If you can, convince the lender that you have prepared yourself thoroughly and looked at the pros and cons in your business plan, and have prepared a well-documented proposal. This will greatly assist your negotiations.

Once you have obtained your loan, your banking relationship of course does not end. It is an ongoing one until your loan is repaid. If you establish and nurture a good working relationship with the branch manager, it will assist you greatly in the long-term relationship. Some tips on maintaining a good relationship are as follows:

- If you run into unexpected problems, don't hide that fact from the lender. After you have determined reasonable solutions that may be available, inform the lender. If you cause the lender to have unpleasant surprises such as NSF cheques, stalling on loan payments, late loan payments or unapproved overdrafts, this will certainly impair your relationship. It could very well cause your loan to be called.

- Establish a reputation for integrity by conducting your banking affairs in a consistent and realistic manner.

- Adhere to the policy set by the bank in regard to terms and conditions of the loan agreement.

- If your bank requests financial data, provide it without unreasonable delay.

- Invite the banker to visit your place of business, and explain your operating procedures and future plans.

- Be confident in your approach, and be prepared to negotiate the terms, by having done advanced planning after consultation with your professional advisors.

- Schedule regular meeting sessions with your banker to provide a progress report on your business plan. If you request these regular meetings as a courtesy, rather than a further attempt to get more money, it will increase confidence in you when you *do* need the money.

Remember, if you are not satisfied with the initial negotiating terms proposed by the bank, or the relationship is unsatisfactory, consider other lenders. The lending process is highly competitive.

5.9 PROFESSIONAL VENTURE CAPITAL

The public's perception of "venture capital" is as divorced from the reality of professional venture capital as a pawn shop is from a Swiss bank, and gaining access to the vault is generally just as difficult. Professional venture capital is inaccessible to over 99% of the business enterprises in Canada. Accordingly, we will not spend a great deal of time on the subject here, other than to let you know that it exists and what are its general terms of reference. However, for that rare business which is at just the right stage in its growth cycle to be both ready for, and receptive to, an infusion of capital from a professional venture capital company (VCC), a VCC can be both a useful investor and valuable ally. The Association of Canadian Venture Capital Companies (ACVCC) publishes an excellent manual on venture capital which also includes a detailed list of most of the sources of professionally managed venture capital in Canada. See "Sources of Further Information," Section F, for information on how to contact the ACVCC.

"Venture capital" refers not to the "adventure capital" of which many entrepreneurs dream, but rather refers to professionally managed pools of capital which have been created by investment professionals and money managers for the purpose of earning an above-average return on the invested money. To understand the motivations and investment approach of venture capitalists, you must appreciate that the venture capitalist is usually a manager of other people's money. His job is to preserve the original capital and make it grow at a faster rate than the source of the money generally could on its own. The sources of capital for venture capital funds include pension funds, banks, insurance companies, certain other financial institutions and very wealthy individuals. There is thus a conservatism inherent in the nature of venture capital with respect to the pressures on the fund managers to preserve the original capital base and also to ensure that a better-than-average gain is achieved. This generally leads to investment policies which, in the eyes of many money-raising entrepreneurs, is more risk adverse than they would prefer and is certainly not the "adventure capital" of their entrepreneurial dreams.

Although each Canadian venture capital company differs in the specifics of its investment policy, the following criteria will give you a general idea of what professional venture capital is looking for:

1. **An established business.** Many venture capitalists will not invest in a company that is less than five years old. Unfortunately, most VCCs in Canada will not invest in start-up or very early-stage companies, although there are exceptions. The manual published by the ACVCC includes information on the investment criteria of most of Canada's venture capital companies, including whether a particular VCC will normally invest in start-ups or early-stage companies. Refer to the Appendix under "Sources of Information" for the contact address.

2. **A high rate of earnings.** Most VCCs look for a projected rate of return on investment in the magnitude of 30% to 40% per annum or more compounded

over five years, and will rarely accept less than 25%. Even for VCCs, picking the winners in the entrepreneurial sweepstakes is more of an art than a science. Historically, the majority of their Canadian investments has not been particularly successful. Accordingly, they must depend on those one or two stellar successes out of every ten investments made in order to preserve their capital and turn an acceptable profit.

3. **Proven management.** It is a truism approaching dogma in the venture capital business that "you invest in management," not products, or companies or opportunities. The reasoning is that good management can make money even in a lagging industry in a bad economy. There is also the logic that if someone has been successful once, he can do it again. A well-balanced management team in place that covers all aspects of the business, such as sales and marketing, production, finance and administration, is also deemed important.

4. **Definite market niche.** Many VCCs look for companies which focus their efforts on a very specific market niche. It would likely be easier for the company to become a dominant player in one specialized corner of a larger market than to attempt to compete across the board.

5. **Proprietary product or technology.** It is considered to be a great competitive advantage if a company owns or has the rights to proprietary technology. The reason for this is that proprietary rights make it more difficult and expensive for competitors to defeat the company head-to-head and therefore gives some assurance to the VCC investors.

6. **Requires $250,000 or more of funding.** For a VCC, virtually the same amount of time and expense will be involved in the due diligence investigation for a $50,000 or a $500,000 investment. Thus a larger investment is preferred in order to absorb the investigation costs and make a profit in the future. Although there are some VCCs which will invest less than $250,000, there are many VCCs in Canada which will not consider investments below $1,000,000. The booklet distributed by the ACVCC lists the minimum investment amount for each of its members.

7. **Money is for business expansion.** VCCs generally prefer to see that the money invested is for the purpose of financing the expansion of a business, either through internal growth or by way of an acquisition, which builds on the company's past record of success. They are generally less likely to put money into a company simply for the purpose of reducing its debt, as there may be an attitude that debt should be retired from earnings which implies discipline and success, rather than through a mere infusion of capital.

8. **The VCC's exit opportunity is clear.** A VCC invests in a business for the purpose of making a profit on its capital. At some point, the VCC will want to realize this profit. There are only a limited number of ways in which the VCC can dispose of its shares in the company, such as in the sale of the company to a third party, the sale of the VCC's shares back to the company or to another investor, or the sale of the VCC's shares to the public as a result of a public offering of the company's shares. The more likely the company is to be able to provide for one of those exits, or the more definite management can be with respect to the VCC's exit, the more likely a deal can be made. Ultimately,

the VCC wants to dispose of its investment at a profit and wants to know that management is in agreement with the VCC's strategy.

The ideal candidate for venture capital in Canada would be a company that has been in business for over five years, has shown a return on invested capital of at least 30% for each of those years, has sales which are several millions of dollars per year, has a solid and complementary management team, has a proprietary product, has a definite market niche, and seeks an infusion of capital of at least $1,000,000 but preferably more with which to finance its market expansion, either internally or through acquisition, and plans to undertake a public offering of the companies shares on the TSE or NASDAQ within three years. If your company meets that description, you would be a prime candidate to receive venture capital funding in Canada today.

5.10 THE INITIAL PUBLIC OFFERING (IPO)

Introduction

While the ultimate dream of many a Canadian entrepreneur has been to take a company public, it is also true that for many who have done so, it has turned out to be close to the ultimate business nightmare. If there has ever been an arena of business activity which absolutely epitomizes the truth of the old saying, "All that glitters is not gold!", it is the lure of the road to riches represented by the Initial Public Offering, otherwise known as the "IPO". With great optimism and high expectations, "I'm going public!" has been the jubilant cry of many an ambitious Canadian businessperson. Two or three years later, with the business ruined and the project dead, the failed entrepreneur's epitaph is: "He went public!"

There is probably no legal area of commerce that affords such a great upside potential, yet at the same time has within it the potential for such disaster, as being involved in the public stock markets and taking one's own company public. This is not a game for the naive or the uninformed. Even if you are crafty, intelligent, well informed and maintain a vigilant outlook, you can still lose all of the marbles that you brought to the game. You are voluntarily leaping into the financial jungle. In many respects, it is like the old adage that "fools go where angels fear to tread."

You will need all of the survival skills that you can both muster on your own and purchase from seasoned advisors. Even then it may not be enough for you to make it. In this sort of deadly game, your problem as a newcomer is that you don't know what it is that you don't know. The infamous "UKV" (unforeseen killer variable) is always lurking, waiting for an opening to strike you between the financial shoulder blades or in the centre of your fiscal kneecaps! There are only two kinds of players in this deadliest of business games, the very quick and the very dead!

How is it that the ultimate dream of so many entrepreneurs undergoes such a tragic transformation into the ultimate business nightmare? It is in the nature of the stock markets themselves, and in the nature of many of the professional market players, such as certain stock promoters, market makers and stockbrokers, that make a very handsome living being very tough and very fast in the financial jungle. And very possibly at your expense.

What Does It Mean to "Go Public"?

"To go public," or "to take a company public," generally refers to the process whereby a formerly privately-owned company arranges to have its shares listed for trading on a recognized stock exchange so that members of the public can buy and sell the shares of that company. The phrase also usually implies that a sum of money has been raised from members of the public as part of the process of "going public." In other words, part of the ownership of the company is now held by the public in the form of shares and these shares may be traded through the facilities of one or more stock exchanges.

Canada presently has five stock exchanges. These are the Montreal Stock Exchange, the Toronto Stock Exchange, the Winnipeg Stock Exchange, the Alberta Stock Exchange and the Vancouver Stock Exchange. A company can go public and undertake an IPO on any one of these stock exchanges. Each exchange has its own rules regarding the requirements of companies to become listed on the exchange, its own price for so doing, and its own unique financial sub-culture and cast of characters.

What Is an "Initial Public Offering"?

As the name implies, an initial public offering refers to the process whereby a company for the first time makes an offering of its securities to the public. There are usually two purposes for undertaking an IPO. The first is to raise money for the company so that it may better pursue its intended business. The second is to provide a means whereby the owners of the company's stock can sell some of their stock holdings; in other words, to provide liquidity and cash to the company's shareholders. Often the company's early stage investors, such as "angels" or venture capitalists, will only provide early stage financing on the promise of management to exert its best efforts to pursue an IPO on one of the country's stock exchanges within a certain time frame.

The "Emerging Company"

The discussion which follows will assume that yours is what is euphemistically currently known in Canadian financial circles as an "emerging company." It is never made clear exactly what such a company is emerging from. It may be emerging from obscurity, from nothingness (it may have been incorporated the day before yesterday), from insolvency, or from all of the foregoing. Occasionally, it may even have been modestly chugging along making fistfuls of dollars and now you want it to leap forward and become a mighty engine of industry. Or, you may be one of the fortunate few Canadians actually involved with a "fast track" or "megagrowth" company, so-called because its sales are growing at a rate of 30% to 50% or more per year and its biggest problem is finding the capital needed to fuel its growth. At the very least, "emerging" means that your company is not yet either established or Establishment. It has not yet "Made It." In any case, you feel that an injection of "OPM" ("Other People's Money") would be just the thing to allow you and your company to emerge into the financial mainstream where the bulls and the bears gambol with the sharks and the schwein, and where some get rich and the rest get experience.

Advantages and Benefits of Going Public

The decision to go public is a very major one, perhaps the biggest one that you will ever make for your company, and it has far-reaching implications. Some of these are positive, perhaps even necessary to ensure the very survival and success of your company, while others are negative, perhaps sufficient to cause its demise and failure.

The advantages and benefits to going public include the following:

A. BETTER ACCESS TO CAPITAL

It is presumed that during the IPO that the brokerage firm that leads your public offering (the "lead broker") will arrange for its own brokers, and sometimes for those in other firms who agree to participate in a selling syndicate with the lead broker, to sell shares in your company to individuals and sometimes institutions beyond your own range of contact and sphere of influence. As we will discuss below, this may in fact not be true. It is assumed, then, that several brokers working to sell your stock to their clients will enable you to access capital otherwise unavailable to you. Subsequently, the more successful your company's business performance becomes, the more attractive it will become for other brokers and brokerage firms to raise additional capital for you. Furthermore, once you have a base of public shareholders, your company will have a greater number of alternative methods of financing open to it, such as a rights offering, which can be accomplished relatively quickly and inexpensively compared to the IPO. A rights offering is a method of raising money for a public company whereby existing shareholders are granted the right to purchase additional shares of the company at a fixed price within a certain fixed period of time.

B. BETTER ACCESS TO BORROWING

As the net worth of your company is increased through the infusion of equity pursuant to an IPO, your company's ability to borrow is enhanced through the increase in your company's working capital. On the other hand, if your company undertakes no additional borrowing, your company's debt-to-equity ratio will have improved. This may enable you to borrow money on better terms in the future. In addition, one of the purposes of an IPO is frequently to provide funds to allow a company to reduce its current indebtedness.

C. LESS DILUTION OF FOUNDERS' POSITION

Assuming that your company needs to raise a certain amount of money to implement its business plan, it is almost certain that the founders will give up less of their equity on a public offering than they would if they raised the same amount of money from a venture capitalist or through a private placement with a sophisticated investor. The reason is that you would normally be able to command a higher price for the shares on the stock market than you would by selling them privately. Depending on the business, a shrewd investor might be willing to only pay 3 to 8 times annual earnings per share to purchase an interest in a company, whereas the stock market frequently values a stock at least 15 times earnings, and occasionally will value a stock at 30, 50 or even 100 times earnings if it is perceived to be a "hot stock" with a big upside potential. Sometimes, on a speculative bio-technology or other high-tech stock, or even on an attractive but undeveloped mineral claim, the valuation may actually be only on projected earnings. Accordingly, you may be able to sell a much smaller proportion of the shares in a public company than in the same company if it were private, in order to raise the same amount of money.

D. STOCK LIQUIDITY AND VALUATION

When your company's shares become listed for trading on a stock exchange, they can be bought and sold with ease provided there is a market for the stock. As long as there are buyers who are willing to purchase the stock, listed shares can be sold and converted to cash. In addition, just as the market places a value on the stock, in other words establishes a price for the stock, so can you place a value on your own holdings as well. Banks, mortgage companies and other lenders usually do not make loans against collateral of shares in a private company. However, if that same company is taken public, it is usually much easier to use the shares as collateral because the shares now have an identifiable value.

E. EMPLOYEE INCENTIVES

The ability to obtain stock options in a publicly traded company can act as a strong incentive to capable managers and employees which can give a young company a competitive advantage in the hiring process as compared to competing private companies. It is usually impossible for an emerging company to compete directly against established businesses on a dollar-for-dollar, benefit-for-benefit basis. However, highly capable managers and other employees with a personal entrepreneurial leaning may be persuaded to take a chance with a young company when they are granted a generous program of incentives, the most important component of which is the stock options. The ambitious employee may know that the only hope that he has for becoming wealthy is through capital gains. By obtaining sufficient stock options in your company, he does not have to take the risk of starting his own company. Instead, he becomes a shareholder, an owner, in yours.

F. FACILITATION OF MERGERS AND ACQUISITIONS

As mentioned above, a ready valuation of your company's shares is available in the stock market. This enables you to know their worth and to use them to purchase shares in other companies instead of using cash by exchanging your company's stock for their company's stock. It would also enable your company to acquire assets, or to merge with another company. The exchange of shares with another company is made much easier when there is a market for, and a method of valuation of, those shares, rather than in the case of private companies with illiquid securities where it is much more difficult for both sides of the transaction to arrive at a mutually agreeable valuation of your company's shares.

G. PRESTIGE AND RECOGNITION

Successfully taking a company public is an accomplishment that is generally admired in the business community. There is little doubt that some prestige and recognition accrue to the company founders at the time of a successful IPO. In addition, the financial press may well focus some favourable attention on the company, its founders, its business and products at this time. Also, it often happens that the act of going public generates more interest in a company from its customers and its suppliers, allowing you new opportunities with both.

H. PERSONAL WEALTH FOR THE FOUNDERS

In the end, this is the dream that drives many founders of public companies. They will often attempt to cash out of some of their holdings on the IPO, although this has becoming increasingly unpopular with the brokers leading the IPO, as it is not perceived positively by the public. However, even if the original private company shareholders do not sell any of their stock to the public on the IPO, the value of their holdings on paper is likely to have increased substantially. They are then able to sell some of their stock into the market, little by little over time, subject to any restrictions that may exist on their shares. In addition, their personal ability to borrow should be much improved as they now have better collateral for the bank as security for their own personal banking needs as compared to when their shares were simply those of a private company.

Disadvantages and Drawbacks of Going Public

As is evident from the comments above, there are many attractive, some would even say compelling, reasons to take a company public. However, it is not for nothing that New York financiers are credited with coining the phrase, "There's no such thing as a free lunch." Nowhere is this more true than in the stock market and the world of corporate finance. We will now examine some of the "dark side" of becoming a public company.

The disadvantages and drawbacks to going public include the following:

A. EXPENSES — UPFRONT AND ONGOING

There is no doubt that becoming and remaining a public company is an expensive proposition. In order to make a reasoned decision about taking a company public, you must carefully weigh these costs and the other disadvantages against the benefits that you hope to achieve and other financing alternatives that may be available to you. For starters, you can take it as a given that it will cost you at least 20% of the money that you raise on the IPO in order to actually undergo, and pay for, the whole process. Twenty-five percent is not uncommon. This includes brokerage commissions (which are often 10% for an emerging company and can be higher), lawyers' and auditors' fees, other consultants' fees, such as for the preparation of a technical report, and the costs of prospectus printing and distribution. How high a proportion of the money raised is expensed is also influenced by how much money you raise, how raw and undeveloped your project is, and who the brokers and promoters or market makers are that you become involved with. A more detailed discussion of the costs of an IPO is provided below.

In considering the apparent high cost of IPO money, you must compare it to bank financing and other sources of financing potentially available. If you consider the banking system as a source, your emerging company likely is not bankable in any case, so in most instances bank financing will not be a viable alternative. If it were, consider the cost. If you assume for the sake of this example a prime rate of 7% per annum, then adding 2% to 4% to determine your borrowing rate, you would be looking at a 9% to 11% per annum interest carrying charge on your money (which would have been considered very low for emerging companies for most of the past ten years). Assume a lump-sum payback in three years, which would be an optimistic payback on most capital projects, your interest cost would be between 27% to 33% of the amount borrowed. What's more, you still would have to repay the entire principal amount of the loan! So, in comparison, how attractive is nonrepayable equity obtained from a public offering?

In addition to the IPO costs noted above, there are significant annual costs of maintaining your company's listing with a stock exchange, including annual listing fees, annual general meeting expenses, audited financial statements, annual report, quarterly reports and other expenses.

B. CONTINUOUS DISCLOSURE OF MATERIAL INFORMATION

As a public company, the operations and financial position of your company are open to constant scrutiny by the securities commission, the stock exchange, your investors, your employees, your customers, your creditors and your competition. You may experience this as being anything from a mere nuisance and inconvenience to a serious competitive disadvantage. There is no doubt that a large portion of the time of an emerging company's chief executive officer is taken up by public company related matters, such as ongoing regulatory requirements, financial reporting and investor relations.

C. LOSS OF CONTROL

Voting control of the founders will be diluted upon the sale of shares through an IPO. Retention of 51% of the shares within a control block would ensure continuing control by the current owners, but as ongoing financing requirements demand additional sales of shares and further dilution, the danger will always be present of eventual loss of control. Indeed, as the shares of the founders become more and more diluted, the chances increase of a takeover of the company by other parties.

D. PUBLIC ACCOUNTABILITY FOR DECISION-MAKING AND LOSS OF PRIVACY

The senior executives and directors will lose the anonymity of a private company. Minority shareholders of public companies are becoming increasingly more vocal and demanding. Poor corporate decision-making by public company management does not go unnoticed. Business setbacks are no longer a private affair. More and more executives of public companies are being held responsible for the quality of their decision-making and may lose their jobs if they do not meet shareholder expectations. You can easily come to feel as though you were conducting corporate operations in a huge fish bowl with the whole world looking in at you.

E. SHAREHOLDER EXPECTATIONS

Investors generally expect continually rising corporate performance in all areas. Management will be subject to continual pressure to do better. Sales, profits, growth, market share, product development and share price must all improve. Failure to perform leads to loss of faith in management and the company, with the result that people do not want to hold your company's stock. When that happens, the value of your company's shares decreases. Then no one is happy.

F. INCREASED TAXATION

After the IPO, as your company will no longer be a "Canadian controlled private corporation" as defined by the Income Tax Act of Canada, it will no longer qualify for the small business income tax deduction. Tax advice should be obtained.

G. DIRECTORS' LIABILITY

The directors and officers of a public company have serious and onerous legal responsibilities to the company and to its shareholders. In a private company, the money and assets that the owner invests and risks are his own. In a public company, the money that is invested in shares of the company comes primarily from other people — the shareholders (hence the phrase, "Other People's Money," or "OPM"). Each public company director is accountable to the shareholders and may be held liable for any breach of his fiduciary obligations. A new director or officer of a public company is well advised to request from his lawyer a current summary of directors' legal duties and obligations in Canada. One useful book on this topic, intended for the layman, is entitled *The Responsible Director* and was written by an experienced Canadian corporate lawyer, James A. Millard, Q.C.

H. COLLAPSE OF STOCK PRICE AND INABILITY TO RAISE FURTHER CAPITAL

If the price of a company's stock collapses, it may be totally prevented from raising additional capital. This could result in the death of the company if the company is still in the development stage and is dependant on injections of capital to continue operating. This is not an uncommon scenario. There are many reasons why this stock collapse could happen, one of which is the intentional perpetration of outside parties. For example, the intentional driving down of the price of an emerging company's stock to almost nothing by professional short sellers for their own profit can be the utter ruin of such a company. The share price of a junior company can be very vulnerable as well as very volatile. It is ironic and tragic that the very step which was intended to enhance the company's ability to access the capital markets, namely going public, can ultimately result in its complete inability to raise further capital.

Company founders and directors need to educate themselves in regard to stock market machinations and attempt to develop strong market allies with an interest in the ongoing health of the company and its stock. This is much easier said than done. There are a number of eye-opening books available today which discuss the very sharp, sometimes illegal, practices which have been perpetrated by professional players on Canadian and American stock exchanges. The revelations of scandals, insider trading and outright fraud committed with respect to public companies listed even on the New York Stock Exchange, supposedly the most senior and reputable of all the stock exchanges in North America, is sobering reading indeed.

After weighing all of the factors involved, including those outlined above, the decision to take your company public must be based on the conclusion that it is the best solution to the financial challenges currently facing your company. Part of the decision-making process has to also include an analysis of how long it will actually take for your company to go public. It is essential to make an accurate estimate of the time involved because it will show you how soon you are likely going to be able to have access to the funds obtained through the public offering.

Principal Elements of Going Public

It is not at all unusual for the process of going public, from start to finish, to take at least one year. For most emerging companies, six months would usually be considered fast. A major reason for the length of time involved is the inexperience in securities and public company matters of the average company founder promoting an emerging company in his first public offering. Everything is being done for the first time in his experience, and he has yet to develop the team and the working relationships necessary to solve all of the challenges that lie ahead. In addition, the regulatory approval process can be very time consuming, depending especially on the nature of your proposed project and the preparation of the copious legal documentation which requires detailed regulatory review and approval.

The principal elements of the going public process are as follows:

A. BUSINESS PLAN

This topic has been thoroughly discussed in Chapter Two: "Preparing Your Business Plan." Depending on the capabilities of you and your management team, as well as on the complexity of your business, it may take you from one to six months to produce a suitable business plan and may cost you anywhere from $5,000 to $25,000 or more to produce it. The business plan is essential because in most provinces it will be required by both the consulting firm that must be retained to produce a technical report evaluating your business proposal (see comments directly below) and also by the brokerage firm which agrees to take the lead in taking your company public.

B. LEAD BROKERAGE HOUSE

Under the rules of the stock exchanges, a brokerage firm must sign the prospectus and agree to act as the company's agent to sell its shares if you are using the facilities of a stock exchange to raise money. In fact, it would normally be your hope that a brokerage firm becomes interested in you and your company, see the potential of your business, and want to take the lead in your public offering. You will have to make presentations to various brokerage houses in an effort to find one that wants to work with you.

It is important to note that many first-time company founders become bitterly disappointed with the lack of performance of their broker and the broker's failure to raise the money that the company was planning on. It is essential for you to understand that in the IPO of an emerging company, the cold hard reality is that it is usually the company founders who must accept the primary responsibility of seeing that the company's stock is sold. While it is the brokers that make the selling commission, it is really the founders who are very actively approaching all of their friends and every person who has ever seen their face — and some who have not — to promote the purchase of their company's stock (see comments below in Chapter Six on "Working Your Warm Market.") In most instances, you will be sadly and bitterly disappointed if you naively expect the brokers to actually sell your company's stock for you on your initial public offering.

This is in direct contrast to the stock issues of major corporations such as Bell Canada Enterprises Inc., or the Royal Bank of Canada, where all of the stock is actually purchased by the broker and then sold to the investors. That is called an "underwriting," as opposed to the "best efforts offering" which we have been discussing. In an underwriting, the broker puts up his own money and is actually at risk. In a best efforts offering, the broker puts up no money, takes no risk, and what is surprising to many novices, in many instances actually seems to make no effort.

In the case of many small emerging companies, the broker may agree to sign the prospectus for a fixed fee, often varying from $10,000 to $25,000 just to sign, then leave it to the company founders, other shareholders, and promoters to bring in the buyers for which the brokerage firm will charge a commission, normally at least 10%, for handling the paperwork involved in the purchasers making their investments. It is not difficult to find a brokerage house that will simply sign your prospectus for a fee and charge a commission on the stock purchases made by the investors who you bring in. It is much more difficult to find a brokerage house that becomes interested in what you are doing, will charge no up-front fee for taking the project on, and will actually go and sell your IPO for you.

C. TECHNICAL REPORT

As part of the due diligence process, in most cases the companies undertaking an IPO will be required to engage a recognized firm of consultants to prepare a document known as a technical report which comments on the company's business plan, management, business and prospects. The major accounting firms in their management consulting divisions perform this task, as do specialized smaller firms who prepare technical reports as a major component of their business. The smaller firms tend to be less expensive than the major firms. However, the credibility attached to the name of a large, international accounting and consulting firm has significant intangible value. You should shop around, discuss your project with a number of firms, get a feeling for who you would like to work with and compare prices. Most technical reports cost between $10,000 at the lower end to $25,000 at the higher end. They may take from one month to up to three months or more to prepare, depending mainly on the state of your own preparedness, such as the state of your business plan, management team, company operations and financial statements and projections.

D. AUDITED FINANCIAL STATEMENTS

These are required as part of the prospectus. The cost of their preparation will be a function of the quality of your accounting records, how long you have been in business and the complexity of your business operations. This could cost as little as $5,000 or even less for a start-up with no business history, to $50,000 or more if the company has poor accounting records, has raised and expended significant amounts of capital, and has operations in more than one city. Depending on the state of your company's records and the complexity of your operations, the initial audit could be accomplished in less than a month, or it could take six months or more if you have a large number of deficiencies in your accounting records to rectify.

E. PREPARATION OF LEGAL DOCUMENTS INCLUDING PROSPECTUS AND THE REGULATORY APPROVAL PROCESS

Your choice of securities law counsel will be one of the most important decisions that you make in the process of your IPO. Competent legal counsel, although seemingly expensive at first glance, can open many doors for you, find you appropriate resources, and in fact save you a considerable amount of time, effort and grief. You should retain counsel at the very beginning of your investigations and preparations with respect to going public. This is because your lawyer can steer you towards the appropriate brokers, often getting you in the door that you couldn't open easily yourself, direct you to appropriate technical consultants for your type of project, and provide you with some of the "street-smart" advice that is critical to your survival in the financial jungle. The writers of this book take great professional satisfaction in enabling an entrepreneur to successfully undertake a financing project which he could never have done on his own. A good financing lawyer is like an experienced guide in a hostile wilderness who can keep you safe from the quicksand, the snakes and other predators lurking in the darkness.

The sheer volume and complexity of legal documentation required in an initial public offering on a Canadian stock exchange is amazing and mystifying to most first-time IPO participants. So are the legal fees. A simple and straightforward public offering (most lawyers insist there is rarely such a thing) taking place in just one province, with one brokerage firm, can cost from $35,000 to $50,000 in fees. In contrast, a complex offering in two or more jurisdictions, with two or more brokerage houses and listing on two stock exchanges, could cost five times that amount in legal fees. It should be self-evident then, that the amount of money that you intend to raise on your IPO needs to be large enough to justify the expense of not only the legal fees, but those of the accountants and other consultants as well.

In addition to the costs referred to above, there are considerable printing costs associated with going public. You will require a prospectus and may also utilize a preliminary prospectus. You may prepare a fact sheet, summarizing details of the offering for the brokers. You may prepare product information literature with respect to marketing your company's product. At the minimum, the printing costs are likely to be at least $5,000 and could go as high as $10,000 to $15,000 without taking into consideration the cost of any product literature that you may prepare.

There are a number of other miscellaneous expenses, such as stock exchange filing fees, cost of share certificates, and the fees charged by the registrar and transfer agent to be the financial intermediary between the investor putting up the money, the brokerage firm collecting the money and your company receiving the money. These fees could easily amount to $10,000 to $25,000, depending on the size of your stock offering.

F. SELLING THE SECURITIES

Everything done up to this point has only been preparation for the Main Event: the sale of the securities of your company to the public. This is the Initial Public Offering. Most public offerings are completed within just a few days or at most weeks of when they are legally allowed to be sold. The securities cannot legally be sold until all preliminary matters are concluded and the securities commission has "cleared" the prospectus. However, well prior to the prospectus being cleared, the company founders and promoters will be busy soliciting expressions of interest with respect to purchasing the securities. Ideally, they will have arranged commitments to purchase the entire public offering as soon as selling is authorized by the securities commission.

If your brokerage house is getting behind you in your marketing efforts, it will arrange a number of so-called "dog and pony shows" for you. These "dog and ponies" (so named because the company's sales representatives and promoters are, like acts at the circus, deemed to be putting on a performance for an audience) are meetings in the boardrooms of various brokerage houses where a representative of your company makes a presentation on the company, its prospects, and the specifics of the shares that you are selling. Your purpose in these meetings is to solicit buying support from brokers in the various firms. Whether these dog and pony shows on their own really accomplish anything is debatable. It is a little bit like the old business story about advertising. It is said that 50% of every dollar that is expended on advertising is wasted. The only problem is, we don't know which 50%. Much the same can be said about these broker meetings. You think that you can do without them, but you are not sure. It seems that where they are actually useful is when any particular brokerage house has already committed to you to sell a certain amount of the IPO, then the dog and pony show is the way in which that house educates and interests its brokers in your deal. Another similar case is where one of the biggest producing brokers in a particular house, known in the trade as a "size broker," has agreed to sell your deal. He may want a few of his colleagues to also sell some of the stock and therefore wants you to educate and excite them with a dog and pony show. Both of the cases just mentioned are useful for you because you already have a certain amount of commitment and support. However, where you simply go into such a meeting cold, with no prior contact with, or commitment from, that house, it is probably not going to be very productive. Many, many novice company promoters have spent a lot of time in dog and pony shows without selling their IPO. It is somewhat analogous to a political convention, where the noise and colour is out on the floor, like a dog and pony show in a broker's boardroom, but the actual deal-making is done behind closed doors apart from the rank and file. Again, you would be very well advised to have someone experienced in the ways of successfully marketing a public issue work closely with you in this matter.

To summarize, depending on the nature of your project and all of the circumstances surrounding your IPO, once the lawyer has been retained and starts working on the project, it will likely take a minimum of four months and commonly six months or more, to steer your IPO through the regulatory maze including the stock exchange and the securities commission. The total length of time required to conduct your IPO from start to successful completion will also vary from one stock exchange to another, and from time to time on any one exchange. Your lawyer will be able to give you a timing estimate under the currently prevailing market conditions after taking into consideration the actual state of your business. For purposes of your initial planning, six to eight months is not an unrealistic figure to use for the total length of time to conduct an IPO from concept to completion. You should have a war chest of cash set aside of a bare minimum of $75,000 to undertake your IPO and that is only for a bare bones offering of the simplest nature. It is highly recommended that you have at least $150,000 set aside for your IPO in order to be able to handle contingencies and unforeseen elements. If these funds are not currently available to you, they could possibly be raised by way of a private placement utilizing your own warm market preparatory to undertaking the IPO (see Chapter Six).

Requirements of a Successful IPO

How do you make the final determination as to whether you currently have what it takes to undertake a successful IPO? First, you weigh all of the various factors, the advantages and benefits, the disadvantages and drawbacks, and on balance decide that the interests of the company and its shareholders will be best served by raising money through offering shares of the company to the public and becoming listed on one of Canada's stock exchanges. Second, you prepare a budget for the public offering and determine that you will be able to fund the IPO from your own or other people's money. Third, you determine that once commenced, you will be able to pursue your IPO through to the successful conclusion of achieving the money raised and the stock listed for trading on a Canadian stock exchange. The discussion to follow will deal with how you make the determination as to whether or not your project in its current state is likely to be successful in its pursuit of an initial public offering.

A. YOUR COMPANY — IS IT READY?

There are no longer any firm guidelines as to what constitutes a company that is ready to undertake its initial public offering. Perhaps the most realistic gauge would be that it has a likely story. In other words, the company's business plan must seem "plausible," "credible," "feasible" or "believable." That's it.

All of the criteria normally used to evaluate a company simply serve as ingredients of the likely story. Such factors as sales, orders on hand, margins, inventory, production, employees, overhead, and net profit mean nothing by themselves. Their unique combination, along with company management, the current atmosphere prevailing in the stock markets, and the buying that you can bring forth to the IPO will determine whether you will be successful or not in undertaking and completing your initial pubic offering.

Today, you could have the wildest idea on the planet and the markets could be in their greatest depression since 1929, yet if you have arranged $500,000 worth of buying through your friends and associates, you will definitely find your lead broker and you will be successful in your IPO. In fact, even less buying than that can still see you proceeding successfully with a small initial public offering.

Ironically, if your company has a tremendous business opportunity, yet if the markets are depressed and you have no buying arranged for the IPO, it is unlikely that you would be successful in your IPO. The exception would be if you could convince a brokerage house or powerful market player to commit to ensuring that the offering is purchased in the market. This can be an extremely hard sell. Your chances for success in this regard will be much higher if you have a well-established company with a profitable track record, or a natural resource property with geophysical results so powerful and persuasive that the property's future profitability would be beyond doubt.

Stock Exchange Minimum Listing Requirements

As a final comment with respect to your company's readiness for an IPO, each of Canada's five stock exchanges has certain minimum requirements which must be met by every new company being listed. These minimum requirements deal with such matters as minimum capitalization, annual sales, required number of registered shareholders at the close of the public offering, and other matters. Current listing requirements for each exchange may be obtained directly from that exchange, the addresses and telephone numbers for each are listed in "Sources of Further Information," Section G. Your securities lawyer will also have this information.

B. THE MARKET — IS IT READY?

Market conditions have a strong impact on the do-ability of an IPO. As is true in much of life, timing is everything. In a raging bull market, where the prices of stocks are high, investors' optimism is high and their net worth is up along with the price of the stocks they hold. Under these conditions, it is much easier to convince would-be investors to participate in your IPO. The converse is also unfortunately true. For example, in the immediate aftermath of the October, 1987 stock market crash, the number and size of IPOs in Canada and in the United States in 1988 was dramatically slashed compared to 1986 and 1987.

In addition, the stock market is highly influenced by the prevailing state of all other markets. When property values soared in southern Ontario through the 1980s, the net worth of property holders increased substantially. There was a mood of optimism which, in some circles, seemed to approach invincibility. Under these conditions, individuals were often willing to put money into emerging companies which some would refer to as highly speculative. Such buoyancy and euphoria has a finite lifespan. When the economy changes — and the economy always goes in cycles — property values drop and unemployment increases, even among executives and professionals. This has a real effect on the saleability of an IPO, even though our Canadian stock exchanges, like the larger New York Stock Exchange, could be enjoying stock price averages near their historical highs.

You must always remember that in money raising your task is to persuade the potential investor that the stock certificate in your company is much more valuable than the cash in his pocket. In a mood of fear and pessimism as is found in a deep recession, this is much more difficult to achieve. On the other hand, when there is optimism in the market place, that is the time to swing out and make big strides forward in your company's financing. The advice of brokers will be important on this issue as they are on the front lines between public companies and investors. Astute brokers will have a strong sense of what kind of stocks, what kind of companies and what kind of industries are currently popular and are selling well or, in a recession, can be sold at all.

C. YOUR SUPPORT — IS IT READY?

A successful initial public offering is very much a team effort and will severely strain the resources of almost all emerging companies. The key players on this IPO Team are your company's management team, your board of directors, the brokers working on your IPO, your professional advisors and your investors — existing and incoming. The critical thing to remember is that a successful IPO is about Selling, Selling and More Selling. It is a push. A press. A strain. In almost every case it is a matter of employing Winston Churchill's maxim: "Never, never, never give up!" In almost every case, you will be "pushed to the max!" Again, one more time: your job in the IPO, like in all money-raising, is *to convince the potential investor that the stock certificate in your company is worth more than the cash in his pocket.*

Every member of your IPO Team must be willing to actively participate. You've got to arrange dozens and dozens of individual and group meetings. Every member of your board of directors must prepare a list of dozens of people to contact, preferably at least 100 names each. See our comments in Chapter Six on working your warm market. These comments apply to every single member of your company, your board, your employees and your body of investors. This is a press. A push. You've got to pursue every possible opportunity with potential investors. You've got to make them believers! You and all of your team must become evangelists in the cause of financing and moving your company forward!

If any member of your board, your management team and your employees is not willing to provide dozens of names and help arrange meetings with potential investors, there is a strong argument that an emerging company cannot afford that person's services. As extreme as this may sound, in a small, struggling company, the referrals and contribution of a single person can mean the difference between corporate life and death. If any employee, whether production, administrative or management, cannot see that the future of the company depends on the successful financing of the company and therefore so does his job, he may be too myopic or too emotionally uninvolved to be of any long-term real value in building a company. Admittedly, the difficulty with this viewpoint is that an emerging company often has grave difficulty in attracting skilled workers and professionals in areas vital to the company's progress. Management may justifiably feel that the company is highly vulnerable in particular skill areas and consider that it cannot push employees too far in an area, namely money-raising, that employees do not feel is within their job description. The point here is simply that completing an initial public offering is usually extremely hard work, the outcome of which is often uncertain. Management usually feels that its back is pressed tightly against the wall. An attitude of full mutual cooperation and participation throughout the company will help to slant the odds toward success, whether in an IPO or any other aspect of corporate activity.

An emerging company needs committed players, not people who are merely supportive and who collect a paycheque twice a month for being so. The difference between committed and supportive is critical to the success of your company. It is illustrated by the following story.

> Once upon a time, a traveller arrived one early morning at a Saskatchewan farm. With typical prairie hospitality, the farmer invited the stranger to join the family for a traditional breakfast of bacon and eggs. Over coffee, after a delicious and filling breakfast, the farmer, being something of a prairie philosopher, advised the traveller that the ingredients of his breakfast that morning demonstrated the difference between being "committed" to a cause and being merely "supportive." This difference often means the difference between the success or failure of any worthwhile undertaking.
>
> Asked if he could explain the difference based on his breakfast, the stranger, being a Bay Street financier from Toronto and never wishing to appear mistaken about anything, refrained from answering. "It's really very simple, my seersucker-suited friend," said the farmer. "Think about the bacon and eggs which you just ate with such gusto. In order to put that food in front of you, the pig was truly *committed* but the chicken was merely *supportive!*" And it came to pass that even the Bay Street financier understood.

Accordingly, prior to your making the final decision to pursue your IPO, you must satisfy yourself that you have a sufficient degree of committed players on your IPO Team to ensure a good chance of success. Above all others, the people who have genuinely proven their commitment to your company to-date are your existing shareholders. They are a key resource in your IPO, each of whom has a very personal and tangible reason for wanting to see your company succeed with its proposed share offering — the amount of money that is currently invested by him in your company. If it is $10,000, those are 10,000 good reasons to help you find more investors to complete your IPO. You will find that current shareholders will be some of the most committed and helpful people in introducing you to prospective investors and also in persuading them to purchase stock in your company. Do not overlook this resource of proven, committed supporters of your company.

Making the Decision to Go Public

In the final analysis, your decision to undertake an initial public offering will be a highly subjective one based on a number of factors as discussed above in consultation with the best advisors that you can access. As is the case with almost all extremely important management decisions, this one will likely have an un-comfortable degree of uncertainty as to the outcome. Based on our own experience and those of numerous clients, after you have carefully and conscientiously weighed all of the factors and made your decision to proceed, the crucial element in determining whether you succeed or fail in your IPO will be your will to succeed, your own commitment. This is not the arena for the faint of heart. Once you have set your course, you must play for keeps. And keep your head up!

5.11 METHODS OF INTERNAL FINANCING

Many business owners who are unable to access money in terms of debt or equity capital may be forced to reassess their needs, resources and business management. For example, quick handling of accounts receivable, effective inventory control, customer prepayments, and cutting down on unnecessary expenses can free up funds not otherwise available. It forces your business to operate in a more efficient fashion. This will lessen your need to look outside the business for financing.

Some of the various methods of internal financing include the following:

Customer Prepayments

A business can encourage customers to make a deposit, prepayment or payment on delivery. This is a very common technique in the mail-order business and in service-type businesses.

Employees

Employees with access to capital may be willing to invest in the company because they understand its products and services and trust the management. A financial stake in the company's future could have a positive influence on the employee's work habits and commitment to the business. Conversely, it could prove difficult to replace, remove or retire the employee if the employee becomes unproductive or uncooperative. Therefore, any such form of investment should be written up in a contractual form through the assistance of your lawyer. Make sure that you have buyback or payback provisions built into the agreement as a precaution and to protect the business.

Inventory Control

Effective inventory control will ensure there is just the right amount of stock to satisfy customer demand. Determine guidelines for proper inventory purchases. Adjust your purchases to meet the peaks and valleys of your annual business sales. Too much money tied up in slow-moving inventory, debt servicing payments on inventory loans, or lost customer loyalty due to insufficient stock are costly to your business.

Collecting Receivables

Receivables can be reduced by tighter credit-granting policies, better monitoring of accounts, and more effective collection policies. You may wish to consider credit cards or cash only as a means of sales.

Delayed Payables

Establishing a good working relationship with your suppliers can result in extended payment terms. Make certain that they are aware of your loyalty to that firm and of your repeat business. You may be able to negotiate a discount on volume or regular purchases.

Restructuring Payment Arrangements

There are times when a business is not able to maintain monthly payments plus interest on loans or repayment to creditors. By using creative negotiating techniques, there are ways of getting around short-term problems. Some alternative repayment plans that you may consider include:

- A period of grace for principal loan payments during the start-up period of your business operation.
- Blended payments that feature a long amortization period resulting in low payments of principal in the early years.
- Graduated payments; that is, low payments or principal in the early years and higher ones later on.
- Payments of principal during the high season only, so that the business does not have a cash-tight period during the low sales volume season.

Selective Product Lines

Only handle product lines on which you get the most favourable terms from the supplier and which have the highest sales turnover and profit margin.

Fixed Assets

You may wish to sell your assets to a leasing company and lease them back, thereby freeing up cash for working capital purposes. On reviewing your assets, you may feel that some of them are not necessary to the business and may be sold to free up additional cash. By purchasing second-hand equipment and machinery, you can reduce financial outlay.

Renting or Subletting

You may decide to rent space for a store or factory rather than buying, to improve your leverage and your cash flow. By subleasing space you can offset your monthly rent payments, thereby increasing your working capital. If you have a service business, you may wish to rent an office on a month-to-month basis from a "packaged office" or "executive suite" centre. These places offer fully furnished offices, support services, receptionists, telephone answering, and use of a boardroom. You save on leasehold improvements and the risk of having a long-term lease that you may want to get out of in case you downsize or expand your office needs. Look in the yellow pages of your telephone directory under "office for rent."

Operating as a Subcontractor

You may wish to operate as a subcontractor, which could save overhead expense and risk for you. Conversely, you may also wish to subcontract your services to other companies, which saves on employees and overhead.

Stringent Management

By reviewing the points discussed above to determine how to conserve on capital and save on expenses, financial resources can be freed up and the business risk minimized. The business owner should analyze the financial condition of the business on an ongoing basis.

- Are salaries too high?
- Is the owner taking out too much from the company for personal earnings rather than keeping it in the company for working capital?
- How do the company's costs of goods and other expenses compare to other companies in the industry?
- Is the lease too expensive?
- Are supplies being wasted?
- Do actual expenses compare to budgeted expenses?

The business owner knows best where expenses can be trimmed from the operation. In addition to controlling expenses, the owner should always be looking for ways to increase profits, sell surplus inventory or assets, and maintain an effective receivables collection program. If the owner needs further help in improving profits and viability, an FBDB (Federal Business Development Bank) CASE counsellor may be able to provide management assistance. A private sector business management consultant may also be of assistance. Look in the yellow pages under "consultants" or "management consultants." Also, consult with a professional accountant. Many college and university business departments have business consulting assistance available.

5.12   CONCLUSION

As you can see, there are many options open to you when looking for money. Explore all the ones that you feel comfortable with, that are appropriate for your particular needs, at the various stages of your business' life: start-up, growth, upgrading, expansion, diversification or special, temporary or seasonal requirements. Refer to the "Sources of Financing Checklist," "Money-Rai$ing Master Checklist" and "Sources of Further Information" section, all located in the Appendix, to stimulate further creative ideas on financing. For seminars and other educational services relating to financing, contact the Canadian Enterprise Institute Inc., at #300–3665 Kingsway, Vancouver, B.C. V5R 5W2, Tel: (604) 436-3337. Fax: (604) 436-9155.

CHAPTER SIX

MARKETING AND SELLING YOUR DEAL

*Money never starts an idea; it is the idea that starts the
money.*

W.J. Cameron

6.1 INTRODUCTION

This chapter focuses on *the* source of money for start-up and emerging companies
in Canada: private investors; that is, informal venture capital. Well over half of
all of the risk money for small business entrepreneurs in Canada comes from family,
friends and angels. Accordingly, the aim of this chapter is to coach you on successfully finding and obtaining investment monies from private individual investors.

In many respects, this chapter is the culmination of almost everything that we
have so far covered in this book. The process of contacting the prospective investor,
making the presentation and obtaining the investment funds is the fruition of all
of the preparation to date.

Pursuing the Private Investor

After all of the preparatory work that has brought you to this point, the process
of marketing and selling an investment in your company can be broken down
into stages as follows:

- Determine the amount and form of your financing.
- Review the "Money-Rai$ing Master Checklist" in Appendix B and consult a
  securities lawyer respecting marketing your investment opportunity.
- Identify your three main sources of investors:
  1. Your warm market.
  2. Your cold market.
  3. Financial intermediaries or middlemen.
- Prioritize your lists of potential investors.
- Contact prospective investors to arrange meetings.
- Meet with your prospects and make your presentation.

- Ask for the purchase.
- Get the money.

6.2 DETERMINE THE AMOUNT AND FORM OF YOUR FINANCING

Review Chapter Four, "Structuring Your Deal," and in particular, section 4.4, "Putting It All Together, or Making the Deal." At this stage, you must decide how much you are going to raise, and in what form.

For the type of investor that we are now addressing, the informal private investor, consisting of family, friends and angels, we strongly recommend that you do two things with respect to structuring your investment:

1. Create Fixed Terms for the Deal. You are most likely going to raise money from several individuals. Therefore, it would be virtually impossible for you to move ahead by trying to negotiate a separate deal with every new investor. It would be a nightmare if everyone's agreement to the separate deals with the other investors was required. When approaching a number of smaller investors, it is much more likely to lead to success, and it is a much quicker process, if you fix the terms of the proposed investment in advance. In consultation with your advisors, as we have discussed above, choose and set the terms of the deal that you are going to offer. Create a term sheet setting out *the* deal. This is what you offer everyone.

2. Keep the Terms of the Deal Very Simple. Complex deals confuse and/or make unsophisticated investors nervous. People generally understand the concept of common shares in a company. They also understand a loan to a company. With a little explanation, most people will understand a loan convertible into shares. Anything much more complex than that and you lose many of your private investors.

6.3 REVIEW THE "MONEY-RAI$ING MASTER CHECKLIST"

Review the "Money-Rai$ing Master Checklist" found in Appendix B to ensure that you understand the legal framework and compliance requirements within which your money-raising activities must take place. Discuss your intended money-raising activities with a securities lawyer to ensure that you receive up-to-date information on securities law requirements in your province and any others in which you may undertake money-raising activities. By reviewing the Checklist, then reviewing Chapter Three, and finally creating a plan for your money-raising activities along the lines suggested in this chapter, you will then be well prepared for a short but highly useful meeting with your securities lawyer. The better you understand the basic concepts of Chapter Three before meeting with your lawyer, the less he or she will have to explain to you of a basic nature.

6.4 IDENTIFY YOUR THREE MAIN SOURCES OF INVESTORS

As discussed in Chapter Four, it is usually easiest to raise money from the people who have met you. These are the people know you and are interested in you. We will call the individuals who know you, your "warm market," and individuals who do not, your "cold market."

Your "Warm Market"

This large group has occasionally been described as everyone who has ever seen your face. It has been estimated by some researchers that by the time the average person in North America reaches the age of twenty-one, he knows at least 700 people. *This group of people is your greatest asset in the money-raising process.* For most people, this is where they raise all of their initial capital. *You must use your warm market well.* If you fail to raise adequate funds from your warm market, you usually stand very little chance of launching your project. If the people who know you the best, and should have reason to trust you the most, do not invest with you, why should anyone else?

MAKE A LIST OF 150 PEOPLE TO START

In order to identify your warm market, set a target of listing no less than 150 people whom you know or have met. These can be anyone. Make a game of it. You will start remembering people whom you haven't thought of in years. These in turn will trigger memories of still more people. Expand the list to 200 people, then 300, and more. Have your spouse go through this exercise as well and add hundreds of more names. Almost any couple should be able to list 500 people between them if they put some thought and effort into this. This list is crucial to your success in money-raising. Make it a weekend project.

As an effective means of triggering your memory, think of people in categories. Name all of the people that you can think of in each category. Some suggestions are as follows:

1. *Family and Relatives*
   parents
   parents in-law
   brothers and sisters
   brothers and sisters in-law
   aunts and uncles
   children
   cousins
   nephews and nieces
   in-laws' extended family
   ex-in-laws

2. *Places of Education (Use Your Year Books)*
   Pre-school
   Elementary
   Junior High
   High School
   University
   Vocational School
   Junior College
   Teachers
   Fraternities and sororities
   Societies and clubs

3. *Present and Past Employment*
   Employers
   Employees
   Co-workers
   Instructors
   Customers
   Clients
   Suppliers
   Professional Advisors
   Consultants
   Attended courses with you
   Played sports with you on com-
   pany teams
   Golfed with you
   Owns a related business that is
   prospering
   Received a promotion or salary in-
   crease

4. *Organizations and Volunteer Work*
   Church, Temple, Mosque, Syna-
   gogue
   Charities
   Political Parties
   Environmental Action Groups
   Downtown Improvement
   Rotary, Kiwanis
   Junior Chamber of Commerce or
   Chamber of Commerce
   Board of Trade
   Lodges, Moose, Elks, Masons,
   Knights of Columbus
   Missionary Societies
   Alumni Clubs
   Military Groups and Legion
   YWCA or YMCA

5. *Currently Doing Business With*
   Accountant, Lawyer, Doctor,
   Chiropractor, Architect, Engineer,
   Stockbroker, Financial Planner,
   Real Estate Agent, Contractor,
   Barber, Hair Dresser, Beautician
   Merchants, Grocer, Service Station
   Attendant, Mail Carrier, Delivery
   Persons, Insurance Agent, Travel
   Agent,
   Bars, Restaurateurs, Veterinarian,
   Optician, Pharmacist,
   Nurse, Hospital Staff, Technician

6. *Sports and Hobbies*
   People at your health club or work-
   out studio
   People you play sports with
   Owners and employees of sports
   stores
   Instructors
   People you met on a sports holiday
   or sports camp
   People you play cards with
   Computer bulletin board contacts
   People you know through music
   and art
   People you know through dance
   People you know through theatre

7. *Connections through Your Children*
   Young person received an inheri-
   tance
   Has wealthy parents
   Ambitious
   Knows wealthy people
   Has good job
   Know parents through day care or
   school

8. *Places of Residence*
   Former neighbours in various loca-
   tions
   Present neighbours
   People known through community
   associations

9. *List of Acquaintances Already*
   Available
   Club Members, Telephone Book
   Christmas Card List
   Wedding Invitation List
   List of Company Employees
   Small Community Telephone Book
   Sports Organization Members List
   Church Roll

10. *Connections through Your Family's*
    Warm Market
    Ask your parents about their con-
    nections in the categories above.
    Ask your brothers and sisters about
    their connections as above.
    Ask other close relatives about their
    connections as above.

The foregoing categories of your acquaintances are not exhaustive. Think up your own. Remember, this list is crucial to your success in money-raising.

Your "Cold Market"

This group is the rest of the world outside your warm market. At last count, there were over 5,000,000,000 people in your cold market. Certainly enough to fund your project!

The first thing to remember is that everyone in your cold market is in someone else's warm market. In studies about how rumours are able to spread so rapidly, it has been found that you are only three to five people away from being able to contact almost everyone on the planet!

Therefore, ask yourself, who are the connectors that could help you to contact someone that you feel would be a prime candidate to help fund your project? Look for the people connectors.

The other aspect of this, is simply to phone people that you have read about in the business pages of magazines or newspapers, that you have heard about somehow, that you know are in the same industry or that you know of by being in an aligned industry. You would speak almost identically as written in the script we have included here for your warm market, except that you would introduce yourself slightly differently according to the circumstances.

Financial Intermediaries or Middlemen

A final approach to meeting private investors is through professional financial in-termediaries or middlemen. These are sometimes known as matchmakers as discussed in Chapter Five. A number of provincial governments have attempted to promote their own matchmaking services between money-raising entrepreneurs with projects that need financing and investors looking for something to earn them money. While interesting in concept, these tend to be passive, in that the government middlemen wait for potential investors to contact them. The majority of potential angels and prospective investors never call, whereas successful private sector middlemen actively pursue potential investors through their network of contacts. You need to be cautious when dealing with middlemen because many of them do not have an established track record of connecting entrepreneurs with investors. Be extremely sceptical if they attempt to charge you a fee in advance for conducting a search. They should be paid on performance. If they are successful in raising money for you, then they have earned their fees.

An example of a national clearing house for informal venture capital is the National Business Finance Network, Inc., located in Vancouver. This business, which was established by one of the authors, Brian F. Nattrass, provides many services to both entrepreneurs looking for capital and to angels who are looking for an appropriate investment. The National Business Finance Network can evaluate a company or project, develop a financing or business plan, locate funding sources, help negotiate the terms of the investment and organize an IPO. Because it is exposed to a large number of deals, the National Business Finance Network also acts for investors looking for a particular kind of opportunity, in a particular segment of the economy. The company therefore acts as a dependable bridge between attractive projects and qualified investors. For information on how the company may assist you, contact National Business Finance Network, Inc., at #207–1425 Marine Drive, West Vancouver, B.C. V7T 1B9 Tel: (604) 886-3373 Fax: (604) 886-9605.

6.5 PRIORITIZE YOUR LISTS OF POTENTIAL INVESTORS

After you have created your raw list of contacts, it is time to prioritize them. You need to narrow your money-raising search to those prospects who seem to have the greatest capacity or the highest interest in investing in private companies. A simple and effective method is to mark an asterisk (like this: *), beside the name of each person for every one of the following criteria that he or she meets:

- affluent
- has money to invest
- is known to invest in private companies
- is financially ambitious
- wants to put his money aggressively to work
- a risk taker
- successful but dissatisfied
- not directly involved in small business.

The next step is to use the "Prospective Investor List" in Appendix B. Start listing your prospects in the order of how many asterisks they have. In other words, if someone has eight asterisks, put him first; then the sevens; then the sixes; and so on. The people with asterisks by their names are the ones to start your money-raising program with, in the general order in which they appear.

You should also fill in the Potential Investment Size column on the form. You will just have to guess at this. Then add up the total column of potential investment size and compare it to how much you need to raise. Most people will be pleasantly surprised at how much they could potentially raise from their own warm market. If that includes you, then you can make a positive response to a Go-No-Go decision as to whether or not you will proceed with a plan to raise money in this way. If you are disappointed, you should continue working on your lists until you reach the necessary comfort level. If you are in doubt, discuss this with your personal advisors, such as your accountant, lawyer or stockbroker.

6.6 CONTACT PROSPECTIVE INVESTORS TO ARRANGE MEETINGS

Your attitude towards what you are doing at this stage, both on the telephone and in person, is fundamental and crucial to your success:

1. You must be enthusiastic about your project;
2. You must genuinely believe that your project is a winner;
3. You must believe that you are providing the prospect with a wonderful opportunity to make a substantial profit on his money.

If any one of these three elements is missing, you should seriously reconsider what you are involved with and consider a change immediately. If you are not enthusiastic about what you are doing, why are you trying to get other people involved to share your depression? If you do not believe that your project is a winner, why are you doing it? Wouldn't it be misrepresentation to tell people that you believe in the project's success? If you do not believe that the project is going to be financially very profitable, why are you in it? Why should anyone else invest in it?

1. Start with Your Warm Market First

For most investors, it is easiest to begin the process of offering the opportunity to invest in their business to people they know well. Relationship tends to provide a comfort and a confidence factor to entrepreneurs new to the money-raising process. Most people thus find it easiest to begin with the warmest part of their warm market.

2. Telephone Someone to Get a Meeting to Show Him Your Business. Then Do It Again and Again.

Eventually, you are going to have to pick up your telephone and actually start calling people. Always remember the *sole purpose of this call* is to arrange a meeting for you to show him your business investment opportunity. DO NOT ATTEMPT TO EXPLAIN THE DEAL OVER THE PHONE! IT NEVER WORKS! IT NEVER CLOSES A SALE! You are only seeking a meeting through this call.

There are eight important elements to making these calls effective:

a. Give Your Full Name and Jog His Memory   Give your full name, so there is no confusion as to "Jane, who?" If you think that there is the slightest chance that the other person won't immediately remember who you are (particularly as you move away from the warmest part of your list), jog his memory by a short reference (e.g., "You remember, we were classmates at university." or, "You remember, we met at Joan and Fred Dirckson's party last month." or, "You remember, we sat next to each other last week on the flight from Toronto to Vancouver." etc.).

b. Ask, "Is this a good time for you to talk?"   How many times have you been interrupted when you least wanted it? How interested are you in talking, or more important, listening, at moments like that? Therefore, in order to make your call effective, always ask if it is a good time to talk. It will help ensure that you get the attention that you seek and, at the least, it's an appreciated sign of politeness and respect.

c. Project Enthusiasm Remember always that money-raising is a process of enrollment. You are enrolling the person on the other end of the phone in what you are doing and in wanting to meet with you to hear more about it. It has been said a million times and more, and it's true: enthusiasm sells! Voluminous research in the area of communications research has verified beyond question that what is being transmitted to the other person goes far beyond the literal content of the words. "Information" is being transmitted and received according to your attitude, tone, cadence, emphasis, accent and more.

Sales professionals have known for years that the essence of enthusiasm is contained in these four letters: IASM as an acronymn for:

I
Am
Sold
Myself!

This then relates back to section 6.6 above. Enthusiasm provides the magic to make this miracle happen. It's the music in your money-raising dance. If you do not have it, you are playing in the wrong game. No one is going to want to play with you.

d. Give a Compliment Personalize the conversation to that specific individual. Let him know that there is a good reason why you have phoned him in particular. Why him? People are much more likely to respond favourably if they understand that it may be of interest in a personal, particular way to them.

e. Describe Your Business Briefly and Advise that You Are at the Money-Raising Stage Give a one-sentence statement of what business you are in. Then tell him that you are at a stage of money-raising. This is important, because if he absolutely has no money to invest, or absolutely will not invest in anything, you do not want to waste a lot of your time having a presentation meeting, only to find that out at the end. It also will waste the prospect's time. In addition, you want to differentiate yourself from the throngs of people involved in direct sales of various kinds who are also out phoning people trying to get them to opportunity meetings or sell a product. Your prospect may have no interest in buying or selling someone's product, but may consider an investment proposal in a private business.

f. Tell Him of the Business Plan and Projected Profitability Spark his interest by saying that the business looks extremely profitable. For example, that your financial projections show a return to investors of 50% over the next three years! Use whatever your figures do show, or without using figures make an alternative statement as to your projected profitability. Never mislead. Give him a peek at your Great White Shark! Review our comments from sections 4.1 and 4.2. Speak in positive and enthusiastic tones about what stage you are at and mention the business plan because it helps you sound credible with respect to this project and the financial calculations.

g. Provide a Disclaimer and an Exit to the Prospect Can you remember someone phoning you and being really persistent and pushy on the telephone? They kept pushing, and promoting, and selling, selling, selling . . . How did you feel? Did your sales rejection defense mechanisms come alert? Did you notice that the harder they pushed the more you backed away from what they were saying? It is important that your prospect feel that he is not being pressured or somehow obliged to see you. By letting the prospect know that this business isn't for everyone, it disarms him at the same time that it helps to stimulate his interest.

h. Get the Meeting Assume that he is interested, and ask if a particular day (that you have chosen) would be convenient. Then choose the time and place together. If your first choice didn't work for him, offer him another specific day, and then another, until you find one. Never ask whether you can meet. Do not set yourself up for a "no." Always use the assumption of implied consent. Assume that your prospects will want to meet with you to learn how they can make a profit with you. Why wouldn't they want to learn how to increase their wealth? They would be foolish not to! By assuming that the prospects will want to meet with you, more often than not it's true.

3. Sample Phone Script

The following script is simply to give you an idea of how all of the elements can flow together in the telephone conversation. Once you are comfortable with these appointment calls, you will develop your own style and wording to suit yourself. If you are new to this, be sure to practice it several times before phoning your first prospects. Even do a mock telephone conversation with your spouse or a good friend until you feel reasonably comfortable with it. Some people have no reluctance in calling, but for others it is a real trial. Hopefully this process will not be quite so painful for you. By first phoning friends and family about your business, and by being confident that you really do have a worthwhile proposal, you are sure to get a large number of meetings arranged.

"Hello Bob, this is Jane Lawson. You may remember, we met at the Continuing Education Course on Project Management last summer."
     Refresh his memory as to who you are if this is not a recent contact.

     At this point, the other party will usually say something like,
"Oh, hi Jane, how are you?"
     To which you make the shortest possible friendly response and get right to business.
"Just great! Very busy, but great. Say, is this a good time for you to talk?"

"Sure Jane, no problem."

"Bob, the reason that I'm calling you is that . . . I had a very good sense of you as a businessperson when I met you; . . . or, I know that you are a real student of business and enjoy looking at new ventures; . . . I know that you are a centre of influence in your community/hospital/union/company/etc; or, . . . "

Insert something personal and appropriate complimenting the individual.

Pause for an instant to let the compliment sink in.

"You may recall that I have been intensely involved with developing a new business in the _____ industry for the past _____ years. We have done a tremendous amount of work on the project, have produced a very thorough business plan, and it looks extremely profitable. Our financial projections show a 50% profit over the next three years.

"We are now at the seed capital funding stage.

"There's no question this type of investment isn't for everybody. However, I thought it might be a good fit for *you* because of your interest in entrepreneurship; . . . or, I know you enjoy looking at new ventures; . . . or

"Would next Tuesday be convenient for you to look at this exciting project?"

"Sure Jane, Tuesday works fine. How about 11:00 at my office?"

"Sounds great, Bob!"

"Say, what about your business plan? How have you worked up your financials?"

"Yes, I have. Bob, I've got to run. Let's save everything to Tuesday. 'Bye."

"See you Tuesday, Jane. 'Bye."

6.7 MAKE YOUR PRESENTATION AND GET THE MONEY

When you meet with your prospective investor, greet him with a smile and share your excitement with him. Remember this, from Chapter Four, deal with the Investor's SLIP Test. As long as you deal with those four issues, you will be most of the way there.

Deal logically with your presentation as though you were summarizing your business plan. However, always impart the vision of your company as outlined in Chapter One. *Enroll him in that vision.* We cannot tell you what to say, because your own personality must come through. If you have made it this far, you will do fine.

The key issue: *ask for the investment.* Tell the prospect at the end of the presentation that you would really like to have him on board as an investor. Ask him, "Would you like to go for $20,000?" (or whatever figure you feel he can afford). Assume that he will invest, it's only a question of how much. If he demurs, then keep coming back to it after you answer any questions that he may have. *You must ask for the purchase over and over again, if necessary.* Do not leave the meeting without asking specifically for the investment. *You* must ask. Do not expect him to volunteer. This is critical to your success.

Finally, get the investor's cheque at that meeting, if at all possible. You should always come to the meeting prepared with subscription forms and some blank cheques. If he has said "yes" to the investment at that meeting, at the very least get him to sign the subscription form there and then. Leave him with a copy and you take the original. Make arrangements to pick up the cheque the following day, or as soon as possible. Do not wait passively for him to send you the cheque. You take the initiative. By at least signing the subscription form at that meeting, he will feel much less inclined to back out if he is hit with pangs of "buyer's remorse" afterwards.

Your chances of actually receiving the investor's cheque subsequent to the meeting are much higher if you leave the meeting with a signed subscription form.

6.8 CONCLUSION

Tip: Do not despair if, despite your best efforts, the sale is not made at the meeting. All good salespeople know that "No" only means "Not today, under present circumstances." Keep in touch with the prospect, keep him up-to-date on your progress, and eventually make another appointment to bring him in as an investor then. Keep the dialogue going until the investor decides the time is right. Never write anyone off.

Many people only invest after three or four meetings. Sometimes poeple have said "no" a dozen times before finally saying "yes." Always remember that "no" only means "Not today, under present circumstances."

PART II

TRENDS IN BUSINESS FINANCING

CHAPTER SEVEN

MLM/NETWORK MARKETING

Sow much, reap much; sow little, reap little.
Chinese proverb

7.1 INTRODUCTION

The least understood and most overlooked method of financing a business enterprise in Canada today is clearly network marketing. In fact, so misunderstood is this form of doing business that no other major book on the topic of business financing has examined the nature and implications of the commercial phenomenon now known as network marketing. Whether you are an individual seeking to finance the start-up of a business of your own, or whether you operate an established business and seek to finance the expansion of your operations, you cannot afford to ignore the potential that this form of enterprise may provide you. Some of the benefits that this method of business offers the Canadian entrepreneur includes an enhanced ability to secure financial capital, reduced start-up costs, early cash flow, reduced cost of new product introduction and an overall reduction of general and administrative costs.

Sometimes still referred to as multi-level marketing (MLM), an earlier incarnation was known and vilified as pyramid selling. In this chapter, we will use the terms network marketing, multilevel marketing and MLM interchangeably, and sometimes refer to them together as MLM/network marketing. No matter how it is described, network marketing is arguably the most accessible, the fastest growing and offers to the ordinary person the greatest opportunity for very large financial gain of any segment of lawful business activity in Canada today.

7.2 NETWORKS

In order to fully comprehend the importance of MLM/network marketing as an astonishingly rapidly developing business form, we must first understand something of the social transformation occurring in our culture at all levels and the evolving role of networks generally.

The radical transformation of our industrial society to the so-called post-industrial or information society has bred rampant anxiety, alienation and confusion amongst large numbers of people throughout North America as documented by numerous psychological and sociological studies. Whole industries are dying and once great corporations disappear almost overnight, while at the same time, high technology creates new industries and new products which are increasingly difficult for the average person to identify with or to comprehend.

Social analysts as diverse as Marilyn Ferguson in *The Aquarian Conspiracy*, John Naisbitt in *Megatrends* and Alvin Toffler in *Power Shift* have documented the increasing significance of networks throughout society as vehicles for people connecting with other people and to give some sense of meaning and significance to our lives. As Marilyn Ferguson wrote in *The Aquarian Conspiracy*: " . . . the network is the antidote to alienation. It generates power enough to remake society. It offers the individual emotional, intellectual, spiritual, and economic support. It is an invisible home . . . The network is the institution of our time . . . "

Business and the economy are inextricably interwoven with, and are expressions of, the society of which they are a part. One of the strengths of the capitalist system as we know it in Canada is its incredible adaptability. An example of its expression at the micro, or consumer, level would be that of real estate developers modifying their product lines in perfect congruence with the prevailing tastes and needs of the consumers and the tax laws affecting their industry. When substantial tax "write-offs" are available to the end purchasers or investors in multiple-unit residential housing, there will be a proliferation of new apartment construction. If the write-offs are eliminated, the attractiveness of the investment or purchase decreases and so the developer will have less of a demand for that type of product and will be motivated to seek other opportunities. Another example is that as the "greying" of Canada's population accelerates, developers will focus on the housing needs of older citizens rather than those of young people. In other words, an entrepreneur cannot operate effectively without paying careful attention to what is going on around him. A successful businessperson is adaptive and modifies his or her manner of doing business in accordance with the changing rules, trends and needs in society.

One such powerful trend today is the pronounced move away from the values and form of hierarchical social structures to those of the network. Hierarchies, or social pyramids (not to be confused with "pyramid selling"), are the way that we have organized Western society for centuries. From the Roman Army of two thousand years ago, to the Catholic Church in the intervening millennia, to the Government of Canada bureaucracy today, the pyramid structure is how we have organized and managed ourselves. Direction and communication have flowed in a generally predictable manner from the top of the pyramid to the bottom, from the general to the foot soldier, from the Pope to the priest and from the prime minister to the payroll clerk.

Increasingly, however, the hierarchy or pyramid-shaped organizational structure is not satisfying the needs of contemporary men and women in Canada. In an era of "high tech," we increasingly demand "high touch" in our lives. In other words, as we are surrounded more and more by the elements of a highly technological world, we unconsciously have sought out more and new ways of being in direct contact with other human beings. Networking is one such powerful means of being in contact. Networks have always been part of human social life — they have simply been called by different names, whether it be an extended family, a tribe, a sports club or a fraternal society.

What is a "network"? John Naisbitt in his book *Megatrends* describes the phenomena as follows: "Simply stated, networks are people talking to each other, sharing ideas, information, and resources. The point is often made that networking is a verb, not a noun. The important part is not the network, the finished product, but the process of getting there — the communication that creates the linkages between people and clusters of people."

Marilyn Ferguson, in describing personal and social transformation in contemporary society in *The Aquarian Conspiracy*, notes that networking is done by " . . . conferences, phone calls, air travel, books, phantom organizations, papers, pamphleteering, photocopying, lectures, workshops, parties, grapevines, mutual friends, summit meetings, coalitions, tapes, newsletters . . . "

Jessica Lipnack and Jeffrey Stamps in *New Age* state that: "Networks are appropriate sociology — the human equivalent of appropriate technology — providing a form of communication and interaction which is suitable for the energy-scarce, information-rich future . . . "

As we approach the beginning of the 21st Century, networking as an expression of our needs in society is rapidly ascending. As a social form, it richly satisfies many of the emotional and even spiritual needs of millions of individuals in this era of often confusing social change. In its economic aspect, there are abundant opportunities in networking for the Canadian businessperson astute enough to capitalize on this clear trend.

One such economic manifestation is the rapid emergence of MLM/network marketing as a powerful form of business enterprise. Within the last decade, many corporations organized around the MLM/network marketing format have achieved annual sales of hundreds of millions and even billions of dollars. Millions of people are now involved on either a full- or part-time basis as salespeople with MLM companies throughout Canada, the United States, Europe and parts of Asia. It is estimated that in North America alone, over 12,000,000 MLM/network marketing devotees now distribute billions of dollars a year of a vast selection of goods and services. Richard Poe, senior editor of *Success Magazine*, commenting on this business phenomena in that magazine writes as follows: "Experts predict that in the '90s, network marketing — sometimes called multi-level marketing or just MLM — will fuse Americans from coast to coast into one gigantic, pulsating sales amoeba . . . : 'With multi-level marketing, you reach people through their families, their neighbours, their co-workers,' says William Plikaitis, group manager for US Sprint's FON marketing group. 'There's no better way today to get your product right in the consumer's face.' . . . 'Everybody's working together for the same thing,' says Joe Beasy, a Minneapolis distributor for Dallas-based Omnitrition. 'There's a tremendous feeling of trust, of esprit de corps.'"

7.3 THE NATURE OF NETWORK MARKETING

Given the enormous volume of goods marketed each year in North America through MLM/network marketing and the millions of people involved, the extent of the continuing ignorance of this form of business enterprise is rather surprising.

With numbers this large, MLM is now clearly a major industry in both Canada and the United States, as well as being one of the ten fastest growing industries in North America. Yet what is MLM really?

MLM/network marketing is a self-financing and self-reproducing system of marketing, selling and distributing a product or service to the consumer through various levels of managers, sponsors and salespeople. In a typical organization, products are purchased at a preset wholesale price by independent distributors and resold at a higher price to other independent distributors or to the retail consumer. Each independent distributor is encouraged to "duplicate" himself by "sponsoring" new independent distributors to also join his MLM organization. By such sponsoring, he creates levels of independent distributors below him within the hierarchical structure of the MLM system. These individuals which he has sponsored are collectively referred to as his downline. The sponsored people in his "downline" (first generation) sell the product to the consumer and, in turn, sponsor other people who then become the new distributor's downline ("second generation"), who also then retail products to the consumer and, in turn, sponsor other people who then become new independent distributors ("third generation"), and so on.

The hugely motivating factor in all of this is that each independent distributor can earn rebates, bonuses or commissions from all of the sales in his downline depending on the rules of his particular MLM program. Highly successful independent distributors can have tens of thousands of people in their downline and earn well in excess of $1,000,000 per year in rebates, bonuses or commissions. The following chart illustrates the structure:

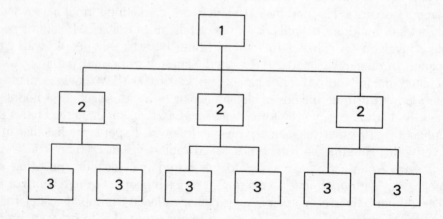

Due to the continuing suspicion by the general public of anything that has the odour of a "pyramid scheme" (see discussion below under section 7.4: "Distinguished from Pyramid Selling"), MLM companies frequently no longer use such a diagram of their hierarchy which, indeed, does resemble a pyramid. Instead, they use a structure which is described variously as "organic," or "molecular" or "cellular" and which emphasizes the "networking" aspect of the MLM/network marketing organization rather than the "multi-level" aspect, as shown below:

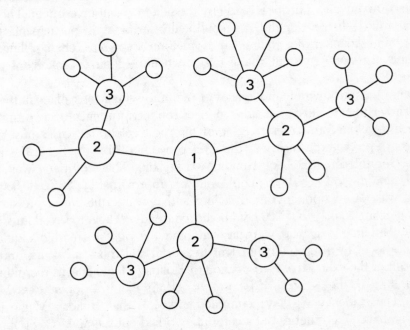

A discussion of financing a business in Canada through MLM/network marketing must differentiate between whose business is being financed: that of the corporation or that of the individual distributor. When a new company is being formed, or when an established firm is seeking to change or enhance its cash flow and/or its marketing program, decisions must be made as to the type of organizational structure that will best satisfy the corporation's goals. Similar issues confront the individual who may be seeking a way to establish a successful independent business. MLM has something of value for both the corporation and the independent businessperson.

7.4 DISTINGUISHED FROM PYRAMID SELLING

Many people continue to confuse MLM with "pyramid selling." The fundamental difference is that pyramid selling is not concerned primarily with the distribution of a product or service but instead seeks the "right to sell the right to sell," as former New Jersey Attorney General George F. Kugler, Jr. articulated in the prosecution of Bestline Products for consumer fraud. The essence of a "pyramid scheme" is that the financial success of the new investor depends on attracting other victims into the scheme as additional investors who pay an "entry fee" for the right to participate, rather than from the sale of products or services to consumers.

The basic distinction is that a pyramid scheme requires an investment for entry into the company and a profit is made by the seller on that investment. The success of a pyramid scheme depends on continually luring new participants into the scheme, in the manner of a chain letter, sometimes known as "chain selling." When the supply of recruits runs out, that is to say, when the chain is broken, the pyramid collapses.

Because the introduction and spread of pyramid selling took place in the United States earlier than it did in Canada, most of the jurisprudence on pyramid selling has been developed in America. One of the most celebrated cases of a pyramid scheme in the United States was the 1974 prosecution by the Securities and Exchange Commission (SEC) of Holiday Magic, Inc. That company was charged with defrauding over 80,000 people out of approximately $250,000,000. Their scheme was based upon pyramid selling and new recruits were pressured into investing from $2,500 to $5,000 with the company. They received the right to recruit other investors, who were also granted the right to recruit additional investors, who in turn received the right to recruit still more investors, and so on. As a result of the exhaustive investigation of Holiday Magic and its recruiting practices in 1972-73, the New York Consumer Affairs Commissioner, Bess Myerson, stated: "The evidence we have compiled indicates that Holiday Magic is not a company that sells cosmetics but a carefully worked out scheme to keep increasing the number of people who can be deprived of their life savings. Victims all over the United States have gone into debt, lost their jobs and their health through participation in these pyramids."

As a result of the public outcry against chain selling and pyramids in the early 1970s, United States federal and state agencies introduced stringent legislation prohibiting this form of marketing. The key principle was established that it is illegal to charge a fee for buying into a marketing opportunity when the organizational structure is such that a profit is made by the sellers on the buy-in. There is now a clear demarcation between the legitimate recruiting of MLM sales people and the illegal pyramid recruiting of investors.

Following the American experience, legislation was introduced in Canada at both the federal and provincial levels to deal with the pyramid problem. In Canada, pyramid sales schemes are prohibited and are punishable under the federal Criminal Code by as much as two years' imprisonment, or under the federal Competition Act, on conviction on indictment by a fine at the discretion of the court, imprisonment for up to five years, or both. On summary conviction, a fine of up to $25,000, imprisonment for one year, or both, may be imposed. However, the Competition Act provides that the prohibition against pyramid selling does not apply to a legitimate "scheme of pyramid selling" licensed or permitted by a province. A number of provinces, but not all, have now introduced legislation regulating the activities of companies and individuals engaged in lawful "schemes of pyramid selling" or, as we refer to them here, forms of multi-level or network marketing.

Today, although MLM/network marketing companies operate within a strictly regulated legal environment in both Canada and the United States, the public memory of such highly publicized illegal pyramid scheme prosecutions as Holiday Magic, Koscot Interplanetary and Bestline Products has left a distasteful aura surrounding the industry generally. This lingering residue of early illegal operations continues to taint the public perception of multi-level marketing and is probably the strongest reason why network marketing continues to be such a misunderstood and much overlooked method of financing a business enterprise.

7.5 FINANCING THE CORPORATION

MLM/network marketing is a method of financing the expansion and growth of a business as well as being a specific marketing strategy. There are at least five very convincing reasons why more and more companies are choosing to start or expand their operations through the use of an MLM system: securing financial capital, reduced start-up costs, early cash flow, reduced cost of new product introduction and reduction of general and administrative costs.

1. Securing Financial Capital

The receipt of cash up-front from the company's distributors to secure their inventories can help to finance the initial growth phase of the company. It can also help ensure that operating expenses can be met. Since all distributors pay in advance for their product, or at the least on a cash-on-delivery basis, MLM companies have no accounts receivable. Everything is either paid in advance or currently. Knowing this, a sophisticated investor or lender who is familiar with MLM may be more inclined to financially support the company which is seeking funding.

2. Reduction of Start-up Costs

This is a very compelling reason to consider an MLM distribution system. Start-up costs can be substantially reduced because an MLM sales force is self-financing. The company incurs no costs for sales offices, no sales overheads, and no sales staff expenses such as draws against commissions. The distributors are all independent businesspeople. What might traditionally have been a fixed cost in an end-user-based distribution company now becomes a variable commission cost. Most of the fixed costs in the MLM firm are transferred to the independent distributors. This also significantly reduces the size and expense of the company's administrative costs.

3. Early Cash Flow

In an MLM/network marketing organization, cash may begin to flow into the company as quickly as new recruits are sponsored into the company. There is no lengthy waiting period while the company negotiates with potential wholesalers, explores various other distribution channels or performs the many time-consuming tasks normally associated with establishing a sales and marketing organization.

4. Reduction in Cost of New Product Introduction

One of the most unique aspects of MLM is that corporations which are organized on the principles of network marketing can avoid many of the costs normally connected with new product introduction. Most of the tasks and expenses necessary to promote a new product are actually passed on to the independent distributor. In many highly successful MLM companies, the cost of product promotions, consumer demonstrations, video tapes, audio cassettes and similar promotional expenses are assumed by the independent distribution network. In many large MLM companies, there are groups of independent distributors who join forces to produce good quality tapes presenting the company's story which provide a real service to all of the company's distributors, cost the company nothing and provide an additional profit centre for the distributors.

5. Reduction of General and Administrative Costs

With an MLM/network marketing company, very few personnel actually need be employed by the firm. This results in the company not having to incur much of the overhead cost typically associated with salaried personnel: Canada Pension Plan payments, U.I.C. contributions, health insurance, income tax withholding and administration, employee record keeping, and so on. In addition, many of the costs normally considered to be fixed costs, such as rental of sales offices, telephone, computer and equipment rental for sales offices, and utilities are transferred to the independent distributors in an MLM firm. These factors, along with the reduced number of company personnel, mean that the relative size of the company's administrative staff can be significantly reduced.

Michael Granfield and Alfred Nicols, in their study entitled "Economic and Marketing Aspects of the Direct Selling Industry," published in the *Journal of Retailing*, express the factors noted above in a slightly different way. While not referring specifically to MLM, they assert that there are at least four advantages to a firm that decides to market its products via the direct selling method:

1. Quick distribution and sales at a relatively low level of fixed cost.
2. Consumer acceptance for a product which is new to the industry.
3. Entrance to a market while avoiding excessive promotional and advertising expenses as well as potential price wars.
4. Potentially higher rate of return on sales by eliminating large outlays for media advertising.

All of these advantages are particularly evident in the MLM system of direct selling.

Don Failla, a widely-known MLM commentator, writing in *The MLM Vision*, sums up the reasons why corporations choose MLM/network marketing very clearly when he writes:

Why would companies with new products choose to multi-level them: There are three primary reasons: simplicity of distribution, speed in developing a large consumer base, and profitability.

Distributing products through MLM is relatively simple, compared to normal channels. Instead of being required to hire salespeople and huge support teams, MLM companies just put together multi-level programs that attract independent contractors (distributors) who are paid for their productivity. Products move directly from the company or manufacturer to these distributors and consumers without several middlemen.

MLM is probably the quickest way to develop a broad consumer base. Traditional distribution requires months, in order to establish accounts with wholesalers and retailers before the product reaches the store shelves. MLM is like having thousands of factory-direct stores, with each one bringing in new ones every day. The more attractive the bonus/commission program, the faster the growth.

Of course, one of the most attractive features of MLM for companies is the level of profitability. Selling direct, on a cash basis, is a quick way to make some big money. Because there are no middlemen and little advertising is necessary, the company's overhead is low. Products may be sold at reasonable prices, yet leave plenty of money to pay distributors.

In summary, all of the reasons shown above demonstrate that the major financial benefits from utilizing an MLM/network marketing system are cost savings and profitability. This includes the cost of financing the operation, the cost of hiring and paying salespeople, the cost of entering a new market, the cost of advertising and promotion and the costs of overhead. For the Canadian entrepreneur with limited capital, or an established firm that is considering the risks involved in entering a new market, MLM/network marketing provides a unique and low-risk opportunity to successfully establish a new firm or a new profit centre.

7.6 FINANCING THE INDIVIDUAL

For the average person in Canada, there is arguably no better vehicle in existence to start and grow a business than MLM/network marketing. Hundreds of thousands of Canadians harbour the dream of owning their own successful independent business. Yet how can they do it? Frequently, a lack of capital, a lack of business know-how, a lack of education, a lack of available time, or a combination of all of those prevent people from pursuing their dreams. With MLM, none of those factors need be a handicap. In many respects, an independent distributorship in an MLM/network marketing company embodies almost all of the elements of an ideal business:

1. **Very low capital requirements.** This is often less than $100. In addition, many MLM companies have made arrangements with a finance company to grant a certain amount of credit without exception to anyone who becomes an independent distributor in order that the distributor can have a larger amount of inventory with which to work.

2. **No experience required.** The company will teach the new distributor about its own unique marketing system and products.

3. No education required. Anyone, almost without exception, can become a distributor for an MLM company. The company will provide product and marketing information.

4. Independence. No boss. People in MLM companies frequently say that you are in business for yourself but not by yourself. No one has the authority to tell you what you do. You get paid on the results that you generate.

5. Set your own hours. Work when you want to work. You set the pace. This allows part-time work to augment one's current income. Interestingly, studies show that approximately 80% of those people involved in direct selling work less than ten hours per week on a part-time basis in order to generate some supplemental income.

6. Totally portable. Take your business anywhere in the world that the MLM company operates. You are not tied down to a particular location as you are with a franchise, conventional business or professional practice.

7. Low risk. You can continue working at your present job while at the same time testing the waters with your MLM company. You do not have to resign or forfeit your present income in order to participate in MLM. It is up to you to choose how much money you wish to invest in inventory and sales aids. You can get started in most MLM companies with an investment of less than $100. You choose your own comfort zone for inventory investment.

8. Tax benefits. Working from home as a self-employed independent businessperson, the MLM distributor may qualify for many tax deductions, such as an allowance for office space in the home, utilities, telephone, automobile, travel and entertainment.

9. Personal choice of business associates. MLM participation allows husbands and wives to work together as a team toward a common goal. Friends and relatives can now choose to work together, perhaps for the first time.

10. Personal choice of type of business. There is now a very wide diversity of products and services available through network marketing. Almost anyone can find something of genuine interest.

11. Lifestyle. MLM is characterized by almost daily opportunity meetings along with frequent training seminars, regional conferences and national conventions. A ready-made social structure is available to those who join any particular MLM company, and you can choose your own level of participation.

12. No employees. By the nature of the system, you do not have employees, only other independent distributors, in your downline. Thus, you have no responsibility for their paycheques, U.I.C. or Revenue Canada withholding and submitting, or any of the other burdens associated with being an employer.

13. Unlimited earning potential. The financial success of top MLM money-earners is the stuff from which dreams are made. All of the largest MLM/network marketing companies have several people making in excess of $1,000,000 annually. Several individuals receive multiples of that. Because of the geometric progression inherent in the MLM structure, it is possible to earn truly stupendous sums of money through the creation of a large downline organization.

An individual MLM distributor can generate profits in three different ways:

1. Sales directly to the consumer (the end-user).
2. Sales at wholesale to other distributors for resale to the consumer.
3. Recruiting other distributors to perform the previous two functions.

It is abundantly clear that there are many appealing elements in the MLM marketing mix. It is also clear that the best way to make a substantial income with the least amount of actual selling of the product or service is to recruit other people to do the work. Income is therefore generated through establishing your own network of distributors, not through your own actual selling of the product or service. The more distributors that you recruit for your "downline," the more may be recruited by them in turn. The better your people sell, the more commissions filter up to you. It is an intriguing method of doing business and probably the most truly egalitarian business opportunity available in Canada today.

7.7 AN INSIDE VIEW OF MLM

As you investigate network marketing organizations and their distributors In Canada, you become aware that there are at least three separate sub-sets of individuals that exist within the larger group of any particular company's MLM sales force.

The first group is comprised of people who come regularly to most of the opportunity meetings, are very friendly to the newcomer, and seem to have lots of time to discuss your questions and talk about the other players in the local game. Since you have mainly been exposed to only the major success stories at the opportunity meetings, you assume that these people are also very financially successful in the business. They are not. At best they may earn a few hundred dollars per month. Yet they are satisfied with their modest financial rewards because money is not the primary reason that they remain involved with their network marketing company. They are there because they like the energy, the excitement, and they can associate with successful people with whom they are on a first-name basis. Equally as important, by staying associated with their organization they are able to hold on to their dreams and to their hope that my ship is going to come in too some day.

This is what MLM/network marketing is for them: a home, a group of friends, relationships and hope. As Charles Paul Conn writes in *The Possible Dream*, when describing some of the people involved with the world's largest MLM company: "But for many people, it obviously is much more than just a business. For some, it seems to be a consuming involvement that shapes conservative political views . . . A leading national magazine called it a socioreligious phenomenon of some sort."

The second group of people is comprised mainly of the individuals who have taken the leap of faith and become full-time distributors. They are intent on making it big financially, with their MLM company as the chosen vehicle, but have not yet made it. They smile constantly and exude confidence to newcomers and to their downline, but get them alone and they are mostly grim and scared. They know that they have to pay the price but they don't know yet what that price will have to be. What is worse and even more stressful, they don't know that they are actually willing to pay that price, whatever it turns out to be. They know that they are very much at financial risk. They know clearly that network marketing is their business, not a social club, and they are very intent on being successful. Relationships within the organization, while enjoyed and appreciated, are very much secondary to their clear business purpose of achieving their dream of financial independence and security.

The third and elite group is very small and comprised of those people who have actually become prosperous through MLM. They have paid the price. They are proud of their accomplishments in getting to where they are and always will tell you that the price was worth it, no matter what it was. They have a stable downline organization which, although it needs care and attention like a lush garden, continues to consistently generate substantial positive cash flow each month. These individuals develop many international contacts through the international meetings of their company and develop a lifestyle considered highly desirable by most of the downline distributors in their company. They receive paid vacations with their spouses each year to interesting cities and resorts to network with the other senior distributors in their organization. They are invited to speak and share their views to gatherings of their company's distributors which are attended by hundreds and sometimes thousands of people. They are also invited to expense-paid meetings with the company's founders and senior executives where their views on the company's operations and future are solicited, and often they are able to become stock holders and profit sharers within their corporation. These are the winners of the MLM financial sweepstakes.

7.8 PITFALLS TO BE AVOIDED

In considering this most contemporary of business forms, there are four ancient adages that need to be kept prominently in mind as you try to determine whether an involvement in MLM/network marketing would lead to success for you.

1. All that glitters is not gold.
2. One man's meat is another man's poison.
3. Let the buyer beware.
4. Know thyself.

There is no doubt whatsoever that dozens of corporations and thousands of individuals have made, and continue to make, a great financial success of their involvement with MLM/network marketing. There is equal certainty that there are many more tens of thousands of individuals who have failed to prosper with MLM than have actually succeeded in attaining personal prosperity or financial independence.

MLM is not a "get-rich-quick" scheme. All too often, over-zealous or under-ethical MLM distributors paint a far too rosy picture of the business and how quickly you can get ahead financially. Frequently, people are told that you can be earning $10,000 per month within three months and similar stories. It is true that some have, but most have not. This is a business like any other; it normally takes serious effort, commitment and time to build a stable and profitable organization. Some of the most common pitfalls to be avoided by future MLM/network marketing distributors are the following:

1. Unrealistic Expectations

Maintain a sceptical attitude toward all representations regarding how soon and how much you will earn as a new MLM distributor. Very frequently the local or national sales leaders are exemplified as models of how well you can do. That is like suggesting to an aspiring young actor that he too can "make it big like Sir Laurence Olivier or Al Pacino." Demand that your sponsor in the business work with you on a detailed plan to show you exactly how much both your sales volume and your recruiting volume would have to be in order for you to meet your financial objectives, or meet the representations made to you. Then you will be in a position to judge whether you are able or willing to do what is required.

The reality is that most distributors in MLM programs make only a few hundred dollars per month. However, for many people that is an adequate financial return for a part-time commitment. Over the course of a year, a few thousand dollars of extra income would enable a family to purchase some major appliances, or take an overseas vacation, or make some other significant purchases, that they would not otherwise have been able to afford.

2. Failure to Use or Like the Product or Service

It is essential that you both like and use the product or service that you are proposing to distribute. Do not enter the business simply for the money that you think you will make. The real heart-felt conviction that is an essential part of both the product or service selling and the distributor recruiting comes only through identifying with the product or service. Many MLM companies state that you actually are not selling their product, you simply share it with other people. As debatable as that assertion is, it is clear that you cannot successfully sell or share anything over the long haul unless you fully believe in it and can speak as a satisfied user.

3. Premature Full-Time MLM

One of the most costly mistakes anyone can make is to prematurely quit his current occupation and plunge full-time into a brand-new career as an MLM distributor. This generally occurs because of the unrealistic expectations raised by a sponsor due to overstatements about what is possible for the new distributor to achieve. This business is no different than any other; there is a learning curve to be experienced. You initially do not even understand what it actually takes to succeed in MLM, despite the common representations that it's easy, all you do is share the product and the opportunity. There is much more to it than initially meets the eye.

Far too much debilitating financial and emotional pressure will fall upon you if you immediately create the situation where you are entirely dependent on your new MLM career for your livelihood. It generally takes from six to twelve months for a new distributor to really learn the basics and build his business to the point where there is some consistent revenue which can be counted on. It usually takes at least eighteen months before you can rely on the revenue from your downline to be consistent. Be highly sceptical of any MLM recruiter who tells you differently.

4. Spread too Thin Geographically

You must build an economic base for your MLM distributorship locally before expanding to other cities. It is very expensive developing and maintaining an MLM business elsewhere, particularly in Canada where the distance between most of our cities is so great. A new distributor requires a certain amount of training, direction and general "hand holding." You must be prepared to either spend a considerable amount of money and time to be in the city where your potential new distributors are located or else spend a great deal of time on the phone with the full realization that likely you will not be as effective on the phone as you would be in person at this early stage.

5. Reinventing the Wheel

All successful MLM companies have developed a selling system that, by virtue of the fact that they are successful, has worked well for them. Therefore, learn and apply that system. Be coachable. MLM is a different game than the one you are currently playing. Some of your skills may be transferable but many are not. Frequently, salespeople are some of the slowest starters in MLM because they think that they know how to sell. They do not know MLM. There are major differences. Understand and modify your approach accordingly.

6. Looking for the "One Big Score"

One of the keys to success in MLM is being duplicatable by the people in your downline. You must teach people to do what you do. To employ a baseball analogy, base hits are duplicatable, home runs are not. Therefore, you should employ yourself to do the basics of your new business in a way that other people can observe and duplicate. It is not effective or efficient to spend a lot of time trying to close a major corporate account when your own people could do so, leaving you to work with individuals to sell their product and to do more recruiting. Stick to the business at hand which is described in the training materials of your company.

7. Not Understanding that MLM is Principally about Recruiting

If McDonald's Restaurants had concentrated only on producing and selling hamburgers from its original location in California instead of expanding to thousands of locations around the world, it is unlikely that many of us would have ever experienced their food or been entertained by Ronald McDonald. Even if they had built one super-large single outlet, they would have nothing like the annual sales in the billions of dollars which they enjoy today with over 10,000 outlets. John Paul Getty, once the world's richest man, is reputed to have said, "I would rather have 1% of the labour of 100 men than 100% of the labour of one man."

Similarly, at its most fundamental level, MLM/network marketing is based on duplication. This requires constant recruiting. To be very successful financially in MLM, you must constantly recruit, recruit, recruit. It is stated repeatedly by many of the most successful distributors in the business that you must spend more than 90% of your time recruiting. Observing leaders in this business, you will see that they often make over 100 telephone calls per day. Followed by business opportunity presentations to groups or individuals. Followed by a certain amount of training and coaching. Followed by the rare and occasional retail sale. It is fundamental to understand that despite what you may have heard, the essence of becoming prosperous in this business is constant recruiting — it is not retailing your product or service. You must understand and be prepared for this. Most people are not.

8. Not Willing to Pay the Price

This is the great unsaid. It is the topic that is rarely discussed with the new distributor. It is no exaggeration to say that most of the people in Canada now earning incomes of $200,000 per year or more in MLM/network marketing were willing to do absolutely whatever it took to succeed. This may involve working for eighteen to twenty hours a day for months at a stretch; it may be going months without a day off; or it may mean totally sacrificing your relationship with your family for months or even years. One Canadian couple we know is now earning in excess of $1,000,000 per year after nine years of MLM. For the first six years they crisscrossed this continent many times in their car and trailer, building and rebuilding an MLM organization. They felt that it was no life for their young son to be on the road, and so had him live with his grandmother for six years. The son went without his parents from the time that he was ten to the time that he was sixteen years old. Today they are together again in a beautiful home with all the extras and advantages that a million-dollar income can provide. Was it worth the price? What price are you willing to pay for your financial success?

7.9 CONCLUSION

In the 1990s, business and society continue their accelerating pace of change in Canada and in most of the world. The socioeconomic phenomenon now known as network marketing is both a contributor to, and a product of, the transformation of our society and our business practices. Just as many of us are ambivalent and even wary about many of the changes to our customary way of life that are now taking place all around us, MLM/network marketing itself is the subject of much ambivalence and suspicion. How do you describe this powerful business phenomenon? One which is considered to be among the ten fastest growing industries in North America today, touching the lives of many tens of millions of individual North Americans, either as a buyer or a seller, yet at the same time continues to be seen by many people as slightly immoral, if not downright illegal?

These negative attitudes toward MLM/network marketing are now rapidly dissipating as more and more professionally trained and educated people enter the MLM business in pursuit of their personal financial dreams, and as more and more corporations utilize MLM as their marketing system of choice for sound financial reasons. Several business analysts have gone so far as to predict that, by the year 2000, over half of all goods and services in North America will be delivered by some form of network or multi-level marketing.

For the individual seeking to establish and finance his own successful independent business in Canada, he would clearly be remiss in not investigating network marketing as one highly viable option. Almost every conceivable product or service is now offered through network marketing, from instant printing to health cookies, from mutual funds to lingerie, from water filters to life insurance. Each of these MLM vehicles shares many of the attractive qualities of network marketing, such as low capital requirements, minimal entry qualifications, ready-made system of operations and an independent lifestyle. At the same time, the individual must do his homework and carefully consider both the particular MLM program and company that he is investigating, and his own suitability for the business.

From the perspective of the corporation considering adopting an MLM/network marketing system, a successful MLM sales force is a marvel indeed. As a recent article in *Success Magazine* states: "Even staid corporate America is catching MLM fever. Industry sources say that the *New York Times* has been considering selling subscriptions through MLM. Even AT&T might be taking notice of network marketing after losing approximately 26 percent of its long-distance market share to MCI and US Sprint — companies that use MLM sales forces . . . An MLM sales force is self-replicating, self-motivated, and self-financed."

However, there can be many landmines on the road to MLM/network marketing success. A Canadian corporation that is seriously considering a move into the world of multi-level marketing would be strongly advised to retain a professional consultant as well as a lawyer who is familiar with all of the legal complexities, financial implications and marketing realities of establishing a viable and profitable MLM system.

MLM/network marketing in Canada is clearly an idea and a reality whose time has come. As long as you are very clear from the outset as to firstly, what your goals are, secondly, that constant recruiting is the essence of creating a financially successful network marketing business, and thirdly, what price you are prepared to pay, this form of enterprise may afford a financial opportunity and a business vehicle that you should not ignore.

CHAPTER EIGHT

FRANCHISING

The buyer needs a hundred eyes, the seller not one.
George Herbert

8.1 INTRODUCTION

Franchising is a unique and important method of entrepreneurial funding of a business. Franchising has a proven track record of success much greater than competing non-franchise methods in many industries. From the perspective of the franchisor as well as the franchisee, franchising has many attractive features, not only in terms of minimizing risks and enhancing revenue, but also in terms of accessing financing.

For the company which has a profitable and well-managed operation, and wants to further develop its concept, product or service (the franchisor), there are many financial benefits. The costs of financing the expansion of various outlets is borne by the franchisee (the person who buys the franchise). This allows the franchisor to expand without the inherent potential financial risks and possible limitations on access to debt or equity financing that otherwise might be present. Other financial benefits include: converting established goodwill into a new source of cash flow and capital, reducing fixed overhead costs due to increased sales and efficiency, as well as reducing labour and management costs, and enhancing efficiency and economies of scale.

There are other potential tangible benefits for the franchisor. Private investors, angels and banks are attracted to a concept that enjoys a positive reputation. This may enhance future interest by financing sourses in the company's plans for expansion, and provide a more attractive context for debt or equity financing.

For the prospective franchisee, one of the advantages of dealing with a credible, experienced and respected franchisor, is that banks are often more amenable to lending money, as the calculated risk is less. Refer to the discussion in Chapter Five on the criteria that banks use for lending money for businesses in general. In addition, potential investors are more interested, as the risk is reduced when dealing with an established franchise system.

Another advantage to the franchisee is that many franchisors partially finance a franchisee, or have made arrangements with a major chartered bank to finance any prospective franchisees, subject to normal bank lending criteria of course. Banks expect and require a portion of owner's equity, the amount depending on the type of franchise and other factors. As noted in the last section of this chapter, many major banks have special franchise departments that lend to franchisor and franchisees.

As many people are not familiar with the structure of the franchise concept, we will expand in more detail in this chapter, in order to provide a conceptual framework when considering this financing option.

There are several forms of franchise. The two most common types are known as (a) the "product format" and (b) the "business format." A franchisor who owns an established product name, logo, and/or trademark and sells the right to use its name, logo, trademark to another party is known as a product/trade name franchisor. The right is actually an exclusive or nonexclusive licence to market the product name to wholesalers and retailers. An example would be a company that has the rights by licence to manufacture and to use the name Coca-Cola. With a business format franchise, the franchisor provides not only a product, name and logo, but also the management and marketing support to create a "turn key" business operation. Examples of this type of franchise include McDonald's, Dairy Queen and Century 21. The remaining discussion in this chapter deals primarily with business format franchising.

The business format franchisor may assist with site selection, owner and staff training, product supply, trademarks and logos, advertising and marketing plans, management and accounting services, system controls, and possibly financing. Besides the initial purchase price of the franchise, there is usually a percentage of the gross sales which is paid to the franchisor for the ongoing support. Under the franchise agreement the franchisee is given the right to sell the goods or services within a certain geographic area or territory. The franchise agreement details the legal and commercial relationship between the two parties. The franchisee may sell goods or services supplied by the franchisor, or it could sell goods or services that meet the franchisor's quality standards.

The guidelines and conditions established for the franchisee can be very comprehensive, and can include sources of supplies, standards of cleanliness, pricing policy, hours of operation, staffing requirements, and many other factors. The franchisor requires strict adherence to the guidelines to maintain consistency of image, quality and service, and to ensure the success of the franchise.

8.2 ADVANTAGES AND DISADVANTAGES TO THE FRANCHISOR

Franchising a business concept or product or service has its benefits and drawbacks. Here are the key ones:

(a) Advantages to the Franchisor

- develops motivated franchisees
- beats the competition to the marketplace
- increases market share
- strengthens market position by improving profitability of locations that are currently marginal operations
- reduces labour costs

- reduces management costs
- reduces fixed overhead costs per sales
- accelerates growth
- improves advertising effectiveness
- improves overall sales
- develops recognizability, credibility and a positive image
- develops an infrastructure and system for potential expansion throughout North America and internationally
- enhances efficiency, productivity and quality control
- provides a new source of cash flow and capital
- develops new sources of profit
- converts goodwill, an intangible asset, into a revenue generator
- spreads business risks.

(b) Disadvantages to the Franchisor

- franchisee might not fulfil obligations
- franchisee might impair reputation of franchise system
- potential litigation by dissatisfied franchisee
- franchisee might be very entrepreneurial and decide to terminate the franchise relationship and attempt to go into competition using similar concepts, systems and strategies of the franchisor
- growth by the franchisor could be too rapid, causing operational problems if the infrastructure and systems were not in place
- if the franchise concept proved to be unworkable or uneconomic, this could cause a serious loss of credibility, image, creditworthiness and investor confidence.

8.3 ADVANTAGES AND DISADVANTAGES TO THE FRANCHISEE

When considering the franchise option you need to review your personal and business goals. How will a franchise benefit you in attaining your goals compared with starting a business from scratch? Are you motivated by the challenge of doing it all yourself? Or does that concept cause you more than a little worry and apprehension? Perhaps you have specialized skills which you would like to turn into a business operation, but all the peripheral aspects of starting a business are somewhat overwhelming and intimidating. If this is the case, then the franchise option may be well suited to your personal and business needs. Some people prefer to have the security and support provided by a large and experienced company. A franchisee has a greater chance of running a business successfully because of the training systems and ongoing support that the franchisor provides. The franchisor obviously has a vested interest in the financial well-being of the franchise, as the more money the franchisee makes, the more money the franchisor makes. However, if your intention is to establish your business and then diversify or expand your operation, you may be restricted from doing so in a franchise situation. Your ability to expand would be based on available territories within your geographic area. In this case, perhaps franchising is not the route you should take.

If you are a potential purchaser of a franchise, you have to clearly evaluate a prospective franchise relationship by looking at both sides of the issue clearly. If after assessing your personal and business needs you decide not to buy a franchise, you may decide at some future point to become a franchise owner. In other words, you may decide to start your business from scratch or buy an existing one, and over a period of time expand your business concept by means of a franchise system. The following outline highlights the advantages and disadvantages of franchises from the perspective of the franchisee.

(a) Advantages to the Franchisee

- having a proven and successful business system
- having a reduced risk of failure
- having an increased chance of profitability within the first few years
- easier to access financing (banks, suppliers, franchisor), than if starting a business from scratch
- being associated with an established company
- having reduced costs of supplies and materials
- having access to extensive advertising (national, regional, local)
- cash flow propositions are more reliable based on the past experience of the franchisor
- having continuing managerial assistance
- possibility of buying an existing operation
- providing greater security for money invested if the franchisor has a successful "track record."

(b) Disadvantages to the Franchisee

- high degree of control, thereby limiting individual initiative
- franchisee may be too entrepreneurial and be frustrated and dissatisfied by franchisor restrictions and inflexibility
- potential dispute of agreement terms
- franchisor might not fulfil promises, for example ongoing managerial, marketing or administrative support
- services and/or products provided by franchisor could be more expensive than comparable services and/or products
- franchise fee comes off the gross revenue
- if franchisor is in another legal jurisdiction, this could create contract enforcement problems for the franchisee if the franchisor breaks the agreement
- profits less than represented or anticipated
- misleading statements by franchisor that could compromise or risk the franchisee's investment

- franchisor could oversaturate market
- franchisor could open a corporate owned an operated outlet or service in same geographic market area
- franchisor company may be poorly managed
- franchisor may cease to operate.

8.4 GOVERNMENT REGULATION OF FRANCHISES

At the present time there is no federal legislation in Canada governing the sale or solicitation of franchises. Of the provinces in Canada, only Alberta has legislation under a Franchises Act, which regulates the sale of franchises in Alberta. This statute is administered and supervised by the Alberta Securities Commission and deals with the issues of full disclosure by the franchisor, as well as registration.

If is important to understand the nature of the Alberta legislation in terms of its intent to protect franchisees. If a franchise is being offered to you, and the company also has franchises in Alberta, you can find out a great deal of public information about the company directly from the Alberta Securities Commission. On the other hand, if the franchise company you are considering is operating in every province except Alberta, that should be a cause of potential concern and more thorough investigation. Possibly the company would not be approved in Alberta, or was rejected or has just commenced operation.

The Alberta legislation requires that any person, firm or corporation which desires to trade a franchise in Alberta must register first by filing a prospectus of Statement of Material Fact containing full disclosure of all data relating to the franchise. The prospectus must provide information as to the franchisor's franchise and business history, any bankruptcy or outstanding litigation affecting the franchisor, balance sheet for the last two complete years of operation, together with statements of income and expense. In addition, the franchisor has to state the source and application of all funds received by the franchisor for each of the three preceding fiscal years. These statements must be accompanied by a statement from the franchisor's auditor confirming that the information set out in the prospectus is derived from the financial statements and in the accountant's opinion, presents the facts accurately and is not misleading.

The registration of a franchisor in Alberta does not imply that the government has approved or recommends the franchise in any way. It simply means the franchise has conformed with the regulatory requirements of the government. If you are thinking of buying a franchise, it is essential that you verify the information disclosed by the franchisor, by speaking with existing franchisees, your lawyer and accountant.

To show the extent of the background detail required to start a franchise in Alberta, here is a list of information required in the statement of material facts:

- name of the franchisor, the name under which the franchisor is doing or intends to do business, and the name of any associate of the franchisor that will engage in business transactions with the franchisee
- franchisor's principal business address and the name and address of his agent for service in Alberta

- business form of the franchisor, whether partnership, corporate or otherwise
- business experience of the franchisor, including the length of time the franchisor has conducted a business of the type to be operated by the franchisee, has granted franchises for that business, or has granted franchises in other lines of business
- a copy of the typical franchise agreement or contract proposed for use or currently in use in Alberta
- statement of the franchise fee charged, the proposed use of the fee by the franchisor and if the fee is not the same in all cases, the formula by which the amount of the fee is determined, together with detail of any continuing royalties
- statement describing any payments or fees, other than franchise fees, that the franchisee or subfranchisor is required to pay to the franchisor, including royalties, payments or fees which the franchisor collects in whole or in part on behalf of a third party or parties, together with the names of the third party or parties
- statement indicating whether the cash investment required for the franchise covers payment for equipment and fixtures
- a statement as to whether the franchisee is able to sell the franchise and if so, what conditions attach to the sale, if any
- statement of the conditions under which the franchise agreement may be terminated or renewal refused, or repurchased at the option of the franchisor
- statement as to whether, by the terms of the franchise agreement, the franchisee or subfranchisor is required to purchase from the franchisor or his designate, products, supplies, services, fixtures, or operation of the franchise business. Detailed description is required.
- statement as to whether the items above are available from sources other than the franchisor
- statement as to whether, by the terms of the franchise agreement, the franchisee is limited in the services or goods which may be offered by him to his customer
- statement of any past or present practice, or future intent of the franchisor to sell, assign or discount to a third party any note, contract or other obligation of the franchisee or subfranchisor in whole or in part
- data upon which any statement of estimate or projected franchisee earnings is based
- a statement as to whether the franchisor has, by contract, agreement, or otherwise, agreed with a third party that the services or products of the third party will be made available to the franchisee or subfranchisor on a bonus or discount basis
- a statement of the terms and conditions of any financing arrangements offered directly or indirectly by the franchisor or his associates
- statement indicating whether the franchisee is required to participate in a franchisor sponsored publicity or promotion campaign
- statement as to whether franchisees or subfranchisors receive any exclusive rights or territory and, if so, the extent of these rights

- statement as to whether any procedures have been adopted by the franchisor for the settlement of disputes between the franchisor and franchisee, and if so, what they are
- statement as to whether any patent or liability insurance protection for the franchisor is extended to the franchisee
- list of other franchises operating in Alberta, and if no such franchises exist, a list of the franchisees operating in the next closest jurisdiction
- statement as to whether the franchisor proves continuing assistance in any form to the franchisee, and if so, the nature, extent, and cost of the assistance
- provisions relating to the right to rescind the franchise agreement
- provisions governing withdrawal for the franchise agreement.

8.5 WHEN SHOULD A COMPANY CONSIDER FRANCHISING?

Not every company, of course, is suited to the franchise concept. There are many examples of companies that started franchising without prudent business and marketing planning, realistic analysis, professional expertise or proper infrastructure and systems. The net effect was business and financial disaster, along with the attendant and expected litigation.

In order for a company to have the basis for exploring the franchise concept further, certain essential ingredients must be present. These would include an existing business which:

- is established, financially viable, and with an attractive net profit
- has experienced, realistic and committed owners and management
- is capable of being cloned, in terms of being operated in different locations by different people, utilizing standardized systems of operation and management, that have already been proven as effective
- has unique features, that make the concept an interesting one to investors, customers and potential franchisees. The features could include distinctive trade-names, trademarks, patents, copyrights, products and/or services.

If these features noted above are present, the next consideration is to obtain as much information as possible to enhance quality decision-making, whatever that decision might be. The last section of this chapter covers the sources of further information. In addition, read the types of issues that are important from a franchisee's perspective, when evaluating a franchise. These are covered in the next section on "Selecting a Franchise Opportunity," and in the "Franchise Assessment Checklist" found in Appendix B.

8.6 SELECTING A FRANCHISE OPPORTUNITY

Selecting a franchise should be approached with the same care, preparation and caution as starting or buying a business. It is important to do a thorough investigation and analysis of the market, the product or service, the competition, the risk, and the potential return on investment. In addition, when buying a franchise one has to thoroughly explore the history of the franchisor, its present reputation in the industry, and the contents of the franchise agreement.

Before starting a thorough review of any franchise, there is a quick test that you can apply to save you time, money and frustration. Simply answer the following questions: Did the franchise representative refuse to give specific answers for any answers to your questions? Refuse to give you a list of franchisee references? Promise you high profits in exchange for minimum effort? Put high pressure on you to make a deposit or sign a franchise agreement immediately? Appear to be less interested in your ability to be successful in the business and more interested in selling a franchise?

If the answer to any of these questions was yes, you should seriously reconsider pursuing that franchise company any further. The franchise company that is truly professional will conduct itself in a fashion that allows an objective and thorough investigation of each party by the other, without adding the stress of time constraints. If you are favourably impressed with the initial attitude of the franchise company, you may wish to contact the owner of one of the franchise locations closest to you. Ask the franchisee if he or she is satisfied with the franchise owner and if not, why not? This should provide you with more insight as to whether you wish to pursue that franchise further.

As noted, there are many key points to look for when assessing the merits of a franchise. The following outline discusses some of the main points that you should address. If you are seriously considering investing in a franchise, complete the "Franchise Assessment Checklist" in Appendix B.

The main areas to examine in evaluating a franchise include:

- **Background of franchise company:** This includes its financial condition, creditworthiness, relationship with suppliers, franchisees and customers, and length of time in business.
- **Management:** Investigate experience, qualifications, reputation, and commitment.
- **Viability of product or service:** Check on whether it is a new, trendy, or well-established product, its suitability in your geographic area, and proven market demand.
- **Potential profit:** Determine the net profit that would be available as a return for your risk of investment and time. Check with other franchisees to satisfy yourself that the figures you have been supplied with in terms of projections are realistic. Are these comparisons based on communities that are similar to your geographic market and economic area? Has there been an allowance for franchisee's salary separate from the profits? Will the projected net profit satisfy your economic and personal needs?
- **Location:** Location is obviously a very critical factor in the success of any business. Satisfy yourself that the location is a viable one for the type of business. The franchise owner may own the premises and lease them to the franchisee, or the franchisee could lease the premises from a third party or purchase the premises outright. The franchisor will have to approve the site.
- **Premises:** Examine strictness of requirements on matters such as appearance, design, layout, colours, fixtures, furnishings.

- **Operational controls:** Check for standardization of character, uniformity and quality of product, value of trademarks, and strictness of operational controls manual.
- **Training and start-up systems:** Check on the duration, nature and extent of training on-site or at franchisor's site, costs, supplemental training, and start-up assistance.
- **Ongoing assistance:** Inquire as to the type of ongoing assistance provided: computer systems for inventory control, purchasing, invoicing and delivery, bookkeeping and accounting, financial management, selection of inventory, research and development, maintenance of equipment, and hiring, training and firing of employees.
- **Advertising and promotion:** Franchises are required to contribute to a fund for national or regional advertising, generally based on a percentage of the franchisee's gross sales. The money from all the franchises is pooled and used to develop promotion and advertising programs, and materials for the entire franchise system. Does the system wide advertising justify the costs involved? Are franchisees required to advertise at local level at their own expense? Does the franchisor supply professional, prepared advertising and promotional material?
- **Franchisor financing:** Can this be done directly through the franchisor, or arranged in cooperation with a bank by the franchisor?
- **Sales or assignment restrictions or latitude.**

There are three areas that are particularly important for you to consider. They are territory, fees and costs, and renewal and termination.

A. TERRITORY

Most franchisors provide some form of territorial protection to the franchisee. The area covered by the territory may be small, such as a few blocks, or as large as a province or number of provinces, depending on the situation. In theory, the exclusive sales territory means that the franchisee has the right to sell the franchisor's service or product exclusively within that area. For example, "area franchising" implies that the franchisee would have exclusivity to a large sales region. The term "master franchise" implies that the franchisee would not only have a large sales area, but would also be able to subfranchise to others within the allocated territory.

Problems can and frequently do arise on the interpretation of the concept of territory. In many cases, the franchisee does not fully understand the implications. The franchisee could possibly go out of business because the franchisor starts up a franchise itself within the territory (either under the same franchise name or indirectly through a subsidiary company) or by selling a location to a new franchisee within the market territory.

Some of the types of problems encountered on the issue of territory include the following:

- The franchisor or other franchisees may sell products in, or ship products into your territory from locations outside your territory. In other words, technically they do not have a location in your territory but they are encroaching into your market share.

- Frequently the term "exclusive sales territory" means that a franchisee merely has the right of first refusal to acquire any additional outlets within the territory before any second franchisee could accept. The company may wish to start up its own operation or sell it to a franchisee. The problem is that the size, cost and timing of the location may not be at all attractive or financially feasible to you. Therefore, technically you have waived your right of first refusal, allowing someone else to establish a location that could erode your market share and therefore income and profit potential.

- Some exclusive agreements are tied to external factors such as population size within the sales territory. Over time, if the population exceeds the specified number, the company would be able to start up or sell a franchise location in your territory.

B. FEES AND COSTS

There is a wide variation in the structure of fees and costs that the franchisor receives from the franchisee. You should make sure that the contract specifically states the fees that are included in your initial franchise fee and royalty, and the fees that are paid separately, periodically or optionally on the part of the franchisee. Some fees and costs may be reasonable compared with the normal expenses an independent business would incur for the same services. In other cases the franchisor may be making considerable profit on the fees and costs which could be unreasonable in the circumstances. Your professional advisors would obviously be able to provide you with more insight on that important issue.

It is very important to know in advance the exact amount of all costs that you will have to pay, including initial and ongoing costs and what benefit you are receiving for your money. Make sure that you get specific details on all cost items such as the amount, financing arrangements, time of payment, and other consideration.

If you are a franchisee who is considering an entire business system franchise, as opposed to just having a franchise that sells a specific product or service, there are numerous areas where payments may be required. Here is an outline of the main areas of areas and costs:

- **Initial franchise fee:** This fee is usually paid at the time that the franchise agreement is signed. The amount varies depending on the type and size of the franchise. The fee normally includes the franchisor's costs incurred in selling the franchise, such as promotion, screening, selecting and training potential franchisees. It also includes the franchisee's right to use the operating procedures and system as well as trade name and trademark of the franchisor.

- **Training cost for franchisee or staff,** either at the franchise location or at the franchisor's training centre. The cost could include room and board, transportation, meals and tuition.

- **Cost for ongoing training and management assistance.**

- **Start-up assistance and promotion charges.**

- **Periodic royalties or service fees:** Royalties are usually calculated as a percentage of the franchisee's gross sales, although it could be on a fixed-fee basis. The royalties may be required to be paid on a quarterly, monthly or weekly basis and the percentage can vary considerably depending on the type of franchise business. In general, retail operations have a higher royalty than service operations. The royalties may or may not cover the ongoing service provided to the franchisee.

- **Product pricing fees:** The franchisor builds a profit margin into the price of all the products sold to the franchisee. In order to make a guaranteed profit, the franchisors require that the franchisee purchase all or most of the goods and supplies from the franchisor.

- **Average contribution to advertising:** This may be based on a specified percentage of the franchisee's gross sales and is usually payable on a weekly or monthly basis. This contribution is normally for the franchisor's advertising pool and is separate from local advertising that the franchisee pays for.

- **Local advertising:** Some franchisors require that the franchisee pay a certain minimum amount on advertising on a local basis, with the nature and form of advertising to be determined either by the franchisor or the franchisee.

- **Equipment:** Cost of buying or leasing equipment supplies and opening inventory from the franchisor.

- **Lease:** Costs of paying the monthly lease on the premises or mortgage if the premises were purchased.

- **Accounting:** Cost of paying for centralized bookkeeping, accounting and data processing services.

- **Cost of site selection and development.**

Some or all of the above may be included in the initial franchise or licence fee or ongoing royalty, or may have to be paid separately.

C. RENEWAL AND TERMINATION

A franchise agreement has a specific term at which the agreement ends. The term is normally between ten and twenty years, but it can vary considerably depending on the circumstances. The contract is automatically terminated at the end of that period unless there are provisions in the contract for renewal. If there are no renewal provisions, then of course you would not be able to sell the franchise business to anyone else. This is why a renewal provision is very important from a resale and return on investment viewpoint. When a franchise agreement is renewed, the franchisor normally requires a new contract to be signed which may have different terms and conditions than the original one. For example, there could be an increase in advertising contributions or royalty payments, and a franchisee may be required to make substantial improvements and renovations to the franchise premises to conform with current standards.

Every franchise agreement has provisions that permit the franchisor and the franchisee to terminate the agreement in certain circumstances. It is common for the termination rights of franchisors to be far more extensive than those of franchisees. From the franchisor's perspective, it is important to be able to protect the reputation and credibility of the franchise system for the benefit of other franchisees as well as the franchisor. Any franchisee who impairs the reputation of the system and its standards could cause serious damage to the reputation of the franchisor. If the default is a minor one, there may be a thirty-day notice period in which the franchisee has the option to rectify the default. If the default is of a more serious nature, termination is normally given without notice.

Some of the common reasons outlined in franchise agreement termination clauses that the franchisor may invoke include the claim that the franchisee:

- made an assignment in bankruptcy
- was petitioned into bankruptcy by creditors
- ceased to do business on the premises
- became insolvent and could not pay creditors
- was placed in receivership
- submitted financial reports that were inaccurate or misleading by understating gross sales on which royalties were based
- sold unauthorized products or services
- refused to cease activities that might damage the reputation of the franchisor's name and trademark
- breached the terms of a lease or sublease relating to the franchise operation
- failed or refused to pay amounts owing to the franchisor
- constantly made late payments to the franchisor
- failed to comply with established franchise operating procedures and standards.

The franchisee may have rights to terminate the franchise agreement in certain circumstances. Some of these may include:

- failure of the franchisor to acquire the location specified in the contract
- inability of the franchisor to develop the site for operation
- failure of the franchisor to meet his contractual obligations to the franchisee
- serious illness of the franchisee
- full payment by the franchisee of all its outstanding debts and other financial obligations to the franchisor.

8.7 THE FRANCHISE AGREEMENT

The franchise agreement is an important legal document. There is no standard franchise agreement, as they can vary widely depending on the type of franchise operation, the size and sophistication of the franchise system, or whether a new location is being established or an existing franchise being purchased. There are as many different types of franchises as there are types of businesses.

The agreement should be as clear and detailed as possible. It is important that it be prepared by a lawyer experienced in franchise law. There are lawyers who specialize in acting for franchisors and those who prefer to represent franchises. Select a lawyer who best meets your needs, and protects your interests. You want to have an agreement customized to cover the unique type of operation of the franchise business.

Here are the typical areas covered in a franchise agreement:

- Date of agreement.
- Parties.
- Grant of franchise and licence to use trademarks, logos, signs, symbols of franchisor.
- Franchisor's obligations to:
  - financially assist franchisee (e.g., in obtaining line of credit, granting direct loans, etc.)
  - aid in the selection and leasing of the site for the business, and in construction of the facilities
  - provide management assistance, including advice respecting the establishment of accounting and bookkeeping systems to ensure a proper flow of relevant financial information to both parties
  - train franchisee and give advice regarding hiring and training of personnel
  - aid in the selection of merchandise
  - advise with respect to opening-day procedure
  - carry out national and regional programs of advertising and publicity.
- Franchisee's obligations to:
  - follow franchisor's specifications in constructing, decorating and furnishing the facilities
  - use products specified by franchisor
  - purchase supplies from franchisor or from approved outlets
  - conduct the business in accordance with franchisor policies
  - conduct no other business on the franchised premises
  - obtain amount and types of insurance specified by franchisor
  - use prescribed accounting and bookkeeping system
  - make books available to franchisor for inspection
  - submit periodic financial statements and reports
  - use prescribed employee uniforms
  - participate in the advertising programs of franchisor and contribute to their cost
  - submit all local advertising to franchisor for approval
  - observe covenants on part of franchisor contained in its lease of franchised premises
  - make financial withdrawals within limits specified by franchisor
  - maintain working capital of the business at a specified level
  - devote full time and attention to the business
  - assume all liabilities for any claims arising out of the franchised businesses and indemnify franchisor.
- Full disclosure of payments required by franchisor:
  - initial fee
  - annual royalties
  - fee for use of premises owned/leased by franchisor

–monthly consulting or management service fee

–franchisee's proportionate share of franchisor's advertising and promotional programs

–payment for supplies or inventory purchased from the franchisor.

- Termination of franchise: grounds for termination:
  –notice by either party
  –default under the agreement
  –failure to meet minimum sales or earnings quotas
  –deviation from quality standards
  –bankruptcy or death of franchisee
  –end of term.

- Winding up of franchisee's business on termination:
  –return of franchisor's trademarks, all materials bearing its insignia, manuals and so forth
  –purchase of fixtures, equipment and inventory by franchisor
  –assignment of lease, or deed of franchised premises, to franchisor
  –settlement of accounts.

- Non-competition covenants:
  –from franchisor: not to cause or assist the invasion of the assigned business territory by other franchisees or any franchisor-controlled competitive business
  –from franchisee: to refrain from engaging directly or indirectly in any business similar to the franchised business during the term of the franchise and for a specified period thereafter
  –to take reasonable steps both during and after the term of the franchise to protect confidential know-how of the franchisor that was unknown to the franchisee prior to the contract
  –not to hire employees of the franchisor or other franchisees or induce such employees to leave their employment during the term of the franchise and for a specified period thereafter.

- Prohibition against assignment of franchise by franchisee without prior approval of franchisor. Agreement to be freely assignable by franchisor.

- Guarantee by principals of franchisee.

- General contract provisions:
  –franchisee an independent contractor and no agency relationship created
  –all payments to be in Canadian currency
  –arbitration provisions
  –all representations, promises or agreements embodied in agreement
  –agreement to be construed in accordance with the laws of specified province
  –severability of clauses
  –time to be of the essence
  –address for service of notice, and method of giving notice.

- Signature of parties.

8.8 WHERE TO FIND INFORMATION ABOUT FRANCHISING

There are numerous sources of general information about franchising as well as specific information on franchise opportunities. To improve the quality of your comparisons and decision-making, review as many as possible of these sources outlined below. The following is helpful whether you are wanting to start a franchise or buy one.

- **Books:** Check with the business section of your local library for books on starting or selecting a franchise, as well as for franchise directories. Also check with your local book stores. Request *Low-Risk Franchising* by Doug Queen (McGraw-Hill Ryerson). Also see *The Complete Canadian Small Business Guide* by Douglas and Diana Gray.
- **Government small business centres:** All provincial governments have offices to assist the small business owner. Most have business resource centres containing book and other information about franchising. Refer to "Sources of Further Information" for provincial contacts.
- **Banks:** If you are considering starting a franchise or buying one, contact the franchise department of the major chartered banks. These departments specialize in the franchise industry and can give excellent feedback and advice. If you are considering buying a franchise, the bank will advise if it considers the franchise a risk sufficient to refuse financing, regardless of your creditworthiness. Many banks track and assess franchise companies.
- **Franchise associations:** There are several national and provincial franchise associations in Canada for franchisors. Refer to the Appendix under "Sources of Further Information" for a listing of them. For example, the Canadian Franchise Association (CFA) is a trade association representing firms in a wide variety of industries who use a franchising method of distribution. CFA has several excellent publications for prospective franchisees and franchisors, as well as a list of members which includes franchise lawyers, accountants and consultants.
- **Franchise directories:** There are several directories available which list Canadian and/or American and international franchisors, distributors and licensors. They describe any of the features of the franchise concept and details for each of the companies listed. Franchise companies are segmented under various categories. The directories also include a listing of franchise consultants in Canada and/or the U.S. You can obtain copies through your local newsstand, public library or provincial business resource centre. The main directories are:
  - *Opportunities Canada*. Published semi-annually by Prestige Promotions of Toronto. Concentrates on current Canadian listings.
  - *The Franchise Annual*. Published by Info Press of St. Catharines, Ontario. Contains Canadian, U.S. and international franchise companies.
  - *The Info Franchise Newsletter*. Published by Info Press and includes Canadian and American franchise information on legislation litigation, trends and details on new franchisors.

–*Franchise Yearbook*. This is published by *Entrepreneur* magazine of Los Angeles, California. Includes U.S. and Canadian franchise listings under various section headings.

- **Franchise shows and expositions:** The various Canadian franchise associations often sponsor franchise shows. For example, shows are regularly held in Toronto and Montreal. The International Franchise Association (IFA) sponsors various shows in the U.S. In addition, there are many regional and local trade shows held in Canada, that are referred to as franchise and/or business opportunities shows. Refer to the annual *Directory of Canadian Trade Shows and Expositions* (published by MacLean Hunter) for upcoming events in the area of franchising. This directory is available in the business section of many public libraries. Also contact Prestige Promotions of Toronto, organizers of various franchise shows offered throughout Canada.

Valuable information can be obtained and comparisons made on all aspects of franchising, such as financing, buying, contracts, advantages and obligations. In addition, most shows offer seminars, workshops and discussion panels. You would also benefit from on-site consultations with franchise specialists, such as lawyers, accountants, bankers and consultants. If you are considering starting up your own franchise, it gives you an opportunity to check on your potential competitors.

- **Franchise lawyers:** As mentioned earlier, it is very important that you consult a lawyer experienced in franchising. The risk is too great to do otherwise. To obtain names of legal specialists, contact the franchise association closest to your area, or the Canadian Franchise Association. These associations are listed in the Appendix. You could also contact the franchise department of the regional office of one of the major chartered banks. In addition, you could contact the lawyer referral service in your province and ask for the name of a franchise lawyer. Ideally, speak to a minimum of three lawyers before deciding which one you would prefer to act for you.

- **Chartered accountants:** Most of the major chartered accountancy firms have experts in the area of starting up a franchise. Contact the office in your area for a consultation. Obtain an opinion from more than one accountant.

- **Franchise consultants/brokers:** A franchise consultant generally advises a prospective franchisor on how to franchise a business, and frequently assists in the marketing and sale of the franchises on behalf of the franchisor. Check with the Canadian Franchise Association and, if one exists, a provincial franchise association for names. To protect yourself, speak to more than one consultant before deciding who to retain. Ask for, and check out, professional references (e.g., lawyers and accountants and other clients) obtained from the consultant.

CONCLUSION TO
RAI$ING MONEY

Everything comes to him who hustles while he waits.
                                    Thomas A. Edison

Several years ago there was a *Harvard Business Review* article on the subject of "Hustle as Strategy." It shows that in comparative analyses of companies with similar resources and products competing in the same market, the critical element that separated the winners from the rest of the pack was the "hustle" of their employees, particularly in sales and service.

Salespeople with hustle always go the extra step: they'll drive at night to a prospects's house far out in the suburbs to get an order signed; they'll work all weekend to perfect a presentation scheduled for a prospect on Monday morning; they'll break through their "comfort zone" and call on prospects who intimidate them; and so on. They are always looking for new opportunities to make a sale, they work harder and smarter, they have a "we can do it" attitude. This is hustle.

It's an attitude of alertness, readiness, of being keen, committed, enthusiastic. It's not being afraid of work. As our grandparents said, it is "not putting the wishbone where the backbone ought to be." It is about actively and aggressively pursuing your goals.

We have given you a full road map of how to make that journey which will finance your business dreams. Yet now it is you who must leap into action. You have a vision to realize, and that means getting into motion. You must now take that first step, then the second step, then the third step, and all the following ones that constitute the path of realizing your dreams.

So, where do you start? At the beginning. Now. Review the steps that we outlined for you and then get into action. Hustle. Your major steps will include the following:

1. Begin by reviewing our "Money-Rai$ing Master Checklist."
2. Create your enrolling business vision.
3. Analyze and be confident of the feasibility of your project.

4. Prepare your business plan including draft financial projections.

5. Review the legal elements of a money-raising program.

6. Determine how much of the business you are willing to give for the investment capital that you receive.

7. Refresh your memory as to the four elements of the SLIP Test which every investor needs satisfied.

8. Create the basic financial structure for the investment.

9. Prepare a term sheet of the proposed investment.

10. Make a list of your warm market using our "Prospective Investor Form."

11. Ensure that you are in compliance with all legal requirements including a proper subscription form and an offering memorandum if considered necessary by your securities lawyer.

12. Begin calling prospective investors for appointments.

13. Make your sales presentations to prospective investors.

14. Sign up the investors by executing the subscription form and deposit the investment funds in the corporate bank account.

15. Raise sufficient money to make your business dreams a reality.

A parting word of advice: As soon as you have an investor in your business, make certain that you create a policy of nurturing your relationship with that person, and every subsequent investor, very conscientiously and very regularly. Your investors want to be well informed and deserve to be well informed. They have proven their commitment to you by putting money into your project. Now it is up to you to consistently demonstrate your commitment to them.

Your relationship with your investors can be a mutually satisfying one for many years, despite the normal ups and downs of business, provided that you are honest, timely and regular in your communications with them. If they are happy with the way that they are treated in this project, there is a strong likelihood that they will be there for you the next time that you are raising money for another business.

At the beginning of *RAI$ING MONEY*, we stated that our vision in writing this book is to empower Canadian entrepreneurs to succeed in business by funding their projects successfully. We hope that your project is one of those. We wish you great success. Remember that hustle can make all the difference.

APPENDIX A

Example 1
MODEL BUSINESS PLAN OUTLINE
(See Chapter Two)

A. Plan Preliminaries

1. Cover page:
   a. Should include name, address and phone number of the business
   b. names and phone numbers of the key principals to contact.
2. Table of contents.
3. Legal disclaimer.

B. Executive Summary

1. Compelling summary statement, including competitive advantages of the business, its outlook, projected profits and return to investors.
2. Summary description of the business, including the purpose of the business, its history including date of formation, and what is distinctive or unique about the business, service or products of the enterprise.
3. Current position and future outlook of the business, emphasizing the commercial opportunity and strategy for exploiting it.
4. Description of the market and the competitive edge and advantages of your business and its products or services.
5. The total team, including key employees, directors, major shareholders and key commercial relationships with customers, vendors and joint ventures.
6. Funds sought and their usage.
7. Investment economics, harvest strategy and projected return on investment (ROI) to investors.

C. The Company

1. Purpose of the company and the business.
2. Incorporation, history and background.
3. Organization and management.
4. Products or services.

D. The Industry

1. Present status.
2. Trends.
3. Company's opportunity.

E. Products and Services

1. Uniqueness and differentiation.
2. Unsatisfied market need.
3. Proprietary elements:
    a. Patents
    b. Trademarks
    c. Copyrights.
4. Product improvement and new products.
5. Research and development plans.
6. Risks and difficulties.

F. Marketing and Sales

1. Market definition, size and overview.
2. Market trends and growth potential.
3. Customer profile.
4. Barriers to market entry.
5. Geographic market factors.
6. Competition.
7. Company's competitive advantages.
8. Marketing strategies: entry and growth.
9. Estimated market share and sales.
10. Reaction and advance orders from prospective customers.
11. Sales and distribution.
12. Advertising and promotion.
13. Ongoing marketing and sales analysis.

G. Production and Operations

1. Geographic locations.
2. Description of facilities.
3. Production process and capacity.
4. Policies and procedures.
5. Subcontracting and licensing.
6. Personnel and training.
7. Regulatory compliance and environmental issues.
8. Technological issues.
9. Development strategy and plans.

H. Management Team and Corporate Organization

1. Organization and structure.
2. Founder's team: qualifications, contributions and responsibilities.
3. Key personnel.
4. Directors.
5. Significant shareholders.
6. Compensation, incentives and percentage of ownership.
7. Professional advisors and consultants in support.
8. Philosophy and objectives of the team.

I. Financial Plan and Information

1. Overview of financing plans and profitability forecast.

2. Current financial status:
    a. Balance sheet
    b. Profit and loss statement.
3. Historical figures summarized (3 to 5 years).
4. Sources of funds:
    a. Initial seed capital
    b. Initial working capital
    c. Major funding to date.
5. Future projections (3 to 5 years):
    a. Cash flow projections: first 12 months detailed by month, second and third years by quarter and subsequent periods by year.
    b. Profit and loss projections: first 12 months detailed by month, second and third years by quarter and subsequent periods by year.
    c. Notes to the projections should contain clear definitions and explanations of all assumptions necessary to support the figures in the projections, including salaries, expenses and breakdown of cost of goods.
    d. Sensitivity analysis: best, worst and likely financial scenarios.
    e. Other analyses, such as breakeven, and key industry ratios such as debt/equity, current, receivables turnover and inventory turnover.
6. Your financial plan:
    a. Strategic objectives: Why are you raising money?
    b. Cash flow projections: How much money do you need?
    c. Use of proceeds: What are you going to do with the money?
    d. Timing: When are you going to raise the money?
    e. Selling team: Who is going to raise the money?
    f. Contingency planning: What if you do not raise enough money?
    g. Profitability forecast: What are the details of the venture's profitability projections (3 to 5 years)?

J. Appendix (Supporting Documents)

1. Historical financial statements and corporate tax returns.
2. Detailed biographies of the principals.
3. Intellectual property documentation, such as patents, copyrights and trademarks.
4. Marketing support materials, such as letters of intent from prospective customers, third-party testimonials, market studies and articles from trade journals.
5. Copies of additional documents relevant to the plan, such as licensing agreements, leases and other contracts.

Example 2
CASH FLOW PROJECTION
(See Chapters Two and Four)

Month #	1	2	3	4
Cash Receipts (Cash In)				
1. Cash sales	$_____	$_____	$_____	$_____
2. Collection from accounts receivable (credit sales payments)	$_____	$_____		
3. Term loan proceeds	$_____	$_____	$_____	$_____
4. Sale of fixed assets	$_____	$_____	$_____	$_____
5. Other cash received	$_____	$_____	$_____	$_____
6. Total Cash In	$_____	$_____	$_____	$_____
Cash Disbursements (Cash Out)				
7. Rent (for premises, equipment, etc)	$_____	$_____	$_____	$_____
8. Management salaries	$_____	$_____	$_____	$_____
9. Other salaries and wages	$_____	$_____	$_____	$_____
10. Legal and accounting fees	$_____	$_____	$_____	$_____
11. Utilities (heat, light and water)	$_____	$_____	$_____	$_____
12. Telephone	$_____	$_____	$_____	$_____
13. Repairs and maintenance	$_____	$_____	$_____	$_____
14. Licences and municipal taxes	$_____	$_____	$_____	$_____
15. Insurance	$_____	$_____	$_____	$_____
16. Other operating expenses	$_____	$_____	$_____	$_____
17. Payments on purchase of fixed assets	$_____	$_____	$_____	$_____
18. Interest paid on loans (short-term loans, lines of credit, overdrafts)	$_____	$_____	$_____	$_____
19. Payments on mortgages/ term loans	$_____	$_____	$_____	$_____
20. Income tax payments	$_____	$_____	$_____	$_____
21. Cash dividends paid	$_____	$_____	$_____	$_____
22. Payments on accounts payable/inventories	$_____	$_____	$_____	$_____
23. Other cash expenses	$_____	$_____	$_____	$_____
24. Total Cash Out	$_____	$_____	$_____	$_____

Reconciliation of Cash Flow	1	2	3	4
25. Opening cash balance	$_____	$_____	$_____	$_____
26. Add: Cash In (line 6)	$_____	$_____	$_____	$_____
27. Deduct: Cash Out (line 24)	$_____	$_____	$_____	$_____
28. Surplus or (deficit)	$_____	$_____	$_____	$_____
29. Closing cash balance	$_____	$_____	$_____	$_____

EXPLANATION

Lines 1, 2 and 22 of the Cash Flow Projection are derived from the information obtained from Examples 2A and 2B which follow (Projected Cash Sales and Accounts Receivable plus Projected Accounts Payable).

Line 3 **Loans** If you take possession of borrowed money during the month, list this cash receipt.

Line 4 **Sale of fixed assets** If you sell a fixed asset such as a piece of office furniture or a vehicle, list the cash income in the monthly column when payment is received.

Line 5 **Other cash** List all other cash income such as interest, rent, shareholders' loans, etc.

Line 6 Total of lines 1-5.

Line 7-16 **Operating expenses** Enter the amount of cheques that you write for your monthly expenses. This is actual cash outlay for the month; for example, if you write a cheque in January for the full year's insurance, the amount of the cheque would be put in the January column and nothing would be entered for the rest of the year.

Other operating expenses The expense items listed in the format may not be applicable to your business. The headings should be changed so that they are applicable to your situation.

Line 17 **Payments on purchase of a fixed asset** If money is spent for the purchase of fixed assets such as a vehicle or a filing cabinet, list the amount for the month when the cheque is written.

Line 18 **Interest paid on loans** This is the interest paid monthly on short-term loans such as bank overdrafts or lines of credit. Since you are in the process of working out the amount of money you will need to borrow, this interest figure may be very difficult to estimate. Consequently, you may decide to leave the line blank for now. If it is likely to be a small amount, you may decide to omit it altogether.

Line 19 **Payments on mortgage/loans** Indicate the monthly payment for the principal and interest on long-term loans. For example, if you borrow $15,000 to purchase a half-ton truck and monthly payments are $450 with the first payment due in March, then $450 will be entered at line 19 for each month beginning in March.

Lines 20-21 **Income tax payments** and **cash dividends paid** The amounts you expect to pay, if any.

Line 23 **Other cash expenses** The expense items listed in the format may not be applicable to your business. The headings should be changed so that they are appropriate for your situation.

Line 24   **Total cash out** Total all possible cash payments for the month.

Line 25   **Opening cash balance** The amount of money you started out the month with.

Line 28   **Surplus or deficit for the month — cash in minus cash out** If line 28 is a deficit, the operating bank loan should be increased to cover the deficit. Sometimes a bank will require a minimum balance to remain in the account at all times. If line 28 is a surplus, excess funds should be applied on the operating loan.

Line 29   **Closing cash balance** The amount of money you started out with plus (or minus) the amount of cash surplus at month's end. The closing cash balance becomes next month's operating cash balance.

Example 2A
PROJECTED CASH SALES AND ACCOUNTS RECEIVABLE

Month #	1	2	3	4
Projected sales	$_____	$_____	$_____	$_____
Cash sales (line 1)	$_____	$_____	$_____	$_____
Collection of previous month's sales	$_____	$_____	$_____	$_____
Collection of sales from two months previous	$_____	$_____	$_____	$_____
Collection of sales from more than two months previous	$_____	$_____	$_____	$_____
Collection from accounts receivable (line 2)	$_____	$_____	$_____	$_____

Example 2B
PROJECTED ACCOUNTS PAYABLE

Month #	1	2	3	4
Planned purchases	$_____	$_____	$_____	$_____
Payments on current month's purchases	$_____	$_____	$_____	$_____
Payments on purchases from two months previous	$_____	$_____	$_____	$_____
Payments on purchases from more than two months previous	$_____	$_____	$_____	$_____
Payments on accounts payable (line 22)	$_____	$_____	$_____	$_____

Example 3
BALANCE SHEET
(See Chapter Two)

As of (Current Date/Year)

Assets	19____ (Current Year)	19____ (Previous Year)
Current Assets		
Accounts receivable (attach aged list)	$_____	$_____
Less: Allowance for bad debts (net)	$_____	$_____
Cash & balance in bank accounts	$_____	$_____
Prepaid expenses (e.g., insurance, rent, etc.)	$_____	$_____
Inventory at market value	$_____	$_____
Other current assets	$_____	$_____
Total Current Assets	$_____	$_____
Fixed Assets (net book value after depreciation)		
Land and buildings	$_____	$_____
Furniture, equipment & fixtures	$_____	$_____
Other fixed assets	$_____	$_____
Total Fixed Assets		
Other assets (nonfixed, e.g., automobiles)	$_____	$_____
Total Assets	$_____	$_____

Liabilities		
Current (due within 12 months)		
Accounts payable	$_____	$_____
Bank loans	$_____	$_____
Loans — other	$_____	$_____
Employee deductions and sales taxes payable	$_____	$_____
Income taxes payable	$_____	$_____
Current portion of long-term debt	$_____	$_____
Other current liabilities	$_____	$_____
Total Current Liabilities	$_____	$_____
Long Term (over one year)		
Mortgages payable	$_____	$_____
Less: Current portion noted above	$_____	$_____
Loans from shareholders & partners	$_____	$_____
Other loans of long-term nature	$_____	$_____
Total Long-Term Liabilities	$_____	$_____
Total Liabilities	$_____	$_____
Net Worth (Total Assets — Total Liabilities)	$_____	$_____

Shareholders' Equity

Share capital	$_____	$_____
Retained earnings	$_____	$_____
Total Shareholders' Equity	$_____	$_____
Total Liabilities & Shareholders' Equity	$_____	$_____

Example 4

INCOME STATEMENT

Also referred to as profit-and-loss statement, P & L statement, or operating statement

(See Chapter Two)

For Month and Year-To-Date Ended _____, 19___

	Current Month		Year-to-Date	
	Amount	Relative to Total Income %	Amount	Relative to Total Income %
Sales				
Gross sales	$_____		$_____	
Less returns and allowances (discounts)	$_____		$_____	
Net Sales	$_____	100%	$_____	100%
Cost of Goods Sold				
Beginning inventory	$_____	___%	$_____	___%
Plus inventory purchases	$_____	___%	$_____	___%
Plus plant & other manufacturing costs	$_____	___%	$_____	___%
Less closing inventory	$_____	___%	$_____	___%
Total Cost of Goods Sold	$_____	___%	$_____	___%
Gross Income (Subtract total cost of goods sold from net sales) **(A)**	$_____	___%	$_____	___%
Operating Expenses				
Advertising & promotion	$_____	___%	$_____	___%
Bad debts	$_____	___%	$_____	___%
Bank service charges	$_____	___%	$_____	___%
Depreciation (e.g., equipment)	$_____	___%	$_____	___%
Employees' wages	$_____	___%	$_____	___%
Insurance	$_____	___%	$_____	___%
Owner's salary	$_____	___%	$_____	___%
Repairs & maintenance	$_____	___%	$_____	___%
Supplies	$_____	___%	$_____	___%
Taxes and licences	$_____	___%	$_____	___%
Telephone and utilities	$_____	___%	$_____	___%
Miscellaneous expenses	$_____	___%	$_____	___%

Other (itemize)	\$_____ ____%	\$_____ ____%
Total Operating Expenses (B)	\$_____ ____%	\$_____ ____%
Net Operating Income (Subtract **(B)** from **(A)**)	\$_____ ____%	\$_____ ____%
Less: Income Taxes	\$_____ ____%	\$_____ ____%
Net Profit (Loss) after Taxes	**\$_____ ____%**	**\$_____ ____%**

Example 5

PERSONAL COST-OF-LIVING BUDGET

(See Chapter Five)

A. Income (average monthly income, actual or estimated)

Salary, bonuses, commissions, dividends	\$_____	\$_____
Interest income	\$_____	\$_____
Other: _____	\$_____	\$_____
Total Monthly Income		**\$_____**

B. Expenses (average monthly, actual or estimated)

1. Regular Monthly Payments

Rent or mortgage payments	\$_____	
Automobile loan	\$_____	
Personal loan	\$_____	
Credit card payments	\$_____	
Insurance premiums (medical, life, house, auto)	\$_____	
Investment plan deductions (RRSP, etc.)	\$_____	
Other: _____	\$_____	
Total Regular Monthly Payments		**\$_____**

2. Household Operating Expenses

Telephone	\$_____	
Heat, gas, and electricity	\$_____	
Water and garbage	\$_____	
Repairs and maintenance	\$_____	
Other: _____	\$_____	
Total Household Operating Expenses		**\$_____**

3. Personal Expenses

Clothing, cleaning, laundry	\$_____	
Food (at home, away from home)	\$_____	
Medical/dental	\$_____	
Day care	\$_____	
Education	\$_____	
Gifts, donations, and dues	\$_____	
Recreation and travel	\$_____	
Newspapers, magazines, books	\$_____	
Automobile maintenance, gas, and parking	\$_____	
Spending money, allowances	\$_____	
Other: _____	\$_____	
Total Personal Expenses		**\$_____**

4. Tax Expenses

Federal and provincial income taxes $_____

Home property taxes $_____

Other: _____ $_____

Total Tax Expenses $_____

Total Monthly Expenses $_____

TOTAL MONTHLY DISPOSABLE INCOME AVAILABLE $_____

(Subtract total monthly expenses from total monthly income)

Example 6

PROJECTED FINANCIAL NEEDS FOR THE FIRST THREE MONTHS

(See Chapter Five)

This worksheet will help you to estimate the amount of money you will need for the first three months of a relatively small business operation. It is intended to illustrate the need for accurate and realistic budgeting. Note: This worksheet relates to your business expenses only. You will also have to calculate your personal cost-of-living expenses on a separate sheet (see Example 5), making certain not to duplicate income or expense items.

Cash Available

Owner's cash on hand $_____

Loan from relative or friend $_____

Other: _____ $_____

Total Cash on Hand $_____

Start-up Costs

Repairs, renovations, and decorating $_____

Equipment (including installation costs) $_____

Furniture $_____

Insurance (homeowner's rider, personal and product liability) $_____

Inventory $_____

Product materials and office supplies $_____

Advertising and promotion (Yellow Pages, business cards, stationery, flyers, newspaper ads, etc.) $_____

Other: _____ $_____

Total Start-up Costs $_____

Operating Costs

Wages of owner $3 × \$_____ = $_____

Utilities   3 × \$_____ = $_____

Supplies and inventory   3 × \$_____ = $_____

Advertising   3 × \$_____ = $_____

Auto and travel   3 × \$_____ = $_____

Contingency   3 × \$_____ = $_____

Other: _____ $_____

Total Operating Costs $_____

Total Start-up and Three-Month Operating Costs $_____

TOTAL MONEY NEEDED FOR FIRST THREE
MONTHS OF BUSINESS (Approximate Only) $_____

Example 7

PERSONAL NET WORTH STATEMENT

(See Chapter Five)

Format Commonly Requested by Lenders

Name   Date of birth   Social insurance number

_____

Street address   City   Province   Postal Code

_____

Home phone   Residence   How long at address?

(   )_____   ____Own   ____Rent   _____Other   ____years ____months

_____

Occupation   Currently employed with: How long with employer?

                                          ____years ____months

_____

Employer's phone   ____ Married   ____ Unmarried   ____ Separated

(   )_____   _____Number of dependents

_____

Your principal financial institution and address

_____

Personal Data on Your Spouse

Under the laws of Canada and of some provinces, your spouse may have a legal interest or obligation arising from your business dealings and may also have an interest in your personal assets.

Spouse's name   Spouse's occupation

Spouse currently employed   How long with   Spouse's work
with: employer?   phone

                              ____years ____months   (   )_____

_____

Financial Information

As at   _____   _____,   19____.

        Day   Month

_____

Assets (List and describe all assets).   **Value**
Total of chequing accounts $_____
Total of savings accounts $_____
Life insurance cash surrender value $_____
Automobile: Make_____   Year_____ $_____
Stocks and bonds (See Schedule A attached). $_____

Accounts/notes receivable (Please itemize):

_____ $_____
_____ $_____
_____ $_____
Term deposits (cashable) $_____
Real estate (See Schedule B attached) $_____
Retirement plans:
_____ RRSP $_____
_____ Employment pension plan $_____
_____ Other $_____
Other assets (household goods, etc):
_____ Art $_____
_____ Jewelry $_____
_____ Antiques $_____
_____ Other $_____
TOTAL ASSETS (A) $_____ (A)

Liabilities

(List credit cards, open lines of credit, and other liabilities including alimony and child support).

	Balance Owing	Monthly Payment
Bank loans	$_____	$_____
Mortgages on real estate owned (See Schedule B attached)	$_____	$_____
	$_____	$_____
	$_____	$_____
Monthly rent payment	$_____	$_____
Credit cards (Please itemize):		
_____	$_____	$_____
_____	$_____	$_____
_____	$_____	$_____
Money borrowed from life insurance policy	$_____	$_____
Margin accounts	$_____	$_____
Current income tax owing	$_____	$_____
Other obligations (Please itemize):		
_____	$_____	$_____
_____	$_____	$_____
_____	$_____	$_____
Total monthly payments	$_____	
TOTAL LIABILITIES (B)	$_____ (B)	
NET WORTH (A-B)	$_____ (A-B)	

Income Sources

Income from alimony, child support, or separate maintenance does not have to be stated unless you want it considered.

Your gross monthly salary $_____
Your spouse's gross monthly salary $_____
Net monthly rental (from Schedule B below) $_____

Other income (Please itemize:)

_____ $_____

_____ $_____

_____ $_____

TOTAL INCOME $_____

Additional Personal Obligations

Please provide details below if you answer yes to the following question:

Are you providing your personal support for obligations not listed above (i.e. cosigner, endorser, guarantor)?

_____Yes   _____No

Details of any of the above including total contingent liability:

_____

_____

Schedule A: Stocks, Bonds, and Other Investments

Quantity	Description	Where Quoted	Market Value	Pledged as Collateral? Yes No

TOTAL $_____

Schedule B: Real Estate Owned

Please provide information on your share only of real estate owned.

Property address (primary residence)	Legal description

Street	City	Province

Type of property	Present market value $	Amount of mortgage liens 1st $ 2nd $

Monthly taxes, insurance, maintenance and miscellaneous $	Net monthly rental income $

Name of mortgage holder(s)	First mortgage	Second mortgage

Percentage ownership %	Month/year acquired	Purchase price $

General Information

Please provide details if you answer yes to any of the following questions.

Have you ever had an asset repossessed?	_____Yes	_____No
Are you party to any claims or lawsuits?	_____Yes	_____No
Have you ever declared bankruptcy?	_____Yes	_____No
Do you owe any taxes prior to the current year?	_____Yes	_____No

Details:

The undersigned declare(s) that the statements made herein are for the purpose of obtaining business financing and are to the best of my/our knowledge true and correct. The applicant(s) consent(s) to the Bank making any enquiries it deems necessary to reach a decision on this application, and consent(s) to the disclosure at any time of any credit information about me/us to any credit reporting agency or to anyone with whom I/we have financial relations.

_____   _____
        Date   Signature of applicant(s) above

Example 8

BUSINESS LOAN APPLICATION

(See Chapter Five)

Format Commonly Requested by Lenders

Please check:

☐ Proprietorship   ☐ Corporation   ☐ General Partnership   ☐ Limited Partnership

Business Name:

Nature of Business:

Business Address: (Street, City, Postal Code)

Business Telephone   Year Business Established

(   )

How long under present ownership?   Number of employees?

Amount of loan(s)   1. Please describe below how you
                                               plan to use your business loan(s)

$

2. What will be your primary source of repaying the loan(s)?

3. What are your usual terms of sale you offer your customers?

4. What are the usual terms of sale offered by your major suppliers?

5. Do you wish this loan(s) to be insured?

   ☐ YES   ☐ NO

6. Please describe any seasonality or business cycle requirements related to your business.

Principals/Owners

Full Name and Address	% Ownership	Title/Position

Historical/Projected Summary

- Existing businesses please provide financial information for the last 3 fiscal years.
- New businesses please provide projected financial information.

Financial Statements Prepared by ☐ Self
☐ Accountant
☐ Other

Year Ending (Date)	19_____	19_____	19_____
Sales	$_____	$_____	$_____
Gross Profit	$_____	$_____	$_____
Net Profit after Tax	$_____	$_____	$_____
Depreciation/Amortization	$_____	$_____	$_____
Current Assets	$_____	$_____	$_____
Total Assets	$_____	$_____	$_____
Current Liabilities	$_____	$_____	$_____
Total Liabilities	$_____	$_____	$_____
Business Net Worth	$_____	$_____	$_____

Credit Relationships

- Please provide details of your business credit relationships below.

Name of Creditor and Address	Purpose of Loan/Credit	Original Amount/ Limit	Amount Presently Owing	Repayment Terms	Maturity Date If Any
_____	_____	$_____	$_____	_____	_____
_____	_____	$_____	$_____	_____	_____
_____	_____	$_____	$_____	_____	_____

Sundry Obligations
- Please provide details below if you answer yes to any of the following questions.

Is the business providing support for obligations not listed on its financial statements (i.e., co-signer, endorser, guarantor)? ☐ YES ☐ NO

If yes, please indicate total contingent liability $_____

Is the business a party to any claim or lawsuit? ☐ YES ☐ NO

Has your business ever sought legal protection from its creditors (i.e., bankruptcy, receiver, receiver-manager)? ☐ YES ☐ NO

Does the business owe any taxes for years prior to the current year (i.e., sales tax, income tax, property tax, municipal business taxes or provincial corporation taxes)?
☐ YES ☐ NO

Amount $_____   Owed to _____

Amount $_____   Owed to _____

Amount $_____   Owed to _____

Details of any of the above:
_____
_____
_____

Business References
- Trade creditor, personal, etc., in addition to those noted.

Name	Address	Business Phone
Banker		
Accountant		
Other		

Insurance Coverage
- Existing businesses, please provide details of present coverage.
- New businesses, please state planned coverage.

Type of Coverage	Insurance Company	Amount of Coverage	Annual Premiums
_____	_____	$_____	$_____
_____	_____	$_____	$_____
_____	_____	$_____	$_____

The undersigned declare(s) that the statements made herein are for the purpose of obtaining business financing and are to the best of my/our knowledge true and correct. The applicant(s) consent(s) to the Bank making any inquiries it deems necessary to reach a decision on this application from a credit reporting agency or otherwise, and consent(s) to the disclosure at any time of any credit information about me/us to any credit reporting agency or to anyone with whom I/we have financial relations.

Per: _____   Per: _____
                 Signature   Signature

_____   _____
                 Date   Date

_____   _____
                 Title   Title

Example 9
LOAN/FINANCING PROPOSAL OUTLINE
(See Chapter Five)

A. Summary

1.   Nature of business.
2.   Amount and purpose of loan.
3.   Repayment terms.
4.   Equity percentage of borrower (debt/equity ratio after loan).
5.   Security or collateral (listed with market value estimates and quotes on cost of equipment to be purchased with the loan proceeds, if applicable).
6.   If private investor, the amount of equity offered.

B. Personal Information

(On all corporate officers, directors, and individuals owning any equity in the business)

1.   Education, work history, and business experience.
2.   Credit references (if requested).
3.   Financial net worth statements.

C. Company Information

(Whichever is applicable below: 1 or 2)
1.   New business:
     a) Business plan (attach copy of your business plan).
     b) Projections (this may have already been covered in your business plan):
        • income statement, (profit and loss) projection (monthly, for one year), explanation of projections and assumptions
        • cash flow projection (monthly, for one year), explanation of projections and assumptions
        • balance sheet projection (one year after loan), explanation of projections and assumptions.
2.   Purchasing a business/Expanding an existing business:
     a) Information on existing business or business to be acquired:
        • copy of offer to purchase agreement (if applicable)
        • business history (include seller's name, reasons for sale)

- current profit-and-loss statements (preferably less than 60 days old) and previous three years
- cash flow statements for last year
- business income tax returns as submitted to Revenue Canada (past three to five years)
- copy of sales agreement with breakdown of inventory, fixtures, equipment, licences, goodwill and other costs
- description and dates of permits or licences already existing
- lease agreement
- other relevant material.

b) Business plan (attach copy of your business plan).

c) Insurance coverage.

d) Partnership, corporation, or franchise papers, if applicable.

Example 10

LOAN PROPOSAL LETTER PREPARED BY LENDER

(See Chapter Five)

From: XYZ Bank
To: ABC Limited

Term Sheet
(for discussion purposes only)
Confidential

Borrower   ABC Limited
Lender   XYZ Bank
Amount $70,000 Demand Operating Facility
              $3,000 Corporate VISA
Availment Operating facility may be availed of by way of overdraft.
Purpose   To assist with general corporate financing and specifically to finance day-to-day operations and purchase of inventory.
Repayment Demand facility to fluctuate.
Interest Rates Demand overdraft facility - Bank Prime + 1% payable monthly.
Fees, etc. Operating overdraft will be subject to an administration fee of $25 per month; service charge will be at the standard rate plus $10 per month; night deposit service will be at the standard rate of $1.10 per deposit bag.
Security   General assignment of accounts receivable registered in (province). Assignment of inventory under Section 178 of the Bank Act, with fire insurance over inventory, loss payable to the Bank firstly.
Covenants 1. Total debt to equity shall not exceed 1:1. Equity shall be defined as the sum of paid-up capital, retained earnings, shareholders' loans and deferred management salaries less advances made to shareholders or associated companies.
2. Operating overdrafts will not exceed 50% of total assigned inventories and eligible assigned accounts receivable.
3. There are to be no dividend payments, unusual withdrawals, redemption of shares or shareholder loan paybacks without the prior written consent of the Bank.

4. Capital expenditures in any one year shall not exceed $10,000 noncumulative without the prior written consent of the Bank, such consent not to be unreasonably withheld.
5. Monthly inventory declarations and receivable listings will be provided during those periods where an operating facility is in effect.
6. Annual financial statements prepared consistent with generally acceptable accounting principles by an accredited accounting firm shall be provided within 120 days of the borrower's fiscal year end.
7. Monthly profit-and-loss statement prepared internally by the borrower shall be provided monthly to the lender.
8. The Bank may request any other financial information it considers necessary for the ongoing administration of the credit facility.
9. The Bank agrees to pay interest on credit balances in excess of $10,000 in your current account #0000 at the rate of the Bank's Prime Lending Rate less 3% per annum to be calculated on the average daily credit balance and payable monthly.

Events of Default The usual events of default shall apply.

Review of Credit The credit is subject to periodic review relative to the financial information to be provided, as well as an annual review by no later than May 30, 19—, in light of the annual statements.

This Term Sheet is for discussion purposes only, is not an offer and represents no commitment, express or implied, on the Bank's part. During our further analysis, information could come to our attention which would detract from the merits of the application and we reserve the right to discontinue the application at any time.

R.B. Jones
Manager
XYZ Bank

Example 11

TERM SHEET: PRIVATE COMPANY MORTGAGE LOAN
TRIPLE PEAKS REAL ESTATE DEVELOPMENT CORP.

(See Chapters Two and Five)

$350,000 SECURED 20% SECOND MORTGAGE LOAN
December 31, 19—

BORROWER: Triple Peaks Real Estate Development Corp. is a highly-regarded developer of residential townhomes. With over 40 townhomes successfully developed, built and sold to date, Triple Peaks is the largest developer of quality townhomes in Tundra County, Ontario.

PURPOSE: Interim financing to facilitate completion of construction of the first phase of the South Winds adult townhome development consisting of 10 new adult townhomes, located immediately adjacent to the borrower's previous successfully developed project of West Winds.

AMOUNT OF
LOAN: $350,000

TERM OF
LOAN: Minimum of 3 months to a maximum of 12 months.

RETURN TO   20% consisting of: a) 5% placement fee (to be paid at closing) and
INVESTOR: b) 15% interest (to be paid monthly in advance).

REPAYMENT: In phases. As the borrower's inventory of new townhomes is sold, $35,000
             of the proceeds from each sale will be allocated to repayment of this
             loan. (The full 5% bonus plus 3 months' interest at 15% will still be paid
             even on loans required within 3 months from the date of the loan).

SECURITY: This loan will be fully secured, with several different components:
   1. General Security Document (floating charge debenture) of Triple
      Peaks Real Estate Development Corp., subordinated to the rights of
      third party commercial lenders, including the XYZ Bank Mortgage
      Corporation.
   2. Second mortgage on the entire South Winds property subject to the
      first mortgage in favour of the XYZ Bank Mortgage Corp.
   3. Collateral mortgage on the personal residence of Mr. Phillip Stone,
      the owner of the company.
   4. Collateral mortgage on the personally owned lot of Mr. Stone in the
      adjacent West Winds residential subdivision.
   5. Personal Guarantee of Mr. Phillip Stone with executed Consent to
      Judgment with amount left open to be held in trust by Mr. Stone's
      solicitors under specified instructions.
   6. Assignment of Proceeds delivered to the company's solicitors
      directing them to forward to the lenders a specified portion of the
      proceeds of each sale of the company's new townhomes. This
      allocation will be $35,000 per townhome sold.
   7. Statutory Declaration of Mr. Stone swearing to the exact financial
      condition of the company prior to receiving the loan including a
      detailed list of all creditors. All loan funds will be specifically
      designated as to their use and Statutory Declaration confirming their
      specific usage will be obtained.
   8. Life insurance on the life of Mr. Stone for a maximum of $350,000 with
      reducing coverage related to the outstanding amount owing at the
      time of death.

Example 12

TERM SHEET: PUBLIC COMPANY CONVERTIBLE DEBENTURE
NORTH CANADIAN MANUFACTURING, INC.

(See Chapters Two and Five)

$1,500,000 11% CONVERTIBLE SUBORDINATED DEBENTURE
PRIVATE PLACEMENT
December 31, 19_

INSTRUMENT: An 11% convertible subordinated floating charge debenture due
              December 31, 1998. This debenture is secured by a floating charge

on all of the company's assets and is subordinated to the rights of third party commercial lenders, including the XYZ Bank of Canada. The company reserves the right to issue additional equal ranking debentures.

AMOUNT: 11% payable June 30 and December 31 in each year of the term. Payable in cash, or stock, if elected by either the purchaser or the company. Stock payments will be calculated on the volume weighted average price of all the company's stock trading on the Vancouver Stock Exchange during the preceding 20 business days.

TERM OF DEBENTURE: December 31, 1998. The company has the right to retire all or part of the debenture at any time.

TERMS OF CONVERSION: Anytime at $1.25 per common share until December 31, 19 , from then until December 31, 19   anytime at $1.65, and from then until December 31, 1998 anytime at $2.00.

TERMS OF CONVERSION CALL: After one year from the date of purchase of debenture, the company can call for conversion of the debenture to common stock at the conversion price described above provided that the stock has traded at a weighted average price of not less than $2.50 for 20 days during the preceding 40 days.

TRADING STOCK: Shares acquired upon the conversion of the debenture will become fully tradeable on the Vancouver Stock Exchange at the expiry of the statutory one year hold period which is one year from the date of the purchase of the debenture.

APPROVALS: The placement is subject to the approval of the Vancouver Stock Exchange.

APPENDIX B

Checklist 1

MONEY-RAI$ING MASTER CHECKLIST

(See Chapters Three and Six)

Private Placement for a Non-Reporting (Private) Issuer

A. Determine the financial needs of your company ("the issuer"):

1. Prepare a business and financial plan for your company.
    a. Analyze your business now and projected growth for the next 3 to 5 years.
    b. Prepare financial projections including cash flows.
2. Calculate how much money you will need to raise now to implement your business and financial plan for the future.

B. Create a list of potential investors from your Warm Market as described in Chapter Six by using the "Prospective Investor List" (Checklist 2) as a guideline and estimate how much each person could invest in your company.

C. Make the "Go-No-Go" decision as to whether or not you will proceed with a plan to raise money for this particular company and project after consulting with your key advisors, based on such factors as amount of money needed, total amount that you have estimated that you may be able to raise and estimated profitability of the project.

D. Decide what kind of securities your company will issue over what time period and whether you will set a minimum subscription amount for the total offering.

1. Consult with your key advisors, including an investment or money-raising professional, an accountant and a lawyer to determine both what kind of securities are saleable in the market as it exists today and also are suitable for your company.
2. Create a sensible timetable within which to accomplish your money-raising objectives (it invariably takes much longer than you plan).
3. Determine whether you will impose on your company the requirement that it raise a certain minimum subscription amount by a certain date. (The consequence of this is that if this amount is not raised by a date specified by you, all monies invested must be returned to the investors.)

E. Prepare a summary of the proposed issue of securities (a "Term Sheet") providing details of the proposed money-raising project as follows:

1.   Total dollar amount to be raised ("proceeds of issue").
2.   Planned use of the money raised ("use of proceeds").
3.   Type(s) of securities to be offered (i.e., common shares, debentures, etc.).
4.   Price and total number of securities to be offered.
5.   Minimum corporate subscription amount for the total issue, if any.
6.   Minimum individual subscription amount, if any.
7.   Type of information to be supplied to prospective investors.
8.   Provinces in which an offering of the securities will be made.
9.   Specific person(s) in each province responsible for selling the securities and the relationship of each person to your company.

F.   Prepare a list identifying which statutory exemptions are available to your company in each province in which it is proposed to raise money. Determine how many individual prospective investors in total can be approached (solicited) with your investment proposal under each exemption category and then how many individual investors can actually invest in the issuer under each category of exemption.

G.   Determine what size the average investment will have to be in order to raise the total amount desired from the total number of investors permitted under the exemptions available to the issuer. (This functions as a guideline in your soliciting money as to the average amount that you will need to raise from each investor. Any investor may, in fact, invest more or less than that amount, unless you have specified minimum or maximum investment amounts.)

H.   Ascertain what, if any, offering material is required by law to be given to the prospective investors. (The requirements differ under the various categories of statutory exemptions and also as between provinces.) Determine what, if any, additional material you will give them, including photographs and videotapes, and what the legal consequences of providing such additional material to prospective investors may be.

I.   Create and finalize all offering material which you will give to the prospective investor, including the subscription form, offering memorandum and investor information questionnaire where required.

J.   Determine who will do the actual selling (soliciting) of the investments for you in each province and how each such person is permitted to do so under the law of that province. Ensure that each soliciting person fully understands the statutory exemption categories under which the money is being raised in any particular province, the categories of potential investors who may be approached, and that each soliciting person will comply with the law pertaining to each exemption.

K.   Designate a specific person to collect and be responsible for all of the information and documentation relevant to the solicitation, including:

1.   Number of persons permitted to be, and number of persons who actually have been, solicited under each exemption category in each province.
2.   Relationship of each solicitation prospect (prospective investor) to a representative of the issuer in order to fall within an exemption category.

L.   Revise your list of potential investors to include for each prospective purchaser:

1.   His province of residence;
2.   The exemption category for each purchaser to be relied upon by the issuer, such as:

    a. purchaser will have an acquisition cost of not less than $97,000, or $100,000, or other prescribed minimum amount in his province of residence. If this exemption is being relied upon, obtain further details as follows:
      i Net worth,
      ii Income,
      iii Investment history,
      iv Occupation, and
      v Education.

    b. purchaser has had investment experience or has had access to investment advice;
    c. purchaser has had access to information concerning the securities to be purchased;
    d. purchaser is purchasing as principal and, if applicable, with investment intent and not with a view to resale;
    e. purchaser has been recognized as an exempt purchaser by virtue of an order by the relevant provincial securities regulator.

3. Receipt of representations of fact from the proposed investor in order that the issuer will have evidence to support the specific category of statutory exemption utilized for that investor;
4. The name of your sales person who will approach the prospective investor, who will follow-up, and by when;
5. The results of the contact and follow-up;
6. The amount of the proposed investment.

M. Prior to commencement of distribution (selling) of the securities of the issuer, comply with any statutory notices required at this stage. (For example, there is a requirement in certain provinces that notice be given to the provincial securities regulator in advance of a forthcoming private placement of securities.)

N. As you "sign-up" (close) each investor, ensure that each of the following matters has been attended to:

1. Provide the investor with a subscription form and have it properly executed, leaving him with a copy and keeping one for your company (the issuer).
2. Confirm that the investor has received a copy of the disclosure document, if any, that is required by law to be given to him under his particular category of exemption in his province.
3. Obtain from the investor a signed copy of the purchaser's questionnaire if it is required under his particular category of exemption.
4. Obtain the investment funds from the investor made payable to the proper party (usually the issuer, unless a trustee is being utilized).

O. Ensure that the investment funds are deposited in accordance with the terms of the subscription form. If a minimum subscription amount for the entire issue has been specified, then deposit the proceeds of the issue with a trustee as stated in the subscription form.

P. Arrange for completion of all post-closing filings required by law, and optional matters that you choose, such as:

1. Private placement notification form to securities commission;
2. Issuance of share certificates to each investor;
3. Press release publicizing the completion of your successful private placement.

Q.   Install a system to fulfil any ongoing post-closing obligations required by law, and optional matters that you choose in order to maintain good investor relations, such as:

1. Provision of regular financial information;
2. Provision of annual meeting notification;
3. Provision of an annual report or year-end financial statements;
4. Provision of periodic newsletters to the investors to keep them current on the business of the issuers.

Checklist 2
PROSPECTIVE INVESTOR LIST
(See Chapters Three and Six)

Name	Address	Phone	Potential Investment Size	Relation to Issuer	Category of Legal Exemption	1st Contact Results	2nd Contact Results	3rd Contact Results	Date of Investment	Amount of Investment	Notes/ To Do
1											
2											
3											
4											
5											
6											
7											
8											
9											
10											
11											
12											
13											
14											
15											
16											
17											
18											
19											
20											

Checklist 3

SHAREHOLDER LIST

(See Chapters Three and Four)

ame	Address	Phone	Date of Investment	Amount of Investment	Price of Shares	Number of Shares	Class of Shares	Subscription Documents Signed	Government Filings Made	Notes/ To Do
1										
2										
3										
4										
5										
6										
7										
8										
9										
0										
1										
2										
3										
4										
5										
6										
7										
8										
9										
0										

Checklist 4
SOURCES OF FINANCING CHECKLIST
(See Chapter Four)

	Possible Source	Need Further Info	Further Info Obtained
Conventional Sources of Financing			
1. Banks			
(a) Short-term loans:			
• demand loans	___	___	___
• secured commercial loans	___	___	___
• unsecured commercial loans	___	___	___
• operating loans	___	___	___
• lines of credit	___	___	___
• accounts receivable loans	___	___	___
• warehouse receipt loans	___	___	___
• bridge financing	___	___	___
(b) Medium- and long-term loans:			
• term loans	___	___	___
• conventional mortgages	___	___	___
• collateral mortgages	___	___	___
• business improvement loan	___	___	___
• leasing	___	___	___
(c) Other financing services:			
• charge card for business expenses	___	___	___
• charge card for personal use	___	___	___
• factoring services	___	___	___
• leasing services	___	___	___
• letters of credit	___	___	___
• letters of guarantee	___	___	___
2. Federal Business Development Bank (FBDB)			
• term loans	___	___	___
• loan guarantees	___	___	___
• bridge financing	___	___	___
• equity financing	___	___	___
• leasing	___	___	___
• financial broker program (packaging loans to external lenders)	___	___	___
• joint ventures	___	___	___
• equity participation	___	___	___
3. Trust Companies			
• long-term loans	___	___	___
• mortgage financing	___	___	___
4. Credit Unions			
• term loans	___	___	___
• working capital loans	___	___	___

	Possible Source	Need Further Info	Further Info Obtained
• mortgage financing	_____	_____	_____
• equity participation	_____	_____	_____
5. Insurance Companies			
• mortgage loans	_____	_____	_____
• loans based on insurance policy (cash surrender value)	_____	_____	_____
6. Investment Dealers			
• equity purchase	_____	_____	_____
• private placement	_____	_____	_____
• public issue of stock	_____	_____	_____
7. Commercial Finance Companies			
• equipment leasing	_____	_____	_____
• real estate loans	_____	_____	_____
• factoring	_____	_____	_____
• machinery and equipment loans	_____	_____	_____
• inventory financing	_____	_____	_____
• accounts or notes receivable financing	_____	_____	_____
8. Government Funding/Incentive/Programs			
(a) Federal government:			
• External Affairs and International Trade Canada (e.g. PEMB Program)	_____	_____	_____
• Industry, Science and Technology Canada	_____	_____	_____
• Canadian Commercial Corporation	_____	_____	_____
• Canadian International Development Agency (Crown corporation)	_____	_____	_____
• Export Development Corporation (Crown corporation)	_____	_____	_____
• Small Business Loans Act	_____	_____	_____
• Business Development Centre (Community Futures Program)	_____	_____	_____
• Immigrant Investor Program	_____	_____	_____
• Aboriginal Entrepreneur Program	_____	_____	_____
• Western Diversification Fund	_____	_____	_____
• Atlantic Opportunities Fund	_____	_____	_____
• Loans, Grants and Subsidy Programs	_____	_____	_____
• Other _____			
(b) Provincial government:			
• Small business loans, grants subsidies and programs	_____	_____	_____

	Possible Source	Need Further Info	Further Info Obtained

- Provincial development corporations' (Crown corporations) programs ___ ___ ___
- Venture capital corporations ___ ___ ___
- Small business stock savings plan ___ ___ ___
- Other _____

    _____

    _____

(c) Municipal/Regional governments:
- Economic development commissions ___ ___ ___
- Municipal governments ___ ___ ___
- Small business incubator start-up programs ___ ___ ___
- Other _____

    _____

    _____

Creative Sources of Financing or Saving Money

1. Modifying Personal Lifestyle
   - reducing personal long-distance telephone calls ___ ___ ___
   - minimizing entertainment expenses ___ ___ ___
   - minimizing transportation costs (e.g. car pool, using more gas-efficient car) ___ ___ ___
   - cutting down on tobacco and alcohol ___ ___ ___
   - reducing number of restaurant meals by packing your own lunch ___ ___ ___
   - combining personal and business travel ___ ___ ___
   - taking on a part-time job ___ ___ ___
2. Using Personal Assets
   - using credit cards ___ ___ ___
   - using personal line of credit ___ ___ ___
   - reducing premiums by reassessing insurance policy ___ ___ ___
   - using funds in personal bank accounts ___ ___ ___
   - renting out part of your home or garage ___ ___ ___
   - selling your stocks and bonds ___ ___ ___
   - cashing in pension plans (e.g., RRSP) ___ ___ ___
   - selling unnecessary personal possessions (e.g., second car) ___ ___ ___

	Possible Source	Need Further Info	Further Info Obtained
• selling personal assets to the business	_____	_____	_____
• remortgaging your home	_____	_____	_____

3. Using Private Investors Known to You
- previous employers _____ _____ _____
- previous co-workers _____ _____ _____
- friends _____ _____ _____
- neighbours _____ _____ _____
- doctor _____ _____ _____
- lawyer _____ _____ _____
- accountant _____ _____ _____
- dentist _____ _____ _____
- stockbroker _____ _____ _____
- other (see Chapter Six) _____ _____ _____

4. Using Other Private Investors
- through word-of-mouth contacts (various network groups) _____ _____ _____
- answering ads in newspapers and magazines that read "business opportunities wanted" _____ _____ _____
- placing ads for a private investor in newspapers and magazines _____ _____ _____

5. Family Assistance
- loans from relatives _____ _____ _____
- loans from immediate family members _____ _____ _____
- equity financing from relatives _____ _____ _____
- equity financing from immediate family _____ _____ _____
- employing family members _____ _____ _____
- sharing an office used by family members _____ _____ _____
- using a family investment company _____ _____ _____
- using a family bank _____ _____ _____

6. Using Customers' Funds
- having a cash-only policy _____ _____ _____
- invoicing on an interim basis _____ _____ _____
- asking for advance payments or deposits _____ _____ _____
- providing discounts for prompt payments _____ _____ _____
- charging purchases on customers' credit card accounts _____ _____ _____
- getting signed purchase orders or contracts (collateral for bank) _____ _____ _____
- phoning collect _____ _____ _____
- third-party billing long-distance phone calls to customer's account (with consent in writing in advance) _____ _____ _____

	Possible Source	Need Further Info	Further Info Obtained
7. Employees as Investors			
• asking staff to co-sign on loan guarantees			
• asking staff to invest in the business			
• direct loans from staff			
• paying partial salary in the form of stock			
• create a registered Employee Stock Option Plan (ESOP)			
8. Using Suppliers' Funds			
• supplier loans			
• establishing credit accounts with suppliers			
• buying goods on consignment			
• floor planning			
• equipment loans from manufacturer			
• rack jobbers			
• instalment financing			
• conditional sales arrangement			
• leasing equipment			
• co-op advertising			
9. Selling Ownership			
• incorporating and selling shares			
• taking on partners			
10. Renting			
• sharing or subletting rental space, staff, and equipment costs with another business			
• renting a packaged office (office space, telephone answering, mailing address, secretarial services, equipment, etc.)			
• renting office space, furniture, and equipment			
11. Leasing			
• selling your assets and leasing them back through a commercial leasing company			
• leasing assets rather than purchasing			
12. Factoring Companies			
• factoring with or without recourse			
• company sets up its own factor			
• block discounting			
13. Volume Discounts			
• buying groups			
• agency discounts			
• co-op advertising			
• group rates on insurance			

	Possible Source	Need Further Info	Further Info Obtained
14. Financial Matchmaking Services (Lists of interested private investors)			
• federal government — immigrant investors under Immigration Act	_____	_____	_____
• provincial government small business departments	_____	_____	_____
• regional/municipal economic development commissions	_____	_____	_____
• Federal Business Development Bank	_____	_____	_____
• chartered banks	_____	_____	_____
• COIN investors' network (Canadian Chamber of Commerce)	_____	_____	_____
• National Business Finance Network, Inc.	_____	_____	_____
15. Other Creative Financing Techniques			
• advance royalty deals	_____	_____	_____
• licensing your product or service	_____	_____	_____
• franchisor financing	_____	_____	_____
• franchising your business	_____	_____	_____
• multi-level marketing	_____	_____	_____
• joint ventures	_____	_____	_____
• limited partnerships	_____	_____	_____
• business brokers	_____	_____	_____
• mortgage brokers	_____	_____	_____
• mortgage discounters	_____	_____	_____
• mutual fund companies	_____	_____	_____
• overseas lenders and investors	_____	_____	_____
• pension fund companies	_____	_____	_____
• small business stock savings plans	_____	_____	_____
• small business venture capital corporations (provincially regulated)	_____	_____	_____
• venture capital companies	_____	_____	_____
• local venture capital clubs	_____	_____	_____
• financial consultants	_____	_____	_____
• business consultants	_____	_____	_____
• obtaining services in exchange for equity	_____	_____	_____
• contra bartering (exchanging service/product for service/product)	_____	_____	_____
• RRSP (defer tax)	_____	_____	_____
• assigning exclusive rights to copyright or patent, etc.	_____	_____	_____
• proposal under Bankruptcy Act	_____	_____	_____
• other	_____	_____	_____
	_____	_____	_____
	_____	_____	_____
	_____	_____	_____
	_____	_____	_____

Checklist 5
FRANCHISE ASSESSMENT CHECKLIST

Check when
answered
to your
satisfaction

The Franchisor

1.   How long has the franchise been in business? _____
2.   Is it a well-established company? _____
3.   How long has it been offering franchises? _____
4.   Does it have proven experience of operating a franchise chain? _____
5.   If a new firm, how long has the concept been tested? _____
6.   What are the results of the concept testing? _____
7.   Is it the subsidiary of another company? If so, who is the parent company? Has that company ever franchised other products or services? What is their track record? _____
8.   What business is the company really in? Is it more interested in selling franchises than in marketing a viable product or service? _____
9.   How does the company make its money? From "up-front" fees or from continuing royalties? (Reputable franchisors are interested in the continuing success of their franchisees; money should come from successful franchises and products, not reselling unprofitable franchises.) _____
10. How many franchised outlets are currently in operation? How many outlets are company-owned? _____
11. Have any outlets failed in the past? If so, why? What is the ratio of successful franchises to those which have failed? _____
12. Have you received the franchisor's recent audited financial statements? Is the company financially stable? Has your accountant analyzed the statements? _____
13. Who are the franchisor's directors and officers, and what is their business experience? _____
14. Are these management people employed full-time by the franchise company? _____
15. How long has the present management been with the company? _____
16. What is the depth and quality of the franchisor's management team and supervisory personnel? _____
17. Does the franchisor have a reputation for dealing honestly with its franchisees? With its customers? _____
18. What is the franchisor's standing with the Chamber of Commerce? The Better Business Bureau? Dun & Bradstreet? Its bank? Your bank? Canadian Franchise Association? _____
19. Have you discussed the franchisor's plans for future development and expansion or diversification? _____
20. What effect will development and expansion have on your dealings with the franchisor? _____
21. What innovations has the franchisor introduced since first starting? _____
22. Are there immediate plans for further expansion in your area? Will that affect your sales? _____

23. Where will new franchises be located? _____
24. Has the company shown a pattern of solid growth? _____
25. How selective is the franchisor when choosing its franchisees? Have your qualifications and financial standing been reviewed? _____
26. If the franchise is being offered in Alberta, has the franchise been registered in the province of Alberta? Have you seen the prospectus or Statement of Material Facts filed with the Alberta Securities Commission? _____
27. Has the franchisor shown you any certified figures indicating exact net profits of one or more franchisee firms which you have personally checked yourself with the franchisee? _____
28. Is the franchisor connected in any way with any other franchise company handling similar merchandise or services? _____
29. If the answer to the last question is yes, what is your protection against this second franchisor organization? _____
30. Are there any lawsuits pending against the franchisor or its key people? What is the nature of the claim? Has there been a history of dissatisfied franchisees litigating against the franchisor? _____

The Product or Service

31. How is the firm's image in the community? How is the product regarded? _____
32. Are you prepared to spend the rest of your business life with this product or service? _____
33. Will this product/service sell all year round or will you be out of business for some months each year? Would you be prepared for such a slack period? _____
34. Might this product/service just be a fad? Or will demand increase? Is it a luxury? _____
35. Is it well packaged to promote sales? _____
36. Where is the product/service now sold? _____
37. What assurance do you have that the franchisor will be able to continue getting the product for you at a fair price? _____
38. How many people in the area are potential customers? _____
39. Is the product or service protected by a trademark or copyright? Is it patented? _____
40. What makes the product or service unique, and does it satisfy a particular need in your market? _____
41. Can the product or service be duplicated by your competitors? _____
42. How much of this product or service is presently sold, and have sales been increasing or decreasing? _____
43. Would you buy the product or service on its own merits? _____
44. How long has it been on the market in its present form? _____
45. Is the product or service marketable in your territory? How do you know? _____
46. Is the price competitive with similar products or services on the market? Do you have many competitors? _____
47. Have you reviewed the federal/provincial standards and regulations governing the product or service? _____

48. Are there product warranties or guarantees? Are they your responsibility or the franchisor's?
49. Are you allowed by the franchisor to carry other product lines or provide additional services?

The Location and Territory

50. How well defined is the franchised sales area? Is it outlined on a map? In the contract?
51. Are there proposed changes in traffic patterns or redevelopment which could affect the business in the proposed location? (Check municipal offices about local bylaws.)
52. How expensive are taxes and insurance in the area?
53. Are your franchised rights exclusive for the area? What guarantee do you have? Can the company open its own outlets?
54. What competition is in the area?
55. Can you select your own location?
56. Do you lease, sub-lease or own the premises? What are the terms?
57. Will you receive assistance in selecting a location? Is there a fee for this?
58. Will the population in the territory given you increase, remain static, or decrease over the next five years? Does the franchisor have information on these matters?
59. Will the product or service you are considering be in greater demand, about the same, or less demand than today five years from now?
60. Can you, or the franchisor, change the size of your territory in the future?
61. Do you have a profile of the people in your area, including age, income, and occupation?

The Franchise Contract

62. Does the contract fully explain your rights and obligations under the franchise agreement, and those of the franchisor?
63. Does the contract benefit both parties — you and the franchisor?
64. Can you terminate the contract if, for some reason, you have to?
65. What is the cost or penalty if you do terminate the contract?
66. Will you have the privilege of selling or transferring the franchise and under what conditions or restrictions? Will you have the option of selling it yourself, or must it be handled as a resale by the franchisor? How is the resale price then set?
67. Does the contract give the franchisor the right of cancellation for almost any reason, or must there be good cause? Are the reasons for cancellation outlined?
68. If the franchisor can terminate, will you be compensated for goodwill?
69. Are the payments to the franchisor spelled out in detail? What do they include?
70. Must you purchase a minimum amount or all of the merchandise from the franchisor?
71. Can you use your own suppliers?

72. Must you purchase or lease equipment directly from the franchisor?   _____

73. Are makes and/or sources of supply for equipment, furnishings, and fixtures specified?   _____

74. Who is responsible for repairs to fixtures and equipment? Are warranties provided?   _____

75. Do you fully understand the terms of any leasing agreement you sign?   _____

76. Is there an annual sales quota? Is it realistic? Can the company terminate the contract if the quota is not met?   _____

77. Does the contract prevent you from establishing, owning, or working in a competing business for a certain period after termination? Do you feel this restriction is fair in the circumstances?   _____

78. Before you sign the sales contract, are you sure that the franchise can do something for you that you cannot do for yourself?   _____

79. Does the franchisor provide continuing assistance? Is this specified in the contract?   _____

80. Is training-school attendance required? Is it of a calibre that you and your staff require?   _____

81. Have you examined and seen in operation the company's franchise handbook, the accounting system and all other systems and methods to which you will have to adhere?   _____

82. Will the franchisor help with the financing arrangements? What will it cost you?   _____

83. Are advertising and sales support adequate? What is the cost?   _____

84. If a well-known personality is involved in the advertising, does he/she assist you directly? How? What happens if the celebrity quits or dies?   _____

85. What controls does the franchisor specify in the following areas?
    - operational procedures   _____
    - product/service quality   _____
    - hiring staff   _____
    - advertising   _____
    - accounting   _____
    - insurance   _____
    - prices   _____
    - reporting and records   _____
    - other.   _____

86. Are you allowed to hire a manager, or must you run the franchise yourself?   _____

87. Does the franchisor perform a market study for each potential franchise location?   _____

88. Is the chosen franchise location right for your own needs?   _____

89. What standards does the franchisor specify for the property?   _____

90. If a lease is involved, are you leasing from the franchisor or from an independent landlord?   _____

91. Can you sub-lease, assign the lease, or move the franchise if necessary?   _____

92. Is the franchise contract for a specified number of years, at which time a new agreement must be negotiated? Or is the franchise term indefinite, with automatic renewal privileges, subject to certain mutually agreeable restrictions?   _____

93. Does the franchise agreement provide for arbitration in the event of a dispute or default?

94. Are your payments to the franchisor clearly specified? Are the following shown?
    - the franchise fee
    - any fixed yearly payments the franchisor receives
    - royalty payments based on a percentage of gross sales
    - the monthly percentage of gross sales required for advertising.

95. Are these costs realistic or overly burdensome to profitability?

96. What happens if supplies from the franchisor are interrupted? Can you purchase goods from alternative suppliers?

97. Have you the right to the franchisor's latest innovations?

98. Does the contract cover in detail all the franchisor's verbal promises made during the interview?

99. If leasing the location, will the lease be for the same term as the franchise agreement? Can the lease be renewed if you renew the franchise?

100. Are you responsible for the construction or improvement of the premises? If so, will the franchisor provide you with plans and specifications, and can these be changed?

101. If you default on the contract, how much time do you have to rectify the situation?

102. What happens to the business in the event of your prolonged illness or death? Have questions regarding succession been clearly addressed?

103. Before you sign the contract, are you sure that the franchise can do something for you that you cannot do for yourself?

104. Will the franchisor arrange financing?

105. Does the franchisor call upon you to take any steps which are, according to your lawyer, unwise or illegal in your city or province (e.g., Sunday openings)?

106. Are you prepared to give up some independence of action to secure the advantages offered by the franchise?

107. Do you really believe you have the innate ability, training, and experience to work smoothly and profitably with the franchisor, your employees, and your customers?

108. Have you had your accountant and lawyer carefully check out the agreement, particularly those areas dealing with bankruptcy, termination, renewal, transfer, and sale of the franchise? What are their opinions?

The Experience of Current Franchisees

109. Was the profit projection by the franchisor accurate?

110. What reports to the company are necessary? Are they reasonable?

111. Is there a minimum quota of sales? Is it difficult to achieve?

112. Are the products and equipment supplied by the franchisor satisfactory and delivered promptly?

113. How reliable is delivery from the franchisor?

114. What problems have been encountered with the franchisor?

115. How did the franchisor's income projections compare with the results experienced by existing franchisees? _____

116. What was the total investment required by the franchisor? _____

117. Were there any hidden or unexpected costs? _____

118. Has the franchise been as profitable as expected? _____

119. How long was it before the operating expenses were covered by revenue? _____

120. How long was the franchise in operation before the business became profitable? _____

121. How long was it before the franchise was able to pay a reasonable management salary? _____

122. Does the franchisor respond promptly and helpfully to questions asked? _____

123. Has there ever been a serious disagreement with the franchisor? What about? Was it settled amicably? Is there any legal action? _____

124. What kind of management and staff training was provided? Did it meet expectations? Where was it held? _____

125. Is the marketing, promotional, and advertising assistance received from the franchisor satisfactory? _____

126. What steps have been taken to make the franchise successful with this particular franchisor? _____

127. Do franchisees advise anyone else to start a franchise with this particular franchisor? _____

128. If the contract can be changed, what items require discussion? _____

SOURCES OF FURTHER INFORMATION

Contents

Introduction

Introduction

The cliché that "Knowledge is Power" is a fundamental truism when dealing with the issue of financing. Thorough knowledge will greatly assist you in reaching your financing goals. It will show you are resourceful, enhance the quality of your decision-making, increase your confidence and decrease your stress. Knowledge is a function of research and utilization of available resources. There are many sources and resources to assist your learning curve. The following is a summary of key contact sources to facilitate your search.

Many of the following federal and provincial government departments and agencies have local or regional offices. Check the Blue Pages of your telephone directory. In many cases the government offices have toll-free phone numbers, or they will accept collect calls or phone you back at their expense. This is helpful to keep in mind if you are making general or specific enquiries, or want information sent to you and no local office exists.

The phone numbers given here relating to government departments, and other organizations and associations, change from time to time. If this happens, the correct number can be obtained from directory assistance, or you could call the Federal Business Development Bank (FBDB) toll-free number to obtain information, contact addresses, and phone numbers relating to federal, provincial, and municipal programs that assist small business. You can also phone Reference Canada toll-free to obtain current information on federal government programs, services, and contact addresses and phone numbers. The number is listed in the Blue Pages of your directory under "Government of Canada." It is 1-800-667-3355.

A. Federal Government

Consumer and Corporate Affairs
Place du Portage
Phase 1
50 Victoria Street
Hull, Quebec K1A 0C9
(819) 997-2938

For information on matters relating to federal incorporation, trademarks, trade names, copyright, patent, industrial design, bankruptcy, and consumer protection legislation. District offices in major cities throughout Canada.

External Affairs and International Trade Canada
Info Export Division
125 Sussex Drive
Ottawa, Ontario K1A 0G2
(613) 993-6435
Toll-free: 1-800-267-8376

An excellent and comprehensive information source of all federal government programs, services, assistance, and financial support for the novice or experienced exporter. Also contact for information relating to imports.

Federal Business Development Bank (FBDB)
800 Victoria Square
Tour de la Bourse, C.P. 335
Montréal, Québec H4Z 1L4
(514) 496-7966
Toll-free: 1-800-361-2126

A federal Crown corporation. For information on small business management seminars, CASE counselling, financing, financial matchmaking, and government programs (federal, provincial, and municipal). Branches throughout Canada.

Industry, Science, and Technology Canada
235 Queen Street
Ottawa, Ontario K1A 0H5
(613) 954-2788

For information on federal government assistance and incentive programs for business (e.g., Research & Development programs), counselling on how to apply for those programs, and publications, BOSS sourcing systems, and directories. Offices in major cities throughout Canada.

Statistics Canada
Customer Enquiries
Tunney's Pasture
Ottawa, Ontario K1A 0T6
(613) 951-8116

For information and statistics on geographic, demographic and other population characteristics for business planning and decision-making. Publications and computer data access are available. Offices in major cities throughout Canada.

Supply and Services Canada
Communications Services
45 Sacre-Coeur Boulevard
Hull, Quebec K1A 0S7
(819) 997-6363

For information on how to sell products or services to federal government and Crown corporations, statistical information, and publications. Offices in major cities throughout Canada.

B. Provincial Governments — Small Business

For information on provincial small business financial assistance and matchmaking programs, free counselling, seminars, publications, small business reference material, selling goods or services to provincial governments, and management assistance programs.

British Columbia
Ministry of Economic Development
Small Business and Trade
601 Cordova Street
Vancouver, B.C. V6B 1G1
(604) 660-3900
Toll-free 1-800-972-2255

Alberta
Economic Development and Tourism
Sterling Place
#9940 - 106 Street
6th Floor
Edmonton, Alberta T5K 2P6
(403) 427-3685
Toll-free: 1-800-272-9675

Saskatchewan
Economic Development
1919 Saskatchewan Drive
5th Floor
Regina, Saskatchewan S4P 3V7
(306) 787-2207

Manitoba
Department of Industry, Trade and Tourism
155 Carlton Street
5th Floor
Winnipeg, Manitoba R3C 3H8
(204) 945-7738
Toll-free: 1-800-282-8069

Ontario
Ministry of Industry, Trade and Technology
Small Business Advice and Counsel
900 Bay Street
Hearst Block
7th Floor,
Toronto, Ontario M7A 2E1
(416) 963-0050
Toll-free: 1-800-567-2345

Quebec
Ministère de l'industrie et du commerce
930, chemin Ste-Foy
5e étage
Québec G1S 2L4
(418) 643-5070

Communication - Québec
Bureau régional du Québec
870 rue Charest est
Québec G1K 8S5
Long distance: (418) 643-1344
Zenith for toll-free number

New Brunswick
Department of Economic Development and Tourism
Centennial Building
King Street
Suite 517
P.O. Box 6000
Fredericton, N.B. E3B 5H1
(506) 453-3890

Prince Edward Island
Department of Industry
Small Business Division
Shaw Building
105 Rochford Street
Charlottetown, P.E.I. C1A 7N8
(902) 368-4219

Nova Scotia
Department of Economic Development
1800 Argyle Street
7th Floor
Halifax, N.S. B3J 2R7
(902) 424-7139

Newfoundland
Enterprise Newfoundland and Labrador
136 Crosbie Road
St. John's, Newfoundland A1B 3K3
(709) 729-7000

Northwest Territories
Economic Development and Tourism
P.O. Box 1320
Yellowknife, N.W.T. X1A 2L9
(403) 920-3349

Yukon Territory
Department of Economic Development
Mines and Small Business
P.O. Box 2703
Whitehorse, Yukon Y1A 2C6
(403) 667-5466

C. Provincial Governments — Venture Capital Programs

Many provinces have their own form of venture capital sponsorship program, providing either grants or interest-free loans when specified venture capital investments are made. Alternatively, the government may contribute partial funding to a private sector operated fund or Crown corporation.

The contacts for information in each province are as follows:

British Columbia
Venture Capital Program
Financial Evaluation and Equity Branch
Ministry of Economic Development,
Small Business and Trade
712 Yates Street
2nd Floor
Victoria, British Columbia V8V 1X4
1-800-665-6597

Alberta
Alberta Opportunity Company
P.O. Box 4040
Ponoka, Alberta T4J 1R5
(403) 421-7979

Saskatchewan
Saskatchewan Economic Development
Venture Capital Program
5th Floor, 1919 Saskatchewan Drive
Regina, Saskatchewan S4P 3V7
(306) 787-2252

Manitoba
Vision Fund
2670-360 Main Street
Winnipeg, Manitoba R3C 3Z3
(204) 949-5350

Ontario
Small Business Development Corporation
Ministry of Revenue
33 King Street West
Oshawa, Ontario L1H 8H9
1-800-263-7466

Ontario Investment Fund Initiative
900 Bay Street
9th Floor, Hearst Block
Toronto, Ontario M7A 2E1
(416) 325-6700

Quebec
Société de développement industriel du
Québec
770 Sherbrooke W., 9th Floor
Montreal, Québec H3A 1G1
(514) 873-4375

New Brunswick
Economic Development and Tourism
Centennial Building, King Street
P.O. Box 6000
Fredericton, New Brunswick E3B 5H1
(506) 453-2474

Nova Scotia
Business Development Corporation
Department of Economic Development
1800 Argyle Street
6th Floor
P.O. Box 519
Halifax, Nova Scotia B3J 2R7
(902) 424-6862

Prince Edward Island
P.E.I. Business Development Agency
West Royalty Industrial Park
Charlottetown, Prince Edward Island
C1E 1B0
(902) 368-5800

Newfoundland
Enterprise Newfoundland and Labrador
136 Crosbie Road
St. John's, Newfoundland A1B 3K3
(709) 729-7000

Northwest Territories
Venture Capital Program
Box 1320
Yellowknife, Northwest Territories X1A 2L9
(403) 873-7360

Yukon
Department of Economic Development
P.O. Box 2703
Whitehorse, Yukon Y1A 2C6
(403) 667-3011

D. Provincial Governments - Immigrant Investor Programs

Many provinces have their own programs for encouraging investments by immigrants. Contact your province for details on current programs.

British Columbia
Ministry of Economic Development,
Small Business and Trade
Business Immigration Branch
629 - 999 Canada Place
Vancouver, B.C. V6C 3E1

Alberta
Alberta Career Development and Employment
Immigration Settlement Division
11th Floor
10155 - 102nd Street
Edmonton, Alberta T5J 4L5
(403) 427-0537

Saskatchewan
Economic Development Business Immigration Programs
5th Floor
1919 Saskatchewan Drive
Regina, Saskatchewan S4P 3V7
(306) 787-9212

Manitoba
Industry, Trade and Tourism
Financial Services Branch
5th Floor
155 Carlton Street
Winnipeg, Manitoba R3C 3H8
(204) 945-2475

Ontario
Ministry of Industry, Trade and Technology
Business Immigration Section
900 Bay Street
5th Floor, Hearst Block
Toronto, Ontario M7A 2E1
(416) 325-6986

Quebec
Ministère des Communautes
Culturelles et de l'immigration

360 rue McGill, Chambre 301
Montreal, Québec
H2Y 2E9

New Brunswick
Economic Development and Tourism
Centennial Building
King Street
Suite 549
P.O. Box 6000
Fredericton, New Brunswick E3B 5H1
(504) 444-4294

Nova Scotia
Department of Economic Development
1800 Argyle Street
6th Floor
P.O. Box 519
Halifax, Nova Scotia B3J 2R7
(902) 424-5052

Prince Edward Island
Department of Industry
P.O. Box 2000
Charlottetown, P.E.I. C1A 7N8
(902) 368-4240

Newfoundland
Department of Industry, Trade and Technology
Marketing and Investment
P.O. Box 8700
St. John's, Newfoundland A1B 4J6
(709) 729-4205

Northwest Territories
Economic Development and Tourism
P.O. Box 1320
Yellowknife, Northwest Territories X1A 2L9
(403) 920-3349

Yukon
Department of Economic Development
P.O. Box 2403
Whitehorse, Yukon Y1A 2C6
(403) 667-3011

E. Associations - Franchise Companies

Pacific Franchise Association
#523 - 409 Granville Street
Vancouver, B.C.
V6C 1T2
(604) 669-3177

Alberta Franchisors Institute
P. O. Box 63150
2604 Kensington Road NW
Calgary, Alberta
T2N 4S5

Canadian Franchise Association
5045 Orbiter Drive
#201, Building 12
Mississauga, Ontario
L4W 4Y4
(416) 625-2896

Association Quebecoise de la Franchise
C.P. 156
Succuisale Duvernay
Laval, Québec
H7E 4P5
(514) 669-5044

International Franchise Association
#900 - 1350
Washington, D.C. USA
20005
(202) 628-8000

F. Associations - Venture Capital Companies

Association of Canadian Venture Capital Companies
1000 - 120 Eglinton Avenue East
Toronto, Ontario
M4P 1E2
(416) 487-0519

G. Stock Exchanges

Vancouver Stock Exchange
P. O. Box 10333
609 Granville Street
Vancouver, B.C.
V7Y 1H1
(604) 689-3334

Alberta Stock Exchange
6th Floor
300 - 5th Avenue SW
Calgary, Alberta
T2P 3C4
(403) 974-7400

Winnipeg Stock Exchange
2901 - 1 Lombard Place
Winnipeg, Manitoba R3B 0Y2
(204) 942-8431

Toronto Stock Exchange
Stock Exchange Tower
2 First Canadian Place
Toronto, Ontario
M5X 1J2
(416) 947-4335

Montreal Stock Exchange
Stock Exchange Tower
P. O. Box 61
800 Victoria Square
Montreal, Québec
H4Z 1A9
(514) 871-2424

H. Matchmaking Services

There are various government and private matchmaking services available. New ones are continually formed and existing ones discontinued. Some are free or at a nominal fee. Others are more costly. Check in the yellow pages of your telephone directory under "Financing." Here are some of the organizations involved in matchmaking or who produce matchmaking publications:

Bridge Finance Network Inc
National Business Finance Network, Inc.
#207-1425 Marine Drive
West Vancouver, B.C. V7T 1B9
Attn: Brian Nattrass
      President
(604) 886-2207

Canadian Opportunity Investment Network (COIN)
c/o Canadian Chamber of Commerce
#55 Metcalfe Street
Ottawa, Ontario K1P 6N4
(613) 992-4793

You can also contact your provincial Chamber of Commerce for further information.

Business Opportunity Bulletin
c/o Business Immigration Branch
Ministry of Education and Multiculturism
Province of British Columbia
999 Canada Place, 6th Floor
Vancouver, B.C. V6C 3E1
(604) 844-1800

The Marketplace Bulletin
c/o Domestic Industry Support Branch
Ministry of Industry, Trade and Technology
Province of Ontario
900 Bay Street

7th Floor, Hearst Block
Toronto, Ontario M7A 2E1
(416) 325-6873

Investment Matching Program
c/o Ministry of Economic Development
Small Business and Trade
Province of British Columbia
770 Pacific Blvd South
2nd Floor
Vancouver, B.C. V6B 5E7
(604) 660-4080

Small Business Development Corporation (SBDC) Program
Ministry of Revenue
Province of Ontario
P.O. Box 625
33 King Street West
3rd Floor
Oshawa, Ontario L1H 8H5
(416) 434-7232

Business Opportunities Quarterly
Bank of Nova Scotia
Commercial Banking Services
100 Yonge Street, #602
Toronto, Ontario M5H 1H1
(416) 866-4285

I. Educational Organizations

This organization provides research, consulting and education programs on a national basis, on all aspects of business development. This includes business start up, expansion, diversification, purchase, sale, management, franchising and financing.

Canadian Enterprise Institute Inc.
#300 - 3665 Kingsway
Vancouver, B.C. V5R 5W2
(604) 436-3337 / (604) 436-9155

J. Networking Organizations

Many major cities have venture or enterprise clubs or forums. The purpose of such groups is to provide networking, business opportunities and education programs in an informal setting, designed for investors and those looking for investment.

GLOSSARY

Accounts Payable
Money owed by a business for goods and services received.

Accounts Receivable
Money owed to a business by purchasers of its goods and/or services.

Accrued Interest
The amount of interest accumulated since the last interest payment date.

Acid Test Ratio
Simple ratio of a company's liquid assets to current liabilities. Liquid assets include cash, marketable securities and accounts receivable.

Age of Inventory
Shows how fast merchandise or inventory moves through the business.

Age of Payables
Shows how long a business takes to pay its suppliers.

Age of Receivables
Shows how long a business takes to collect its receivables.

Angel
A term used to describe an individual who puts up money as a private investor in someone else's business. Generally refers to an investor who is not a family member or friend of an entrepreneur; in other words, distinguished from "Lovemoney".

Appraised Value
An estimate of the current market value of an asset, frequently used in evaluating the worth of assets pledged as security for a loan.

Authorized Borrowing Limit
The maximum amount you can borrow against your operating loan.

Balance Sheet
The financial statement that provides a snapshot of everything a business owns and owes at one point in time.

Bank Rate
The rate set each week by the Bank of Canada.

Basis Point
One one-hundredth of one percent.

Bear Market
A market that experiences a period of falling prices, usually brought on by the antici pation of a declining economy. "Bearish" investors are pessimistic about the stock market.

Bearer Form
A security on which payments are made to the party that has physical possession of the security. There is no registered owner of the security.

Bearer
Person possessing a bill or note payable to bearer; i.e., ownership is presumed to be with the person bearing or holding the bill or note.

Bill of Exchange
An unconditional order in writing addressed by one person to another, signed by the person giving it, requiring the person to whom it is addressed to pay at a fixed future date a sum certain in money to the order of a specific person or to bearer.

Blended Payment
A loan payment, consisting of principal and interest, that is the same each month. Because the total payment amount remains fixed, the amount applied against principal each month varies. An example is a mortgage payment.

Blind Pool
Limited partnership or investment fund that does not specify the properties the general partner plans to acquire.

Block Trading
Transaction of large stock lots, usually in excess of 10,000 shares, most frequently among institutional buyers and sellers.

Blowout
Quick sale of all shares in a new offering of securities.

Boilerplate
Standard legal clauses, often in fine print, used in most contracts, indentures, prospectuses, and other legal documents.

Book Value
Value of a corporation or of a corporate asset according to accounting records after allowing for depreciation. Also known as net asset value.

Boutique
Small, specialized brokerage firm that deals with a limited clientele and offers a limited product line.

Break-even Point
The level of sales where revenue equals total costs. Once you reach the break-even point, your business will start earning a profit.

Bridging/Bridge Loan/Bridge Financing
A short-term loan to cover the purchase or construction of an asset until permanent financing, frequently a previously arranged mortgage loan. Can be drawn down against the acquired or completed asset.

Broker
An intermediary in the market who brings two parties together to make a deal, but who himself doesn't take part in the deal and receives a commission for his efforts.

Bull Market
A market in which there is a prolonged rise in the price of stocks and bonds. Characterized by a high volume of trading. People who are "bullish" are optimistic about the future of the stock market.

Business Plan
A document in words and numbers setting out the goals of a business and how, when and by what means the business proposes to reach these goals. Covers issues such as financing, marketing, organizational structure, downside risks and other important matters. The business plan is an essential part of raising money.

Business Cycle
Recurrence of periods of expansion (recovery) and contraction (recession) in economic activity with effects on growth, inflation and employment.

Buy-sell
A legal agreement between two or more shareholders setting out the conditions under which each may sell their shares.

Calling a Loan
A formal demand from a creditor for repayment of a loan.

Capacity
An assessment by a lender of a borrower's ability and willingness to repay a loan from anticipated future cash flow or other sources.

Capital Investment Funds
Money used to purchase fixed assets for a business, such as machinery, and or buildings. Also, money invested in a business on the understanding that it will be used to purchase permanent assets rather than to cover day-to-day operating expenses.

Capitalization
The total amount of debt and equity issued by a company.

Cash Flow Forecast
An estimate of how much money will be coming in and going out of a business over a specified time period, usually on a month-by-month basis for a period of one or two years.

Cash Cow
Business that generates a continuing flow of cash. Such a business usually has well-established brand names whose familiarity stimulates repeated buying of the products.

Character
An assessment of your dependability as a person.

Chattel Mortgage
A charge over goods or equipment of a movable nature, as opposed to real estate.

Cold Market
Refers to people whom you do not know. Term normally used in the context of targeting people who could be sources of financing for you. Opposite of term "Warm Market".

Collateral
Property (whether of a real or personal nature or whether used in your business or otherwise) pledged as security for a loan. Also, any supplementary promise to pay, such as a guarantee, in support of a loan.

Comfort Letter
A letter required by the securities commission from the company's auditors which provides the commission with limited assurance on the unaudited financial statements included in a prospectus, based on the auditors' review of those statements. The same term is used for the auditors' letter to the underwriters reporting the results of performing specified procedures on financial information in the prospectus.

Comment (or Deficiency) Letter
A letter from a securities commission listing the comments noted in its review of the preliminary prospectus. These comments must be cleared to the satisfaction of the commission's staff before the final prospectus may be filed.

Commitment Fee
Fee charged by lenders on the committed loan facility.

Common Stock
Securities which represent ownership in a corporation and carry voting privileges.

Conditions
The limits written into an agreement between a money source, such as a lender or investor, and the recipient. The limits specify exactly what each party is expected to do in exchange for the benefits each will receive.

Contingency Plan

An alternate plan of action to use if circumstances change.

Cost of Goods Sold (or Cost of Sales)

Costs that are incurred because units of your product are sold. To calculate, add the cost of goods purchased or manufactured to your beginning inventory, then subtract ending inventory. In a manufacturing business, cost of goods sold includes labour; in a retail or service business, labour is not part of CGS, but is an operating expense.

Covenant

A promise or legal agreement you make when getting a loan. You must adhere to these covenants for your loan to remain in good standing.

Current Assets

Assets, such as cash, accounts receivable and inventory, that are likely to be turned into cash within one year.

Current Liabilities

Amounts owed, for example accounts payable, wages and taxes, that will normally be paid within one year.

Current Ratio (or Working Capital Ratio)

One measure of estimating how easily a business can meet its current debts.

Debenture

A legal document given in acknowledgement of a debt, containing terms of repayment, and providing a pledge of assets as security. There are usually terms in the document requiring the debtor to do certain things or refrain from doing certain things so long as the debt is unpaid.

Debt

Funds that are borrowed to run a business. These funds would come from yourself, other individuals or financial institutions.

Debt/Equity Ratio

A comparison of debt to equity used as a measure of the financial health of a business. See also Debt, Equity and Ratio.

Debt to Tangible Net Worth

Measures how much a business is borrowing in relation to the amount of equity invested in it. To calculate, divide total liabilities by tangible net worth.

Deemed Realization

A transfer of assets which, for tax purposes, is considered "a sale" by Revenue Canada, though no cash or other consideration may be involved.

Default

Failure to pay as agreed or to meet one or more of the conditions written into an agreement between borrower and lender. To fail to pay an outstanding debt. Also, failure to satisfy any other obligations such as failing to pay municipal taxes, maintaining the property or obtaining insurance.

Demand Loan

A loan on which the bank can demand full repayment at any time.

Due Diligence

The conducting of reasonable investigative procedures by the underwriter and other persons to provide a defensible basis for believing that there are no misrepresentations contained in a prospectus.

Entrepreneur

A person who starts, organizes and manages a business, who invests money in it, and who thus accepts the possibility of either profit or loss.

Equity
The amount of cash a business owner invests in the business. Also, the difference between the price for which a property could be sold and the total debts registered against it.

Escrow
Money, securities, or other property or instruments held by a third party until the conditions of a contract are met.

Factoring
A factor is a financial source which purchases the accounts receivable from businesses at a discount to the face value of the receivables.

Fiduciary Responsibility
The ethical and legal responsibility of someone who invests or manages money, to the people whose assets he or she is handling.

Fixed Assets
Assets such as machinery, land and buildings. Property used in operating a business which will not be consumed or converted into cash during the current accounting period.

Fixed Expenses
Costs of doing business which do not change with the volume of business. Examples might be rent for business premises, insurance payments, heat and light.

Fixed Rate
An interest rate that remains the same for the term of the loan.

Floating Charge
Debt security in the form of a general claim on all of the assets of a corporation existing from time to time.

Franchise
The right to sell products or services under a corporate name or trade mark which has been established by someone else. This right is usually purchased for cash in addition to a royalty fee on or percentage of all subsequent sales.

Franchisee
The person who purchases a franchise.

Franchisor
The owner of the franchise, including the corporate name, who sells licences to others who wish to operate under the corporate name.

Front-End Loading
Charges or fees which are greater at the start of a loan or investment contract than in its later stages.

General Security Agreement
Another form of debt security, similar to a floating charge.

Generally Accepted Accounting Principles
GAAP is the term used to describe the basis on which financial statements are normally prepared. This is codified in the *Handbook of The Canadian Institute of Chartered Accountants.*

Gross Profit (or Gross Margin)
Sales less cost of goods sold. A measure of a business's profitability.

Income Statement (or Profit and Loss Statement or P & L Statement or Income & Expenditure Statement)

A financial statement which reflects overall operating results for a fiscal year. It provides an overview of the results flowing from the assets and liabilities of the business and summarizes sources of income and expenses. It shows the amount of profit (or loss) during the year by comparing the data.

Initial Public Offering

Commonly referred to as an IPO. Refers to the process whereby a company, for the first time, makes an offering of its securities to the public through a stock exchange. The purpose of the IPO is to raise money for the company to better pursue its intended business and to provide cash to the company's original shareholders.

Insider Trading

Trades on the market by persons with access to inside information — that is, information unavailable to the investing public which in circumstances where if the information was generally known would likely considerably change the value of a company's shares in the market. Such insider trading is a violation of the law.

Insiders

Generally the directors, senior officers, and principal shareholders of a reporting issuer. Insiders are required to file publicly available reports on their holdings in the company and changes to same.

Insolvent

Being unable to pay debts as they become due; not strictly the same as bankruptcy.

Intangible Asset (or Soft Asset)

An asset such as goodwill or leasehold improvements that can't easily be sold.

Interest

A charge for the use of money supplied by a lender.

Inventory

Stock on hand in the form of goods ready for sale; or raw material to be made into goods for sale; or material in the process of being manufactured or completed for sale.

IPO

See "Initial Public Offering".

Issue

Offering of securities such as shares or bonds.

Issue Price

Price at which securities are sold on issue. This may be at face value or par, at a discount or a premium. Occasionally an issue may be partly paid, meaning that the price at launch is met by instalments.

Joint Venture

See "Strategic Alliance".

Lease

An agreement to rent for a period of time at an agreed price.

Leasehold Improvement

An improvement to the premises; for example, redecorating.

Letter of Credit
Financial instrument issued by a bank guaranteeing the payment of a customer's drafts up to a stated amount for a specified period.

Leverage
A term used to describe the amount of debt in a business in relation to the amount of equity. To measure the degree of leverage in a business, use the debt to tangible net worth ratio above.

Line of Credit
An agreement negotiated between a borrower and a lender which establishes the maximum amount against which a borrower may draw, as well as other conditions, such as how and when money borrowed against the line of credit is to be repaid. A line of credit usually fluctuates every month as it is often used for payables and then brought down again by the deposit of receivables.

Liquidation Value
The amount for which an asset can be sold. In a distress sale context, therefore usually a lower net value than would be calculated as a replacement value or market value.

Listing
When a securities issue is listed on a stock exchange, it is approved for trading through the facilitaties of that stock exchange.

Loan Margin
The percentage of the total value of the asset being financed (such as accounts receivable, inventory, or a fixed asset) for which the bank will lend you money.

Lovemoney
Refers to the risk capital contributed to a start-up or early-stage company by those who are closest to the entrepreneur; that is, family and friends.

Margin Requirements
A term used to refer to the percentage of total accounts receivable and inventory against which you can borrow on your operating loan. These margin requirements are usually calculated each month and reported to the lender.

Marketing Plan
A statement in words and numbers of how a business proposes to sell its product and/or services and to whom. It is an integral part of the business plan.

Matchmaker
A person, company or government agency who acts as an intermediary in attempting to match investors who have money to businesses that require money, usually for a fee.

Merchant Bank
Originally a bank which specialized in financing international trade and as such developed specialist knowledge of the countries with which it deals. Now it plays a much broader role by acting as an issuing house for stocks and bonds, by raising loans and equity, and dealing in bills and foreign exchange. Merchant banks also act for and advise companies on corporate finance matters — e.g., in merger situations.

Mezzanine Financing
Generally refers to the final round of non-public financing. The next stage for a successful company could be to qualify for an IPO.

Mezzanine Level
Stage of a company's development just prior to its going public.

Minority Shareholders
Stockholders who do not have control of a corporation by virtue of having less than 50% of the cumulative voting shares.

Multi-Level Marketing (MLM)
A self-financing and self-reproducing system of marketing, selling and distributing a product or service to the consumer through various levels of managers, sponsors and salespeople. Also referred to as MLM or Network Marketing.

Negative Cash Flow
When a business spends more cash than it receives through earnings or other transactions in a set period. Money flowing out exceeds money flowing in.

Network Marketing
See "Multi-Level Marketing".

Net Worth
Total assets less total liabilities. Applies to a business or to an individual.

Offering Memorandum
Refers to a document which provides details of a a company's past, present and prospective business operations. The purpose is to disclose all the material factors that a potential purchaser of securities would need to know in order to make a rational decision.

Operating Loan
A loan intended for short-term financing to supply cash flow support or cover day-to-day operating expenses. Loans of this type are part of the line of credit.

P/E Ratio
Price/earnings Ratio. Calculated by dividing the current price of one share of the company's stock by the amount of the company's earning share for the previous 12 months; e.g., 15/1 = $45/$3.

Personal Guarantee
A personal promise made by an individual on behalf of a personal or corporate borrower to repay the debt if the borrower fails to repay as agreed.

Preferred Stock
A class of share capital that entitles the owner to a preferred position over the common shareholders in specified circumstances.

Prime Interest Rate
Also called the prime lending rate or prime rate. This is a variable per annum reference rate of interest (as announced and adjusted by the banks from time to time) for Canadian dollar loans by the banks in Canada. This is also the rate charged by the banks to their most creditworthy customers.

Principal and Interest Payment
A loan payment that consists of a fixed amount of principal, plus an interest portion that varies monthly.

Principal
The amount of money actually owed, excluding interest.

Private Placement
The sale of stock or debt to a limited group of investors. Properly structured, the private placement does not have to comply with all the rules and regulations relating to disclosure that would be required in a normal placement process.

Pro Forma

A projection or estimate. Pro forma financial statements look at your business's expected performance.

Promissory Note

A signed promise to pay a certain amount of money on demand or on a fixed date.

Prospectus

A detailed disclosure document required by Provincial legislation. The purpose is to provide the prospective investor "full, true and plain disclosure" of all information material to the investment. The investment information is to be supplied by a salesperson who is "registered" to sell securities in the province in which the securities are sold.

Proxy

Person or legal entity authorized to represent, and if necessary act and vote on behalf of another.

Ratio

Comparison of two figures used to evaluate performance. One measure of the health of a business is how well it is doing in these activities compared with similar businesses. Examples of key ratios are the Debt/Equity Ratio and Return on Investment.

Ratio Analysis

The process of calculating financial ratios for your business in order to determine trends and to compare its performance with that of other businesses in the same industry. (See Current Ratio, Gross Profit Margin, Debt to Tangible Net Worth, Age of Receivables, Age of Inventory, Age of Payables.)

Recourse Loan

Loan for which a guarantor is liable for payment in the event the borrower defaults.

Return on Investment

The amount of money earned by an investment return. This key number is usually expressed as a percentage obtained by dividing net return received by the original amount invested.

Securities

Negotiable instruments issued by a company, institution or government, such as stocks and bonds.

Security (often called Collateral Security)

Asset(s) belonging to the business or to you personally which are pledged to a lender in support of a loan and which can be sold in the event you do not repay your loan. In the case of term loans, the property (e.g., land, buildings, equipment) being purchased with the loan usually forms the security for the loan.

Seed Money

The initial investment in a company. Funds generally used to investigate the market, develop product technology, or purchase the initial assets. Usually funded by the owner or by lovemoney.

Share Capital

Total of shares authorized to be issued, or actually issued, by a company.

Shot-gun

A clause in a buy-sell agreement or shareholders' agreement whereby if one party offers to buy out the other at a certain price, the other party has, within a limited period, either to accept the price or buy the offeror out at the same price.

Small Business

There are many definitions for this term. Most banks use a version of this: a business owned and operated by one or more persons, which has up to 20 employees, which has annual sales of up to $2,000,000 and which requires loans of up to $500,000.

Spread

The difference between the interest rate paid on depositors' funds and the interest rate charged to borrowers.

Strategic Alliance

Concept commonly falling under other terms such as corporate partnering, business collaboration or joint venture. Term means making a business agreement with another company involved in some aspect of its business which interacts with your needs and interests. The result is to combine resources for greater individual profit.

Subordinated Debt

Where one lender has agreed in writing to rank behind another in claiming against an asset, he will only receive his capital back after the other has been fully paid out. A bank will often insist that shareholder loans be subordinated to the obligations of the bank. This is also known as "subrogation".

Subscription Agreement

A document which sets out the issuer's sale and the investor's purchase of securities. This document creates certain legal rights for both parties.

Sweat Equity

Refers to all of the labour and organizational work that a founder contributes, usually without remuneration, in order to launch a business.

Tangible Net Worth (sometimes called Tangible Equity)

Net worth less intangible assets.

Term

The length of time which a loan agreement covers. The maximum time during which a loan is to be repaid.

Term Loan

A loan intended for medium- or long-term financing to supply cash to purchase fixed assets, such as machinery, land, or buildings or to renovate business premises.

Term Sheet

A summary of the important terms of an investment agreement, usually related to venture capital.

Unencumbered

Property free and clear of all liens (such as creditors' secured claims).

Undercapitalization

Situation in which a business does not have enough capital to carry out its normal business functions.

Valuation

The value of an asset, as assessed by a qualified appraiser, usually expressed as the resale value given current market conditions.

Variable Expenses

Costs of doing business which vary with the volume of business. Examples are advertising costs, manufacturing costs and bad debts.

Variable (or Floating) Rate
An interest rate that varies with the bank's prime rate.

Venture Capitalist
An individual or institution that provides debt or equity capital typically unavailable from traditional sources, for the growth (or in some instances, seed funding) of business enterprises.

Warm Market
Refers to people whom you know. Term normally used in the context of targeting people who could be sources of financing for you. Opposite of term "Cold Market".

Warrant
A financial instrument which authorizes the holder to purchase securities at a predetermined price until a specified time in the future.

Working Capital
Current assets less current liabilities.

Workout
In the case of a bad loan or troubled firm, remedial measures being taken.

Yield
Percentage return on an investment, usually expressed as an annual rate.

READER FEEDBACK, EDUCATIONAL AND FINANCING RESOURCES

We welcome your candid feedback and constructive suggestions for improvement for future editions of the book. Please write to us at the address of the Canadian Enterprise Institute Inc., below:

Educational Resources

If you would like information about educational seminars, books, video and audio tapes and other material relating to financing and business, please contact:

Canadian Enterprise Institute Inc.
#300-3665 Kingsway
Vancouver, B.C. V5R 5W2
Phone: (604) 436-3337
Fax: (604) 436-9155

Financing Resources

If you are interested in consulting services on:

* creating your business or financing plan
* analyzing your project or company
* locating funding sources
* presenting your investment proposal
* developing a strategic alliance
* pinpointing attractive private investments
* organizing an initial public offering
* negotiating a superior deal
* arranging a purchase or sale of a business

Please contact:

National Business Finance Network, Inc.
#207-1425 Marine Drive
West Vancouver, B.C. V7T 1B9
(604) 886-2207
Fax: (604) 886-9605

ABOUT THE AUTHORS

DOUGLAS A. GRAY, B.A., LL.B., is one of Canada's foremost authorities on entrepreneurial development and small business management. He is a retired lawyer and an internationally recognized consultant. In his extensive past experience as a business and real estate lawyer, he represented numerous lenders and business owners in negotiating financing packages, including extensive security documentation. Client financing has been arranged through commercial lenders (banks, trust companies, credit unions), government, private investors, joint ventures and syndications.

As a public speaker and educator, Mr. Gray has conducted seminars and presentations to over 250,000 people across Canada and internationally. Many of these presentations involve financing and money-management strategies. He is frequently interviewed by the media as an authority on entrepreneurship and real estate. Mr. Gray has given over 1,000 media interviews and has been profiled on the three national television networks (CTV, CBC, Global). He has founded ten successful small businesses, and is the President of The Canadian Enterprise Institute Inc.

He is the author or co-author of numerous best-selling business books including: *Start and Run a Profitable Consulting Business; The Entrepreneur's Complete Self-Assessment Guide; Marketing Your Product; The Complete Canadian Small Business Guide; Home Inc.: The Canadian Home-Based Business Guide; Buying, Owning and Selling a Condominium; Making Money in Real Estate: The Canadian Residential Investment Guide; Mortgages Made Easy; Home-Buying Made Easy;* and *The Complete Canadian Home Inspection Guide* (co-authored with Ed R. R. Witzke). He is currently at work on two more books, *How to Prepare a Winning Business Plan* and *Risk-Free Retirement,* a multi-authored work.

Mr. Gray lives in Vancouver, B.C.

BRIAN F. NATTRASS, B.A., LL.B., Barrister and Solicitor, is one of Canada's leading experts in the field of raising money for emerging companies. He has been responsible for raising tens of millions of dollars for entrepreneurial ventures in Canada, the United States and Europe over the past decade, ranging in amounts from $100,000 to over $10,000,000 per project.

Mr. Nattrass combines the insights and skills of a "street smart" fund raiser and businessman with his almost twenty years' experience as an entrepreneurial lawyer and financing consultant, primarily concerned with corporate finance and commercial transactions. He has raised money for his own and other people's projects in many forms including equity, convertible debt and government guaranteed financing. Mr. Nattrass has planned and fully executed dozens of individual financings, ranging from small closely-held corporations to highly complex public offerings requiring months of negotiations with securities commissions, investors, technical consultants, investment dealers and stock exchanges. He is the President of National Business Finance Network, Inc.

The achievements of Mr. Nattrass have been the subject of articles in such publications as *Newsweek, The New York Times, Small Business* and *Venture.* He has also appeared on the Financial News Network (FNN), the British Broadcasting Corporation (BBC), the Canadian Broadcasting Corporation (CBC) and the Canadian Television Network (CTV). Mr. Nattrass gives seminars across Canada on all aspects of business financing.

Mr. Nattrass lives in Vancouver, B.C.

OTHER BESTSELLING
BOOKS BY DOUGLAS A GRAY

The Complete Canadian Home Inspection Guide
(with Ed Witzke)
ISBN 0-07-551-245-9

Making Money in Real Estate: The Canadian Residential Investment Guide
ISBN 0-07-549596-1

Home Buying Made Easy: The Canadian Guide to Purchasing a Newly-Built or Pre-Owned Home
ISBN 0-07-551560-1

Buying, Owning and Selling a Condominium: A Guide for Canadians
ISBN 0-07-549681-X

The Complete Canadian Small Business Guide
(with Diana Gray)
ISBN 0-07-549595-3

Home Inc.: The Canadian Home-Based Business Guide
(with Diana Gray)
ISBN 0-07-549872-3

Raising Money: The Canadian Guide to Successful Business Financing
(with Brian Nattrass)
ISBN 0-07-551490-2

Available at your local bookstore or by contacting:

McGraw-Hill Ryerson Limited
Consumer & Professional Books Division
300 Water Street, Whitby, Ontario
L1N 9B6

Phone 1-800-565-5758

Fax 1-800-463-5885
(orders only)